# Inside
## the Cage

# Inside the Cage

{ A SEASON AT
WEST 4TH STREET'S
LEGENDARY
TOURNAMENT }

# Wight Martindale Jr.

SSE

SIMON SPOTLIGHT ENTERTAINMENT
New York   London   Toronto   Sydney

**Author's Note**
I have changed the names and descriptions of certain people in this book.
The conversations I present in quotations come from my memory, and they
are not meant to be word-for-word transcriptions. These conversations are
intended to convey the general idea and feel for what was actually said.

**SSE**

SIMON SPOTLIGHT ENTERTAINMENT
An imprint of Simon & Schuster
1230 Avenue of the Americas, New York, New York 10020
Text copyright © 2005 by Wight Martindale, Jr.
All rights reserved, including the right of reproduction in whole or in part
in any form.
SIMON SPOTLIGHT ENTERTAINMENT and related logo
are trademarks of Simon & Schuster, Inc.
Designed by Ann Zeak
Manufactured in the United States of America
First Edition 10 9 8 7 6 5 4 3 2 1
Library of Congress Cataloging-in-Publication Data
Martindale, Wight.
Inside the cage : a season at West 4th Street's legendary tournament /
by Wight Martindale Jr.
p. cm.
ISBN 1-4169-0539-1 (alk. paper)
1. Basketball—New York (State)—New York. 2. Playgrounds—New York
(State)—New York. I. Title.
GV885.73.N4M37 2005
796.357'09747'1—dc22
2004027438

# Contents

Part Three: THE OFF-SEASON

# preface

## West 4th Street
## and the Ron Artest Affair

**No good book is** truly original; nothing worthwhile is created from the imagination alone, with no precedent and no tradition. *Inside the Cage* is one of many accounts of basketball and the inner-city experience, and as such, it is about urban life as much as it is about basketball. Its most obvious predecessor is a book called *Heaven Is a Playground,* written twenty-five years ago by a young sportswriter, Rick Telander. Telander focused on street scout Rodney Parker and the Brooklyn kids he was trying to get into college so they could play their way out of the ghetto.

This story, like Telander's, follows a single year of playground basketball in New York City.

In this book, *Heaven Is a Playground* is revisited twenty-five years later. Even some of the same characters, Rodney Parker and Fly Williams, for example, appear here. But this is a story told by an older man about other older men, so it looks at the people who have stayed involved with summer basketball here for three decades and turned a pleasant run into an enduring New York social institution.

The book explores the most broad and fundamental principles of the street game, and it attempts to understand what lies beneath the game's most blatant features—the leaping, the shouting, the tricks, and the physical confrontations—and what is not so obvious: the culture that has been created within the park.

The story has two central characters. The most important person is Kenny Graham, the man who started the West 4th Street Pro-Classic back in the 1970s and who continues to run it today. The second character is the Cage itself, a tiny park between West 3rd Street and West 4th Street on Sixth Avenue in Greenwich Village. Kenny's benevolent dictatorship here, combined with the natural discipline enforced by the configuration of the Cage, has produced some great basketball and even better people.

This account does not romanticize eccentric black athletes who can jump to the moon but cannot function in normal society. Instead, it demonstrates that institutions created in the ghetto by the people who live there do the community more good than something imposed by a remote bureaucracy. *Inside the Cage* is about having fun, sticking with a good thing, and making it better.

Thus, this book should be a welcome antidote to the Ron Artest affair of November 19, 2004. After Artest went into the stands in Detroit to punch out courtside spectators—one of whom had thrown beer on him while he lay on the scorer's table, taunting Detroit fans—Commissioner David Stern said that this was the single worst event he had seen in twenty-one years of running the NBA, and he banned Artest from playing for the rest of the year. The entire episode was played and replayed on television, in slow motion and super-slow motion, until America couldn't stand it any longer.

The violence in city playground games can be even worse. But in the Cage at West 4th Street, it is not. While the culture of the National Basketball Association appears to have been deteriorating over the past two decades, the culture of many inner-city parks has been improving. Why is this so? And why do we not know more about it? Why are inner-city black men better able to take care of themselves than the superorganized and superrich NBA?

Money alone does not solve the problem, and it may even make matters worse. The rage and frustration of men living in what they perceive as a hopeless, oppressive environment has been well documented—in movies like *Straight Out of Brooklyn,* by Matty Rich, and in books like *Native Son,* by Richard Wright. This rage still exists, and it is likely that Ron Artest feels it, despite his annual salary of $6.2 million. Yet because so many big businesses—and unions—have so much invested in the success of the NBA (each separate team is a big business itself), the problem there will be finessed and negotiated; it will be viewed as a business problem that requires a consensus-based business solution. Unfortunately this approach seldom fixes anything.

At West 4th Street, impulsive violence is understood, even sympathized with. But still, it is not accepted. Players who cause trouble are simply not invited back. More likely, they are identified and dealt with before they can do any harm. That's how problems get fixed in real life, and that is what *Inside the Cage* is about. Real life.

# acknowledgments

Anything written with only a slim hope that it may ever be printed requires exceptional emotional and intellectual support. I wish to begin by acknowledging the emotional support of my wife, Sally, and my children.

More directly, I thank Rebekah Berry, without whom there would be no book. She was involved in the original reporting, the writing, the editing, and the organizing of the final manuscript. When I was most discouraged, she remained hopeful. It is her book almost as much as mine. My friend John Carlson urged me to go ahead with my writing, and he supported me throughout the entire project. Blanford Parker, my mentor from graduate school, provided most of the good ideas and insights that, I hope, keep this book from being just another book about athletes. Sterling Lord, a wise agent who has been helping writers for more years than most of you have been alive, focused the book's writing and organization.

I am grateful to Kenny Graham for his friendship and patience over twenty years, and I must acknowledge the many fine people mentioned in the book, including Rick Johnson, Lambert Shell, Mike Williams, Dytanya Mixson, Tony Sherman, Bo Keene, Greg Jackson and Darryl Glenn from the BRC, and Joe and Rosy from West 4th Street. Indeed, I admire everyone who has contributed to the Cage. My life is richer for having known them all.

# introduction

# The Cage

**Nobody at West 4th** Street in New York City is famous.

No one is rich.

No one is important.

Or influential.

Or politically connected.

But a summer basketball tournament has been going on down here for over twenty-five years, and the same guy who started the tournament is still running it. His name is Kenny Graham. He is fifty years old and he drives a limo for a living. He spends almost half the year in Rio de Janeiro and speaks excellent Portuguese. New York City and the Department of Parks and Recreation give him no assistance with his program. They probably never will.

But his summer tournament is known to basketball insiders around the world. Professional scouts come here from Europe. PlayStation, the giant computer game producer, features the West 4th Street Cage in its hottest video basketball games. Nike is selling a BattleGrounds line of clothing and footwear featuring the Cage logo. The recent book *Hoops Nation* (1998), by Chris Ballard, evaluated over one thousand public courts for the quality of their pickup games. The Cage was ranked first, the best there is. This is no ordinary playground.

Greenwich Village is a melting pot of New York cultures, the home of New York University and the New School, as well as the heart of New York's gay community. Partly due to its proximity to Wall Street, real estate values have risen steadily. Retail businesses flourish, and there is no vacant land. Refurbished one-bedroom cooperative apartments start at $300,000, and the zoning board makes it difficult to erect residential buildings. Everything seems to have landmark status.

The Village's population has increased every decade, and now it stands at about 95,000. While Village residents like to claim that their community is broadly inclusive, fewer than 10 percent of those who live here are black or Hispanic, with only 5 percent of the population on public assistance. Its elementary school population is small, since only 8 percent of the population is under eighteen years old. St. Vincent's Hospital, on Twelfth Street, is one of the city's best.

Two of New York's most elegant gourmet food stores, Balducci's and Dean & Deluca, got their start in the Village. The community board here is organized, active, and powerful. It has spun off nearly two dozen subcommittees to keep the city aware of its needs. Tony Dapolito, proprietor of Vesuvio's Bakery Shop on Prince Street, has been chairman of the Parks and Recreation Committee in the Village "for forty-five or fifty years, I can't remember which," he says. (The neighbors tell me that the bakery is a known New York Mafia location. I don't press Tony, who is eighty-two, on the issue.) This collective involvement ensures that public services remain first-rate. The area is politically liberal, but police protection is everywhere.

Village residents are tolerant of the West 4th Street tournament, but every year is a challenge. Local residents seldom play here, so the tournament doesn't serve residents directly. Gangs, black and Latin, often congregate around the basketball court after dark. At times the police have had to close off the side streets that cross Sixth Avenue to make cruising difficult. Although the tournament adds color to the Village, it can be too much Brooklyn reality for the fashionable Villagers. Still, because the basketball tradition is over thirty years old, a move to shut down the tournament would have ugly racial overtones, which the Village doesn't want. The relationship between the tournament and the community is delicate, but care by both parties—Kenny Graham and the locals—has kept the tournament going. Kenny Graham did not create the Cage, but no one has put it to better use.

The site itself is unique. The improbability of its placement (in the middle of Greenwich Village) is one of its charms.

At its roots the Cage is a child of the New York subway system, and subways have been its sustaining lifeblood for nearly fifty years. The city's Department of Transportation purchased the land where the park is located in the 1920s when the city decided to extend the Sixth Avenue subway line south of 14th Street to the Holland Tunnel. Until 1935, when the Department of Transportation first gave the parks department a permit to run the playground, it was simply the land over the Independent line's new West 4th Street station.

From 1935 until 1953 it remained an unremarkable vest-pocket park in the Village, covering 0.42 acres. It had swings and slides for children and a bocce court for men. Throughout the 1930s and 1940s it was unpaved. When the parks department took official title to the park in 1953, no basketball court existed, and the park's principal recreation continued to be handball, horseshoes, and relaxation on the park benches. There was no Cage. The parks department was planning to build a wading pool for kids.

In 1954 the parks department made an effort to increase the playground's size by acquiring all the land between 3rd and 4th streets going east toward MacDougal Street. This acquisition would have more than doubled the size of the park, but it meant condemning a number of occupied buildings. Naturally the buildings' merchants and residents complained.

Tony Dapolito, chairman of the Village Parks and Recreation Committee, had another reason for opposing expansion of the West 4th Street playground. He realized that if it did not occur, he could get another new park—a substitute if you will—built in his own neighborhood in SoHo. That's exactly what happened. The expansion was defeated, and the shape of West 4th Street has not changed since. Small restaurants and shops line West 3rd Street, and the famous Blue Note jazz club is just a few doors away from the park.

According to Kenny (no detailed park records exist), basketball entered in a small way when a single backboard and basket were put up in the mid-1950s. The surface was unpaved, and only neighborhood residents used the court. Then in the late 1950s, the parks department erected two permanent baskets and laid down a crude, gritty, asphalt surface. Since the court ran right up to the sidewalk on Sixth Avenue, a twenty-foot fence had to be constructed. The Cage was born.

Cage configurations are not unusual in big cities. Often a cage is the only way to design a court located on a busy street, where the ball has to be kept away from passing pedestrians. What is unusual about the West 4th Street court is that it got and kept its name from the subway station over which it was constructed. Players naturally provide nicknames to popular courts, and in the Village it's "The Cage at West 4th Street."

The subway lines that stop here make this location important. The F line forms a U-shaped pattern connecting Jamaica, Queens, with midtown Manhattan, then moving down Sixth Avenue, stopping at West 4th Street, and finally crossing over to Brooklyn, going all the way out to Coney Island. The D line begins up north in the Bronx, moves down past Fordham University, and passes by Yankee Stadium on its route to Brooklyn, going through the Village along the way. The A, C, and E trains come down from Harlem and the Upper West Side along Eighth Avenue, continuing all the way to Wall Street on the E branch. The A train swerves east, heading to Borough Hall in Brooklyn and out to the Aqueduct Race Track and the beaches at Rockaway Park. All these systems stop at West 4th Street.

The Christopher Street station for the number 1 and number 9 Seventh Avenue local trains is located one block to the west, linking the Bronx, Washington Heights, and Harlem to Brooklyn and to the Cage. A few blocks north of the park, on 14th Street, the L line runs west to east across Manhattan before reaching its destination in Brooklyn, passing through New Lots Avenue and Brownsville. The subway connects almost every corner of the three-hundred-square-mile city to West 4th Street, making it possible for players from just about any neighborhood to show up and play basketball.

Bigger and better courts than those at West 4th Street are located two blocks down Sixth Avenue at Houston Street, but they don't get nearly as much play and attention as the Cage does. There is no subway stop down there, and fewer people pass by to watch.

The courts at West 4th Street have been resurfaced only twice since the late 1950s, and officially the city has never paid much attention to what goes on there. David Dinkins was the only mayor to visit the park, and he did so only once. Until recently the parks department's official records gave the site no name other than "playground," but in 1996 it was finally recognized for what it is: "West 4th Street Courts."

The Cage is the only outdoor court in New York City that brings the best black basketball players into a white neighborhood where they can perform before a racially mixed crowd. Here both groups can mix freely, yet an unspoken tension is still in the air; they do not really speak the same language. The blacks suspect that they are guests and that they are not wanted. The whites are attracted by the players' strength and agility, but they are constantly on the lookout for black violence, which terrifies them. When a hotly contested game is being played, the tension is electric, and this heightens the excitement of the game for everyone. It is Kenny's job to keep it all under control.

Rivalries between teams here can be as intense as the soccer rivalries in Europe, and the threat of chaos, of everything breaking down, is always present. Sometimes games do get violent and nasty. But Kenny is part of the street culture; he is not above it, so he understands that he can keep respect for his tournament only if he earns respect for himself. If he were not as tough as his players, con men and hoodlums would have taken over this tournament years ago.

Outbursts of violence are frequent because the court is so small. Years ago, on a sweltering hot July afternoon, Prime Time, a top team back then, was fighting to hold a tiny lead in a bitterly contested game. Kenny was watching quietly, seated in his director's chair behind the scorer's table, just a few feet behind the south basket. The crowd was roaring with every shot.

For both teams the defense had become intensely physical; rebounding was an act of war. When a particularly aggressive Prime Time player, an enforcer in a game like this, went crashing into the boards and sent an opposing player sprawling into the fence, the referee quickly blew his whistle and signaled for a flagrant foul, two shots. When the offending player burst out in rage, the ref added a technical foul, one additional shot plus possession of the ball, and he ejected the player from the game.

The enforcer, who was six foot four inches tall with a sculpted 230-pound body and a shaved head, went ballistic. He swore at the refs, and pushed and cursed at anyone near him. Players on both teams began to shove one another. The ejected player wouldn't leave the court, and he kicked over the scorer's table. He threw a paper cup full of water into the crowd. He then heaved the basketball over the fence and into the middle of Sixth Avenue, where it bounced off the hood of a passing car, disrupting traffic.

At considerable personal risk, Kenny confronted the enraged player and told him that he had to calm down, that his behavior was degrading to himself and to the league. "We are a black basketball league playing in a white neighborhood," he began. "We can be shut down in a minute. You've played here a long time, and you know what I'm talking about."

The two of them were nose to nose.

"Let me ask you," Kenny continued. "Is this the way you repay me for what I am doing for you?"

Neither man backed down, but the ranting subsided and the player eventually left the court without further violence. The crowd calmed down, the game continued, and order was restored. After the game, Kenny told the player that he would be suspended for the following season. He is back now, and he's still a tough player but is a well-respected citizen of the league.

Without this kind of support from Kenny, the referees could not operate. "There are some thugs in this league," Kenny says with a sigh, "but we try to stay on top of them and their coaches so that they play under control."

Inner-city basketball is a serious business. Respect, even more than victory, is always on the line. The men who play here don't live in white clapboard houses with soft green lawns and a two-car garage. They live in huge apartment complexes surrounded by concrete and blacktop, and they spend much of their lives on the streets. Without respect, street life is intolerable.

Iron Mike Montague is one of those players drawn to the Cage from far away. Mike lives uptown in Harlem, but he has been playing here for forty years. He is particularly adept at helping Kenny manage the occasional troublemaker. Although it is rare to have a gun incident at the park, a few years ago one of Kenny's staff members showed up with a loaded pistol in his athletic bag. Apparently he had a score to settle. In a boastful moment, he gave one of the kids in the park a glance at the weapon. In seconds Kenny knew about it and he called Iron Mike over and whispered in his ear. When the staff member stood up to change his shirt, Iron Mike quietly sat down in a chair next to the troubled man.

Unobtrusively Iron Mike slid the bag with the gun in it under his chair. The movement of the bag was no more than eighteen inches. The two men's eyes met, and Mike gave the disturbed staffer a half smile and a knowing nod. No one in his right mind tangles with Iron Mike—at least not when he is looking at you. The game commenced. Mike never moved and neither did the bag. Kenny engaged the staffer in discussion; he sent him on important errands; he asked his opinion about other staffers. He gave him attention and treated him with respect. Two hours later, at dusk, when the game was over and most of the players had dispersed, Mike gently handed the staffer his bag. Everything was cool. The staff member is a trusted regular, and he has not stepped out of line since that day. At the time, little was said. A more reflective chat with the staffer would come later, but disaster was averted. No one was embarrassed and no one was put on the spot.

It is amazing that the Cage needs so little security. The operators at Rucker Park uptown use metal detectors, a uniformed security team, and police officers to keep the fans under control. The only time the police have been involved at the Cage is when a player is hurt and the police come because they get through to the EMT team more quickly.

Kenny is not perfect, and saints do not populate the park. Every guy does not go home to his wife every night, and the women who come here regularly are not all librarians and schoolteachers. Some men live off women. Others profit from disability and welfare scams. Some people here do not file tax returns. Lending them money might be a bad idea. I can't imagine Jimmy Stewart as a character in a movie about West 4th Street. But it works; the Cage has developed a successful culture of its own.

Over the years good basketball at West 4th Street has created a coterie of basketball purists who understand basketball and want to see it played well. If games have no team play or no defense, or if they degenerate into shoving matches, these fans lose interest and go elsewhere. If the game is good, there is no better place to be.

Mike Williams, cofounder of the tournament with Kenny in 1977, was a park player and a referee, and he retains great affection for West 4th Street fans. "All sorts of people would come to watch games in the early days," he recalls. "They'd have their spots along the fence. Some people had regular locations. If they weren't there, if they missed a few days, you'd think that something was wrong. You'd become concerned. Often I would say to a person, 'I didn't see you last week. You all right?' People who you thought never knew you would stop you on the street and say hello. I was a boy from the Lower East Side and this was not my neighborhood, so it was heartwarming. Total strangers wanted to speak with you. You always felt right at home there."

Hassan Duncombe, one of the league's great power players of the 1990s and a star at the University of Pennsylvania, could easily look down on games dominated by skittering guard play, but he doesn't. "West 4th Street is better than any other tournament I've ever played in," he says, "and I've played in the Sonny Hill league in Philadelphia and most of the New York and New Jersey summer tournaments. The big difference at West 4th is the relationship with the fans. They are so close; they really become a part of the game. I consider some of them friends of mine."

Because of the court's small size, the action of the game is compact and intense. A regulation court is ninety-four feet by fifty feet, but the West 4th Street court is only sixty-six feet by forty-five feet, and this width is measured from fence to fence. The marked sidelines, which are generally ignored, make the width of the court only thirty-eight feet, too narrow for ten large bodies. The distance from the foul lines to center court is fifteen feet. This means that the short trip up and down the court produces a game with more shooting and more offense with less legwork.

Big people moving quickly in a small area are bound to bump into one another, so the West 4th Street games remain the city's roughest. Lambert Shell, a star here for over a decade, has always played a physical game, so he likes the court. "I'm getting older and I like a small court," he says. "And frankly, I like to hit guys. That's part of my game." Referees must distinguish between the inevitable contact of play and fouling. This is not easy. No court demands more of officials.

Buddy Keaton, who runs his own referee camp and has been calling games at West 4th Street for twenty years, understands the disciplines of the Cage well. "It is a very tough assignment, and many refs don't want to work there. You must earn the respect of the players and coaches. Plus there must be leadership and support from the league. Kenny is a very strong person, and that helps. Working here makes you a better ref and a better person. If you can work here, you can work anywhere."

The same principle applies to the players.

Any small court naturally favors the defense. With ten mobile players on the court, it is easier to double-team the man with the ball, easier to knock the ball out of someone's hands, and easier to intercept passes. The college game of passing the ball around the perimeter quickly, then reversing it, hoping to find the open man, is unnatural for a small court. Defensive players don't have to move much, so they are not easily caught out of position. Furthermore, because the players are such great athletes and move so well off the dribble, it makes less sense to set a screen or a pick for another player; all you do is bring another defender to him. The offense is more likely to clear out for a perimeter player, or dump the ball into the center down low, and then let the man with the ball work for the shot. The small court produces a simpler, more athletic game.

West 4th Street places a premium on good ball handling. "The small court makes you do all the right things," explains Tony Hargraves, the leader of Prime Time during its championship years. "This court improves your game. It is a place where you cannot continue to make mistakes," he explains. "Anthony Mason is a prime example. West 4th Street polished his game. His strength was important to him, but the park competition also taught him that he had to move much more quickly. It improved his ball handling. Mason is one of the best ball-handling big men in the NBA, and the Cage was a major contributor."

It is no wonder basketball purists love the kind of game that the Cage produces. People on the fence can see *everything*. They catch the subtlety of the footwork and find fear in a player's eyes. At times they can be closer to the players than the men they are playing against. Quickness is more important than power, because powerful men can be double-teamed. Spectators feel the intensity of competitive basketball. Players get to show 'em what they've got.

The early history of the Cage was notable for its pickup games. It attracted some of the best players anywhere, including the Power Memorial High School sensation Lew Alcindor, now Kareem Abdul-Jabbar. Pickup games have drawn famous basketball enthusiasts like Bill Cosby and Denzel Washington. Denzel is the only prominent alumnus of West 4th Street to give money back to Kenny for the program. Most successful players, though they speak well of the tournament, do not return to support it.

Iron Mike remembers when the park was discovered by the players uptown. "The first migration of players began in the early 1960s," he recalls. "Players started coming down from the Battleground on 151st Street and Amsterdam Avenue and the Pit on 151st Street and Seventh Avenue. Word got around that you could get a good run at West 4th Street, and it took you out of the neighborhood."

At the same time, players from all over Brooklyn—Bedford-Stuyvesant, Tillary Park, the Hole in Brownsville, and the Fort Greene projects—found their way to West 4th Street. Kenny points out, "There weren't very many tournaments in those days. Everything was a pickup game. So good players were drawn to anything organized."

Unlike every other summer tournament in the city, the same man has remained in control, and this makes Kenny's tournament different. For example, corporate sponsors now run most big tournaments, and money comes with a price of its own. Ray Diaz runs the Nike Pro City tournament, but Nike owns the league. Nike rents the facility, and Nike can hire whomever it wishes. But Kenny's tournament is called Ken Graham's West 4th Street Pro-Classic. It is his, and he will not let sponsors change the way he runs his games. Not even Nike. Nor do Internet and video sponsors orchestrate the tournament to accommodate their filming. No one is allowed inside the Cage's playing area to film. That goes for the TV networks as well. Kenny never seeks publicity, and he pays no attention to how others run their tournaments.

This independent spirit and autocratic management method is not supposed to work. Kenny does not build a consensus or ask others for advice. He calls himself the commissioner, but controls everything and does what he wants. Any management textbook would tell you this method can't succeed over the long haul, but few writers of textbooks spend much time on city streets. And none of them know Kenny Graham.

It might be said that everyone who came to West 4th Street in the 1970s shared a more unified view of life. Martin Luther King Jr. was successful in the 1950s and 1960s because his audience, black and white, shared a common culture. The issues divided people, but the society was whole. This was true even in the segregated South, which was thoroughly Christian. Segregation was shown to be an error because the central ethical assumptions of both blacks and whites were similar. Lester Maddox looked bad because he was hypocritical, and his Bible-toting supporters were shown to violate their own rules. But there was none of today's separatist rhetoric, no "you owe me" entitlement thinking or divisive legal finagling. Now, proclaiming the same message, King would probably fail. He would not be understood. In the 1970s the Cage enjoyed the same broad-based camaraderie. The dilution of this spirit, even though it may have been lessened at West 4th Street, has made Kenny's job more wearing.

The Cage is a symbol for everyone. It is a New York thing. As Buddy Keaton says, if you can make it here, you can make it anywhere. Your past means nothing. Inside the Cage, men get a fresh start every day.

Nike's new BattleGrounds merchandise line has gotten at least one thing right: West 4th Street *is* a battleground. All battlegrounds are sacred places. That is why we remember them so well, and that is why we revisit them. Battlegrounds are where fates are determined, lives are changed, and often, people rise to new levels. People can be perfected here. The Cage at West 4th Street is hallowed ground—for all the right reasons.

Part One
..
EARLY SEASON ACTION

# chapter one

# The Twenty-fifth Season Begins:
# The Tip-off Games

**The tip-off game on** Saturday, June 1, 2002, officially begins the twenty-fifth season. Tip-off weekend is a four-team set of exhibition games featuring the best teams from the previous season. The flags are flying today just as they have since the tournament's earliest days. Iron Mike has placed a huge American flag atop the interior fence that faces Sixth Avenue. On each side of Old Glory is a T-shirt, one from the New York Police Department and the other from the New York Fire Department. Under them are six more banners—three with the Nike Swoosh logo and three from Mistic, the soft-drink sponsor.

This is a beautiful late spring day, sunny and in the seventies. Kenny arrives bright and early, as do Arizona Pearson and Rick Johnson, both of whom have agreed to take over when Kenny is not around. Rick was the commissioner the year before, and he's been with Kenny, generally as timekeeper, for over twenty years. Today he is sitting at his favorite spot for watching a game—atop an eight-foot stepladder reserved for his use.

Rick has good ears; he knows what's happening on the streets. At the end of one season, word spread that a fancy drug dealer from uptown was going to enter a team at West 4th Street. These guys may want to run things, and they may intimidate referees and threaten opposing players when the game is not going their way. For Kenny's benefit Rick kept a recorded call from an uptown coach who cited a number of dangerous incidents that this team had been responsible for the previous year. This kind of information is valuable to Kenny.

Rick understands hustlers because he is a bit of a hustler himself, and he enjoys keeping his private life mysterious. He can be evasive and difficult to get hold of, and he once confided to a friend, "I am a criminal. But I like the way I live. In the entire course of my life I have spent a total of three hours in jail, and that was for driving with an expired license. Every day I get up in the morning I am happy to be here." Rick may or may not be a criminal, but if there is heat around, he never seems to feel it.

Arizona Pearson, now a schoolteacher, played in the tournament for more than ten years, and he finished his playing days with the championship Prime Time teams. Now he runs the boys' youth program. Today the first of two high school boys' games began at 10:00 A.M. This was followed by the season opener for Janice Carter's women's division a little after noon.

As usual, Kenny runs things inside the Cage. He does this with the subtlest gestures: a nod, a wave of his finger, a few syllables. The people who work for him at the park know their jobs, and they seek his approval more than his direction.

People are hanging on the fence and milling around behind the basket in the spectator area, which includes the scorer's table. There are roughly sixty people (forty men and twenty women) in the crowd behind the basket, with another two hundred to two hundred fifty hanging on the fences that define the court, sometimes standing three and four deep, waiting for the game.

In dealing with his inner circle of sixty-odd people standing inside the park, Kenny reveals a subtle mastery of status management. What has been designated as a VIP area behind the basket is only thirty-two feet square, but Kenny rules it like a medieval principality. He allows some people to sit in front next to the scorer's table, while others can stand inside the rope designating the staff area, but behind Kenny in his director's chair. Everyone else must find his spot behind the rope.

All four director's chairs are occupied. One of Kenny's reliable regular helpers, Robert Blue, is sitting in one of them. Today Blue is dressed in a Denver Broncos outfit—shirt, hat, pants, and brilliant orange sneakers. Blue owns dozens of shirts, shorts, caps, and shoes of NBA, NFL, and top college teams. Tomorrow he may come dressed as a Cleveland Cavalier, the day after as a New York Knick. Blue is always in uniform.

Everyone inside the rope has been affiliated with the tournament for years. Kenny will determine which coaches to favor with new Nike shorts, who gets the free Mistic soft drinks, and which of Kenny's workers will sit by the cooler, officially dispensing free soft drinks. Kenny manages all these gradations of approval. He keeps the crowd happy and organized. It is easier to manage people with perks than with punishment.

Five people run a West 4th Street basketball game. The commissioner, if he is present, is in charge of everything that goes on inside the Cage. Kenny is doing that today. At the scorer's table sits the timekeeper, James Kelly, and the official scorekeeper, Vanessa Charles. Vanessa is a capable woman in her twenties who likes the environment and does a nerve-racking job very well. The announcer and the keeper of the scoreboard at midcourt complete the team.

Another distinctive tradition of the Cage is a result of Kenny's refusal to get a decent scoreboard. At midcourt, standing in front of a two-foot-by-eighteen-inch blackboard with a piece of chalk in one hand and a rag in the other, is a tall, lanky keeper of the scoreboard, aptly named Moneybags. (His real name is Bobby Dyson, but no one uses it.) The nickname is ironic, as he is always out of cash. Moneybags is about fifty years old, and at times he lives on the streets, sleeping in shelters for homeless men. His job is to rewrite the score after every point is made, and the announcer refers to him as the electronic scoreboard. When Moneybags doesn't make it to the park, Isaiah Jackson keeps the score in his place. No game begins without someone keeping score in the middle of the court.

Moneybags is part of a traditon of eccentric West 4th Street scorekeepers. During the seventies and eighties a man known only as Omar Khayyam, a mysterious loner, kept score for over ten years until one winter he simply disappeared. Omar's dress was as unconventional as his behavior. A typical outfit would consist of a Thelonious Monk narrow-brimmed fedora with a feather, a bright orange West 4th Street T-shirt, wide black-and-white pin-striped slacks cut off just below the knee, knee-high basketball socks, and the latest Nike footwear. Joe Merriweather remembers him as "a very intelligent man who held a responsible job until he developed his drinking problem."

In this beautiful summer weather, every young woman in Manhattan seems to have made the switch to flip-flops and pedicures. Many of the women at the park are dressed for the beach. For this game people will line up all along the fences on both sides of the court. Many more watch for a few minutes and then move on. The area behind the scorer's table is always crowded. Two trees with sturdy branches overhang the court, and a few kids climb up the trees to watch the game.

Because Sixth Avenue is so badly paved on this corner, the constant traffic produces a dull humming, thumping drone in the background. Horns honk, but no one notices. Down here, fans and players are oblivious to street life. The Cage is its own little world.

Rebekah, another young woman, has taken an interest in the games, and today Kenny formally introduces himself to her and sets her up in a director's chair. Rosy gives her a T-shirt, and Arizona makes sure she has an ample supply of Mistic. The announcer notices the treatment she is getting and can't let it pass without a comment. "Ladies and gentlemen, I want you all to know we have Britney Spears in the house today."

From now on, Rebekah will be hooked on the Cage. She will show up frequently when she gets out of work early. "I know why people love to come here," she says. "All the players are stars and I'm Britney Spears."

The park is full of old-timers, most of whom have not seen one another since last season. Opening day at West 4th Street is a festive social event. Julius Edwards (Honey Bun) and Roland Rooks are the referees for this game; John Clark and Nate Braswell will do the game between Nike One and the Youngsters. They have been refereeing games here for nearly twenty years.

Rodney Parker, the well-known ad hoc scout and basketball polymath, always makes opening day. Rodney has a comment on everyone. Pointing out one of the players warming up, he remarks, "The kid had great talent, but he was chucked out of a Big East college after one year. I told him he never should have gone there. Had an attitude problem. He was good when he was young, but they're all good when they're young. Most of 'em don't realize—you got to get better."

The dean of all high school scouts, Tom Konchalski, is also at the Cage. Tom is a very tall, quiet man with an incredible memory—he never seems to forget a name. He attended Archbishop Molloy High School in the city but was not much of a player there. "Scouting is my revenge on the game," he says with a twinkle in his eye. He was a full-time teacher until about twenty years ago, when he decided to convert the love of his life—watching basketball—into a profession.

He doesn't drive a car, but he still attends hundreds of high school games up and down the East Coast, and he makes a respectable living by selling his basketball-scouting newsletter to 250 college coaches. Point out a good player to him, and he will tell you about the player's family, his personal habits, his grades, and where he is likely to play next year. He knows which players are just immature and which are thugs. When there are no games to watch, he attends high school practice sessions, and perhaps has dinner afterward with the coach. His entire life is comprised of basketball people of all ages and all generations. No scout is more thorough; no scout digs deeper. When Tom tells a college coach that a kid can play at the Division I level, the kid is signed.

Kenny's longtime friend Bill Parker has arrived, and his son, young Bill, known as Smush, stops by with his sister, Joi. Smush has recently passed up his last two years at Fordham to enter the NBA draft. Dee Foreman, often called D-23, the announcer on the megaphone, spots him. "We have Smush Parker in the crowd today, folks. He'll be makin' a run with the NBA this year. Just you wait; he'll be there. Good luck, man."

Smush says seventeen teams have contacted him, and he has already been to four NBA trials (Knicks, Wizards, Raptors, and Magic). Next week he will go to a big NBA-sponsored camp in Chicago. For hopefuls like Smush on the margin of the draft, the camp is a big event. His father says that not only do coaches watch the athletes play, but they observe the players off the court to see how they mix with one another. Smush knows he did badly in one of his tryouts, but he did better in the other three.

Smush is naturally reserved, almost ill at ease talking with older people. He explains the pressure he is under: "It is intense, you know. A team will bring down four guards, put them through drills in the morning, and then have them play two-on-two in the afternoon. Coaches watch every move you make, and they offer suggestions. Then we are flown home that night. We may be asked back, or we may not."

Mike Williams, the tournament's cofounder, stands behind the rope, claiming no special recognition. He likes opening day. Mike has a natural reserve about him, and today he is wearing dark slacks and a starched white shirt open at the neck, more formal than the rest of the crowd. He just left the Bishop Loughlin Memorial High School graduation earlier in the morning. He loves his school (he is the athletic director there) and is always ready to say something good about it. "You know what they told us at graduation?" he asks rhetorically. "They told us that forty-two percent of the class would be attending college on some sort of scholarship. That says something about our kids and the way we prepare them."

Mark Figueroa, coach of last year's winner, Nike One, gets knuckles, arms, hugs, and assorted forms of fives from everyone around the scorer's table. He's a jovial guy, enjoying the limelight he has earned. His team, along with Sid Jones's United Brooklyn, has just returned from a Nike-sponsored Memorial Day tournament in Venice Beach, California. Someone in the crowd hollers at him, "How'd it go, Fig?"

Fig hollers back, "First game against Las Vegas, we win by thirty-eight. Next we play Seattle. Beat them by thirty-eight. Then we get Sid and he beats us. . . . Hey, I'm tellin' ya, New York is tough."

The voice yells back, "Yo, Fig, you could have just stayed home and lost to Sid."

Along with Nike One and United Brooklyn, the top teams in the league this year should be Karriem Memminger's Shooting Stars, B & B Foods, All Out, and the X-Men. The X-Men, coached by Dytanya Mixson, won the tournament a few years ago, and they are loaded with Bedford-Stuyvesant veterans. Karriem Memminger's Shooting Stars are from Queens, and like all the perennially strong teams, they have played together for years. The heart of the team is a group of five guys who played at the University of Bridgeport from 1990 to 1992, led by Lambert Shell.

Kenny has never had a professional public-address system, and there is no music. Basketball here is not a media event. The tournament's finances are simple and straightforward. All teams pay for the referees at each game ($75 per game for each team). This year's $750 entry fee covers shirts, league equipment, and awards. Sponsorship money (from Nike and Mistic) pays the parks department for the right to use the space, which can cost from $5,000 to $7,000 for the summer. For fifteeen years the parks department charged nothing, or the charges were small, just a few hundred dollars. But when Rudolph Giuliani became mayor and the Fila and Nike banners went up, the city decided it was time to collect. Sponsorship money also covers the trophies at the end of the year along with $10 cash paid to each of the staff, which runs between $70 and $100 per game. On weekends Kenny also buys meals for the staff, since they must work all day long. It is a hot, tedious job. If extra money remains, Kenny pays the staff a year-end bonus, and he pays Rick Johnson, who acts as commissioner in his absence. The directors are paid nothing.

Kenny could charge more, but he doesn't want to drive out teams that have been supporting the league for years. Of course $750 doesn't cover all the fees, and it won't buy all the stuff that Kenny would like to give away, so his search for sponsors is unending.

Compared with other tournaments, expenses here are low. For example, Greg Marius has been running the Entertainers Classic tournament at Rucker Park for more than twenty years, and he's close to making a living at it. He's got nine record labels paying sponsorhip money, he has Reebok providing playing gear plus cash, along with Gatorade, Pepsi, and AT&T as sponsors. His expenses are high. He must rent temporary bleachers allowing him to legally admit twelve hundred people. He pays for his security, his announcers, and the rest of his staff. He also has to pay the city to use the park.

Greg films all his games at his own expense, and he sells the DVDs he produces. Last year Reebok bought fifty thousand of his DVDs, and he hopes to sell more this year. Thanks to his connection with the NBA, MSG Network films his games and plays highlights of one game a week on its New York TV station. The Entertainers has a first-rate Web site and a clothing store near the park. Kenny has none of this.

Today at West 4th Street a film crew from France is shooting footage for a documentary about sports marketing. Kenny insists that they stay off the court, but they get enough on film for their purpose. Their film will be shown around Europe before the end of the year. Another guy is shooting footage for himself, bringing a souvenir home to his family. Once I-Hoops, an Internet programming company, pays their annual fee, they will be filming almost every day.

Tony Sherman, a great guard in the early eighties, arrives in baggy shorts and stylish braids. He carries a low-slung, violet Kickback beach chair, complete with storage bags on each armrest and a delicate sun umbrella, all of which he carefully installs in front of the scorer's table. Sherman lives in Harlem but he hangs around West 4th Street four or five afternoons a week, playing interminable pickup games before the league takes over the court. Next to Kenny Graham, Sherman has identified himself with this park more than anyone. He is often called "the mayor of West 4th Street" because he is here so often.

Sherman never played high school ball, but Rodney Parker says that he got him a scholarship to a college in California. Sherman didn't go. At West 4th Street he draws an entourage, and he dominates the pickup games. If a player becomes his friend, he can count on at least one game in an afternoon. If Sherman doesn't know a guy and doesn't care to, that guy may never play. Through sheer force of character, Sherman draws better players to the Cage, and he keeps them under control. Regulars at the court claim that when Sherman doesn't come to the park for a few weeks, the quality of the play declines, and there is more arguing. Young Smush Parker, who grew up under Sherman's tutelage, idolizes him. Sherman says West 4th Street is his park. When Kenny's not around, it is.

### Calling the Game

Seated in a director's chair at the end of the scorer's table, holding the electric megaphone, is Dee Foreman, who will be today's announcer. Big-time public-address systems have never been used here because they are too loud and neighbors would complain. Dee is calling today's game, but he alternates with Eric Chambers, known here as Butter, an especially keen observer of whatever is going on at West 4th Street.

West 4th Street has always had announcers with a special gift of gab. Kenny and Mike Williams were the first commentators, and dozens of others have followed. One announcer early in the league's history was Nathan Jones. As Kenny recalls, "He was so sarcastic we called him Arthur Trash. He could be merciless. But he knew the players and they all knew him, so he could get away with the things he said."

Ron Creth announced many games in the late 1980s, and he still calls playoff games, where tempers can run high. Ron is an amusing guy, and he can use his good humor to control a tough game. The players know him and they will listen to him.

The announcer's commentary is by no means limited to the players on the court. He will comment on who is in the house, who is escorting whom, who has been mysteriously absent recently, who has a new hairstyle, and whose dress is particularly snappy. If a guy arrives with an attractive date, he is "carrying some very fine luggage."

The announcers establish player nicknames; players do not presume to claim one. They could also be called street names, because they acknowledge that you have a place in street culture. As a rule the names are flattering, but always, they are appropriate. Mike Williams remembers them from the tournament's first days. "The park was always somewhat of a family," Mike recalls, "and these nicknames helped create that feeling. They were like pet names, names of affection you would give to your children.

"As a youngster when I first started coming here, all the players had these tremendous sounding names—Helicopter, Turtle, Rhino, and Bear. It sounded like an animal farm," he says.

Some get nicknames because of their style of play: defensive specialist Darryl Glenn is named Homicide and Marvin Stevenson became the original Hammer. Tone Springer, a great leaper for Nike

One, is called Anti-Gravity, and Ron Matthias, a powerful scorer during the 1980s, was named Terminator. Player-coach Les Pines was known as the Beggar because he was always complaining about the referees' calls. Harlem USA's coach Bill Motley was called Double-Burger because of his size, and coach Chaz Dudley is known as Pat Riley because he often wears a suit and tie to the park.

Kenny wants announcers to do more than be clever; he wants them to sell his playground game of relatively unknown players to visitors who are passing by. The announcers do this well.

"With or without nicknames, the idea is to highlight the players. This allows the fans—who may not know anyone—to become familiar with them," Kenny explains. "It builds community instantly. Everyone feels he knows everyone else. It is pathetic when I see that some of our announcers now don't even know the player's real name.

"I always highlight the guys who are playing well," Kenny continues, "because I think it makes them play better, and I know it makes them want to come down here to play. When guys know they will be hyped if they play well, it gets them pumped and they play harder." Darryl Glenn, a longtime Brownsville regular, agrees. "At West 4th Street you can feel like a star without being a star."

Kenny is strict about what announcers should *not* do. "The announcers should not ride the players or embarrass them publicly. Once in a while, when a guy gets beat or his shot is rejected, it may be appropriate to say something, but the announcer cannot ride the players personally. It sets a bad tone and can lead to violence, on the court or after the game."

Kenny goes on, "No one wants to come down here to be called Onion Head, or Buckwheat, or Hollow Man. This is not a comedy show; this is serious. That street talk may sound good to a small audience, but I'm not interested in a small audience."

Perhaps most important, the announcer is in the best position to control a game that may be getting out of hand. The referees can only do so much; they need support from the scorer's table and from the guy with the megaphone. If the announcer keeps things light he can deflate a nasty episode before it develops.

Dee will keep his commentary light for these exhibition games. He does not chatter away like a TV commentator. (Do we need three of them to watch a pro game?) Rather, he is simply an observant fan who knows the players and loves a good game. He is quiet much of the time, and he avoids jive talk, clichés, and blatant hype.

Today the first contest is between Chaz Hoops, coached by Chaz Dudley, and United Brooklyn, coached by Sid Jones.

When a guard new to the tournament playing with Chaz Hoops makes a quick crossover move to the basket, Dee hollers, "That's Joe, comin' at'cha with the one good move that got him picked up for this league."

A jump shot in the paint is violently rejected by a defensive center. "Ooooo! Get that outta here!" Dee exclaims. "When you take that kind of shot, man, you gotta jump *real* high."

A three-point attempt falls far short. "Ug-ly. NBA. Nothin' But Air."

Dee draws the fans' attention to the best players. He spots United Brooklyn setting up a clearout play for one of its premier guards, Duane Woodward. "Here's Duane settin' up against Shawn. . . . He's trying to make a name for himself down here, he knows this is West 4th Street. . . . Oooooo, with a good move to the hoop! Looks like this is goin' to be the matchup here today. . . . Goin' to be hard guardin' ma' man this summer."

He defuses tempers when the fouling gets rough. A hard charging foul is called in front of the scorer's table. "That's your third charging foul. Man, you got to have another speed. [Then with exaggerated slowness] You can't . . . just . . . have . . . full speed. . . . You've got . . . to have . . . a medium . . . and a slow. . . . You can't . . . just . . . be . . . fast."

When a defender who gets beat hacks the shooter artlessly, Dee reacts sympathetically: "He's givin' ya the roughhouse, Keshawn.

Looks like he been playin' up north—at Elmira." (Elmira is the location of a New York State reformatory.)

Late in the game a new, young player loses his temper and curses at the ref over a call. Dee jumps in quickly. "That's a tech, my friend. Welcome to West 4th Street. You've just been branded." The player stands around, not reacting, apparently dazed by the call, so Dee explains it. "Techs are fifteen dollars here, and you don't go back into the game until it is paid."

Dee encourages the older players. Curtis Burnes makes a good block of a layup. "CB been in the league fifteen years. You not goin' dunk on him like that."

He follows one of his favorite players, United Brooklyn's John Thomas, whom today he has decided to call Spider-Man because he seems to be everywhere at once. "That's Spider-Man takin' a shot . . . he misses it. . . . Look at him gettin' back on defense, though! That's my kinda guy. You take a bad shot, you got to be the first one back on defense. That's how I coach. You keep an eye on number twenty-four. This Spider-Man goin' to be big this summer."

Dee brings the staff into the game too. By the second half, Moneybags has brought a small brown paper bag with him to his blackboard at midcourt, and he's taking regular swigs from the bottle inside. This causes him to fall behind on the score. Dee is on the lookout. "Hey, stay with me, Moneybags. The game is not tied. You got to follow this game, not the one you playin' in ya head." Moneybags has been caught at this before. Quickly he puts up the correct numbers.

Dee helps keep the crowd around the table in line as well. When a well-dressed woman, a friend of one of the players, can't find a seat, Dee reacts.

"The lady wants a seat, my man," he says to one of the men in this section. " You got to move." The man moves. "Thank you, man. We appreciate that." The threat of public humiliation reminds men not to forget their manners.

United Brooklyn wins the first game 99–87. On Sunday they play the winner of the second game, Nike One, to vie for the Tip-off Championship.

But this weekend United Brooklyn is not good enough, so Nike One, the defending champ, wins the weekend Tip-off Classic 83–80. The Cage's twenty-fifth season has begun.

# chapter two

# The Early Years

**Kenny first discovered West** 4th Street when he was barely out of his teens, just one more grocery delivery boy pedaling his bicycle around Greenwich Village making a living. He had two other jobs at the time.

At nineteen he had moved out of his family's apartment in the Fort Greene projects and into his own apartment on Jay Street in Brooklyn. Kenny had been working since he was twelve. "I always knew I would have to work to get money, so I always had jobs," he recalls. "I came from a family of nine children. If you didn't work, you didn't have money, and I loved to have money in my pocket. That was more important to me than playing basketball."

Kenny grew up loving basketball. He made the JV team in high school, and he remembers being fascinated by the midday and Saturday afternoon pickup games played in the Cage. "I played in pickup games with guys like Mike Williams and Ron Creth for three years in the mid-1970s before I started running the league. I didn't think of myself as a great basketball player. I thought of myself as an average player with good fundamental skills. Once I started the tournament in 1977, I never played in it."

Kenny's buddy Mike Williams remembers those days well. "As a player, Kenny wasn't great, but he was willing to hang, and he understood the fundamentals of the game. He was a very good defensive player. He had a funny-looking shot, but he could shoot. He wasn't one to try any trickery. Mostly he was tough, and don't let anyone fool you, he laid some of the best shots on people that I've ever seen. For a while I called him the Silent Assassin. When you needed somebody who wasn't afraid to be embarrassed to guard a really good player, he was your man. There were people who would come out there and try to be marquee players—they wanted to make a name here. Kenny was good with those guys; his strength was defense, and his mind was always working."

Kenny reflects on those days of twenty-five years ago with affection. They were the equivalent of college days for a city kid, because here he began to discover life away from the neighborhood.

In 1976 the Office of Neighborhood Services, a city agency, organized a regular youth league that would play games Thursday through Sunday at the West 4th Street Park. The agency paid only for the kids, but a self-supporting men's league sprouted up immediately. A park regular named Tex Barnwell organized a men's division, and Kenny picked up extra money by refereeing. Like many city tournaments, the men's league ran into trouble. In the middle of its first season Tex disappeared, along with the money that the players and coaches had kicked in to run the league. The teams completed their schedule, but it looked as if the tournament was finished.

The following spring the players began asking if the league could be revived, but no one wanted to take on the responsibility of organizing it. That's when Kenny and Mike Williams decided to give it a shot.

"Kenny was just born to step in. He always had a way about him. He was never flamboyant, but he would do things that other people would not do; he was much more of a risk taker than I was," Mike says today. "I think he was a natural leader, but his influence was subtle. For example, Kenny was always eating in McBell's, a bar just down the street on Sixth Avenue. Well, after a while we all wound up eating there.

"It soon became evident that we were friends and that we worked well together. He took over the tournament, but I supported him and helped out. I worked on scheduling, and I gave him all kinds of advice. Kenny knew that he could make a decision and I would always be with him, standing to his right, letting people know that this was the decision of all of us and it was going to stick."

Mike was a much better basketball player than Kenny. He had been an outstanding power forward at Ithaca College, and he was coaching professionally, first at Columbia, and then at Fordham University. Mike was older than Kenny and a bit more settled. As he put it, "I felt like I was Kenny's big brother. I loved to watch good basketball and I never wanted anything else from it. I am a basketball purist. I love the game and I want to see it played right."

The first thing Kenny and Mike did for the tournament was to bring in Sylvester Dobson to manage the officiating. Dobson was a well-dressed, good-hearted man who had devoted his life to becoming a professional referee. Unfortunately, the highest level he reached was to work some NBA games in the 1976 season when the regular refs went on strike. Nevertheless, Kenny and Mike held him in the highest regard. "He was always just a half step away from really making it," Williams recalls. "Dobson was wonderful for West 4th Street because no one wanted to referee at the tiny court, and he was able to get good refs to come down and work here."

For Kenny, taking over the league was a big step. He was asserting himself. He was seeking to establish his place in the street life of New York City. Mike saw this at the time.

"Plenty of guys were jealous of Kenny in those first years. I mean, here was a guy with no reputation running things. Everybody did not realize he was building his base all the time. He was active in the night scene. He would throw parties at clubs in the Village that were all-time greats. People still talk about them today, and the parties were always free to the players."

At the end of the season, over Labor Day weekend, Kenny would organize a trip to the Bahamas for twenty-five to thirty people. Everyone paid his own way, and needless to say, the parties and this travel helped to bring women down to the park. Kenny went on every trip. Part of the West 4th Street group evolved into a social club, and Kenny always welcomed women. Even today park etiquette requires that the dozen or so spectator seats are set up next to the scorer's table for the ladies. If a woman makes a habit of coming to games, the announcer with the battery-operated megaphone may call attention to her arrival.

Keep in mind that in New York City, every major summer tournament has been closed at least once during the past fifteen years. A riot at a rap concert and basketball game in which two people were killed almost closed the pro-am tournament at City College uptown. Shootings have occurred in Coney Island. Referees and visiting players have been threatened so much in Brooklyn that the better teams from the Bronx and Harlem stopped going there. The original Rucker tournament at 155th Street and Lexington Avenue in Harlem was shut down by outright stealing before Greg Marius revived it with the Entertainers Classic about ten years ago.

Bill Parker, who has been hanging out at the park with Kenny for thirty years, acknowledges that the presence of women helps to moderate the behavior of the men on the court.

"Because so many women were around the court, guys would rely on their skills in the game," he recalls. "The gladiator mentality was replaced by a game of finesse. The guys would wash their cars, and if you were in a feature game, you might even get a haircut. Remember,

West 4th Street was always a melting pot. People would come from New Jersey, Philadelphia, even Connecticut for big games."

Joe Merriweather, a director and longtime friend, looks back fondly on the league's beginnings.

"Those first ten years were wonderful ones for West 4th Street," he says. "The tournament was always interracial, and that distinguished it from many of the tournaments in the city. Most of the players had played in high school or college; they were not just street players. I remember the Homeboys from Bedford-Stuyvesant, a remarkable team back then. The White brothers organized the team. There were five brothers, and occasionally all of them would be on the court at the same time, playing together. That was impressive.

"The staff was dedicated too," Joe continues. "They took what they did very seriously. Iron Mike; Janice Carter, who ran the women's division; and Pete Simmons, who helped set the place up every day, were there from the beginning. People looked forward to coming down to the park after work. We couldn't print enough schedules."

The locals, who were mostly white professionals, soon lost playing control of their playground. Mike Williams explains that for the locals to get playing time on weekends, they had to get to the park early. Winners could always stay on the court for the next game, so the local guys would get to the park at the crack of dawn for pickup games.

Mike recalls, "These guys would be there at seven o'clock Saturday morning, and if they got a good group together they could stay on the court until noon, when the P.M. group arrived.

"The P.M. group was made up of the players that finally woke up around ten or eleven A.M. and wanted to go play some good basketball, so they came down to the park. You know," Mike says with a sigh, "the A.M. group just wasn't good enough. So the P.M. group took over. One thing that was unique was that there were many professionals— lawyers, doctors, and teachers—in the early years that would sneak down to West 4th Street to be part of the A.M. group. Then they'd turn around and be spectators of the P.M. group. The park was very integrated back then, probably more than it is now."

## The Influence of the American Basketball Association

While West 4th Street was becoming a center of basketball life in the city, the game itself was going through a temperamental and stylistic renaissance. The driver of this rebirth was the upstart American Basketball Association, which began play in 1967 and stayed alive until 1976, after which the NBA absorbed its strongest teams and best players. The ABA had Hall of Fame talent like Julius Erving, Moses Malone, Rick Barry, Artis Gilmore, George Gervin, Larry Brown, Billy Cunningham, David Thompson, Spencer Haywood, and Connie Hawkins. The league's first commissioner was George Mikan, the star center of the early Minneapolis Lakers. The founding principle of the ABA was that the twelve-team NBA was too small and restrictive. Basketball had grown into too big a game, with too many underutilized players unable to find a place to play and be seen.

The eleven-team ABA challenged the NBA's style. It introduced the three-point shot and the slam dunk contest, and by moving the ball up the court more quickly, the teams produced more scoring. Team scores of 120 points were common, and 140 points was not unheard of. Although the ABA thrived on whatever was spectacular, its players had grown up learning solid fundamentals, so they were equally capable of hard-nosed defense. Hubie Brown, a successful coach in both leagues, points out, "We used pressing and trapping defenses, something you never saw in the NBA. About everything we did in the ABA they do now in the NBA, except they didn't take our red-white-and-blue ball."

Everyone in the ABA had a nickname. In addition to the incomparable Dr. J, there was the coach of the Indiana Pacers, Slick Leonard, and players like Fatty Taylor, Bad News Barnes, Ice Gervin, and Magnolia Mouth McCarthy, who seemed to have lost their first names entirely.

Much less basketball was on television then. The ABA had no TV contract, and the NBA was pretty much limited to Sunday afternoons. Street basketball was a local event, a pleasure appreciated by those who made the trip down to the park to see what the buzz was about.

The same innovations that were going on in the ABA game were happening in big-city parks as well. The playgrounds and the ABA were both underdogs, and together they helped to make the game itself better and more popular. They showcased the players the big colleges and the NBA ignored, and they fought for wider recognition of a game they knew was underrated. The spirit of the playgrounds and the ABA built today's global basketball empire.

Al Bianchi, the coach of the Virginia Squires, recalls that the ABA had become particularly adept at finding talent where the NBA would not look, such as in high schools and junior colleges. "In Virginia we developed a track record of finding pretty good players no one knew about, like Julius Erving and George Gervin," he says. "The NBA started drafting people we had taken, figuring that maybe we knew something. So we would draft guys we knew couldn't play just to see if they would take them, and sure enough, some of those names would show up on an NBA draft list and we'd just laugh."

Almost by default West 4th Street became a developmental league for professional basketball camps, for scouts of European teams, for the Eastern League, for the Continental League, for the newly formed ABA, and even for the NBA. College coaches came by looking for promising freshmen. The NCAA never sanctioned the league, but top college players came anyway, playing under an alias to preserve their eligibility. If you wanted to be noticed, West 4th Street was the place to be.

## The Early Teams

Kenny started the men's league with sixteen teams and the entry fee was $150, which covered shirts, miscellaneous league equipment, and trophies. He recalls, "You could run the league very cheaply then. Shirts were only four dollars. It was not a money thing. The next year, 1978, I decided to name the league the West 4th Street Pro-Classic. The league drew great players right from the start; we had the top players in the area, and a number of pros. The pickup games in the 1960s and early 1970s had enough players on their own to supply a full league." With so much talent around, the tournament quickly expanded to twenty-four teams, and games were played seven days a week.

Dynasties soon emerged. In 1978 the first of the great Harlem USA teams, coached by Bill Motley, won the championship. No team better combined talent with balanced team play. Motley's gang included Leroy Shaw (drafted by the Knicks), Mike Henderson (Harlem Globetrotters, and now an NBA referee), Chris Seace (Syracuse), Marvin Stevenson (University of Massachusetts), Joe Thomas (University of Georgia), Clark Elie (CCNY), and his younger brother, Mario. Mario was a high school standout at Power Memorial, where he teamed up with Chris Mullin. Milwaukee selected him in the seventh round of the draft in 1985, but he was promptly cut. Until he was picked up five years later, Mario played wherever he could, including summer leagues in the city. From 1990 to 2002 he played in the NBA, his longest run being with the Houston Rockets.

Harlem USA combined the two best teams in Harlem. Bill Motley was running a summer tournament in Central Park, and his own entry in that tournament, a team of veterans, was the regular champion. But one summer a new team of younger players, organized by Clark and Mario Elie, almost upset them in the finals. Motley saw that the future lay with these younger players, so he simply combined the best of both teams and entered them in the West 4th Street tournament the following summer. A few years later, when Motley added Sam Worthen, the best player from the Bedford-Stuyvesant section of Brooklyn, his team became invincible.

Clark Elie places Sam Worthen, who had a brilliant career at Marquette and was the second-round draft pick of the Chicago Bulls in 1980, in that category of brilliant playground and college players who, mysteriously, never clicked in the NBA. "I first saw Sam when he was playing with Boys and Girls High School, and I could tell that boy had talent. Then he just grew more," Clark recalls. "He played in a high school all-star game when he was a sophomore. He was about six foot two then, and I'll tell you, he stole the show. He was palming the ball, dribbling behind his back, dunkin' on guys—I mean that boy had skills. Then he kept getting bigger, eventually reaching six foot six and weighing over two hundred pounds.

"I think in his senior year at Marquette he was the best guard in the country. I've seen him drop forty-seven points, thirty of them from down low. The only thing that hurt his game was that he didn't have a twenty-foot jump shot." Clark thinks the company Sam kept upset Chicago management. "He had some bad people around him comin' out of Bedford-Stuyvesant. Those guys would smoke up the world. One of his best friends was a guy they called Water Bug, who'd start smokin' the minute he got up. Sam was not carrying himself right by hanging around with those guys."

Harlem USA won eight championships in eleven years: 1978, 1979, 1980, 1982, 1985, 1986, 1987, and 1988. Harlem's style was simple and beautiful to watch. No team had better mastery of the Cage. They used the fences and the physical configuration of the court as a sixth man. At crunch time Mario Elie and Sam Worthen figured a way to force opponents into the fence—out of bounds and a turnover. Meanwhile, they kept their own offensive play in the middle of the court. They emphasized team basketball. They knew the importance of powerful rebounders, and everyone on the team was a good defensive player. No one got easy shots off Harlem, and fast breaks against them were rare. Point guard Clark Elie and Worthen—a brilliant passer—kept everyone in the game.

The teams they had to beat were tough and talented. Les Pines's Village Mustangs had played as a team even before the league was formed. There was Lloyd Adams, a six-foot-ten player and coach, who named his team the Adams Family. His players came primarily from the Bronx. The Crew, organized by Bill Brady, came from the Farragut Housing projects and Bedford-Stuyvesant in Brooklyn. Segarra's Five was another strong team that made it to the finals in 1981. Arnoldo Segarra himself was from the Village, but his players were from all over the city; the legendary Joe Hammond from Harlem played with him for a few years. Darryl Strickland, his big man, was a star for Essex County Community College. He was probably the best player in the Jersey Junior College system at the time. Johnny Dean, the most spectacular of the early leapers, also played with Segarra.

Doris Green, a woman from New Jersey, brought in the New Jersey Blazers, with Nate and Jeff Granger, Gary Taylor, Jo-Jo Walters, and Beno Cook. This was another physically powerful team that played a methodical, careful game. After Harlem USA they were the strongest team in the league, taking the championship in 1981, 1983, and 1984.

Kenny's Kings, the team that was the subject of the movie *Soul in the Hole* (1997), was in the tournament. Kenny Jones attracted some of the best Brooklyn playground stars, including the legendary Booger Smith and Charles Jones (LIU), who is still a top playground player. But Kenny's Kings could not do well outside of Brooklyn. "I don't think they ever won a playoff game here," Kenny Graham recalls.

In the 1980s new franchises were forming. Bo Keene built a championship-caliber team by dominating the talent in Brownsville, a crime-ridden but basketball-rich neighborhood in Brooklyn. Sid Jones brought in a team he called United Brooklyn, because players came from all over the borough. Eugene Downs got to the finals with the Infocomp Raiders, and his best player, Doug Herring, came down from Schenectady, New York. Herring still brings a team down from Schenectady to play.

While Marty's Crew was officially from Staten Island, his roster included perhaps the highest-scoring pair of guards in the tournament's history, Pete Edwards from Queens and Curtis Sumpter from

Brooklyn. Roland Rooks, a longtime referee at West 4th Street, says Curtis was the best player he ever saw at the park. "There is no way he should not have played in the NBA," Roland says. Adds his running mate, Pete Edwards, "He was simply unstoppable. No one could control his offense." Curtis's son is playing at Villanova, having completed a superb high school career at Bishop Loughlin in Brooklyn. Pete Edwards was a better balanced player than Curtis because he was excellent on defense and he could function as a point guard as well as a shooter. Today Pete runs a year-round high school program in Queens, known as IS 8, which draws the best players from anywhere near New York City.

Kevin Dunleavy, brother of NBA player and coach Mike Dunleavy, entered a strong team after he graduated from the University of South Carolina in 1981. His lineup of predominantly white players included Jerry Hobby (Fordham), Dan Calendrillo (Seton Hall), Frank Gigliardi (Stone Hill), Bill Baino (U Mass, UNLV), Billy Rose, Brandt Johnson (Williams College), and Mike Doyle (USC). "We were all friends and we all had good day jobs," Dunleavy says today. "West 4th Street provided great competition, and you knew the games would be safe and clean. After the games our girlfriends and wives would join us and we would go to a pub down the street, Boxers, and have a burger and a beer. We could play, have fun, and wake up the next day and go to work."

Dunleavy's team generally made the playoffs, but it never won a championship. This in itself tells you something about the league's competitiveness. Clark Elie remembers well Harlem's games against Dunleavy's team. "They would always try to 'fundamental' us to death. They were good jump shooters, they spread the court, and they used lots of screens and backdoor passes. They were very good, but as a rule, I think we prevailed."

The most popular and glamorous team of the late 1980s—a team that never did win the championship—was Vice Squad, which got its name from the popular TV show *Miami Vice*. The team was coached for a while by Kenny's old friend Ron Creth, and it was led by six-foot-nine inch center Alex Roberts (Saint Peter's) and three brilliant guards. Darryl MacDonald (Texas A&M) was the quickest and most colorful passer and shooter. He got a tryout with the New Jersey Nets but he didn't stick. Tony Sherman, who never played in high school or college, was the best defensive player and the team's assist leader. The third guard, Gerald Thomas, known only as Doogie, never said anything to anyone—which is why no one in the park ever knew his real name—but he would quietly score 20 to 30 points a game. Many claim he was the best clear-out, one-on-one player who ever played at West 4th Street. He is still playing on weekends uptown in a forty-and-over league, and on those rare occasions when he returns to the park, he is recognized as a returning hero.

All during this time established collegiate and NBA players would drop by for a game or two during the regular season. Earl "The Pearl" Monroe (New Jersey Nets, Miami Heat), Sidney Green (UNLV), Phil Sellers (Rutgers, Detroit Pistons), Reggie Carter (St. John's), Tracy Jackson (Chicago Bulls), Charlie Yelverton (Portland Trailblazers), Hawthorne Wingo (New York Knicks), Jayson Williams (Philadelphia 76ers and New Jersey Nets), Scooter Barry (son of Rick Barry, Kansas), Lloyd Daniels (San Antonio Spurs), Kelly Tripucka (Detroit Pistons), Rod Strickland (New York Knicks, San Antonio Spurs, Portland Trailblazers), and Fly Williams (Austin Peay, Spirits of St. Louis, ABA) all played at West 4th Street.

Kenny admits that the talent level is not as high today. "Few men playing now would make my top fifty players over twenty-five years," he says. "Athletically they are great. They work out in gyms, and they look terrific. But they don't have the same basketball sense. They don't understand team play. A tradition was established by those early players—Lorenzo Charles and Rod Strickland. They paved the way for those who are here now."

In 1990 a new powerhouse was built on the talents of an apparently washed-up college player no NBA team would look at—Anthony

Mason from Queens. His team, Prime Time, had three outstanding guards: Elmer Anderson (St. Bonaventure), Tony Hargraves (Iona), and Vernon Moore (Creighton). All played at a professional level, and for a few years they were joined by Pete Edwards. Prime Time had a good coach, James Ryans, now a Knicks scout, who led them to championships in 1990, 1991, and 1992.

The style of play became much rougher during those years, and for Kenny this meant that he had to stay personally involved. As Dunleavy recalls: "In the late eighties and early nineties playing in the park was getting dangerous. It was borderline. Anthony Mason, before he caught on with the NBA, was at the park, and in the NBA you had the Pistons with 'The Bruise Brothers,' Bill Lambeer and Rick Mahorn. The tone was rough generally."

By the 1980s Kenny had brought to this tiny court at West 4th Street a tournament that was well organized and orderly and attracted the best coaches and players from all over the city. Fans from all parts of the city soon followed. Professional scouts from Europe would introduce themselves to Kenny and ask his advice about promising players. A youth team from France and another from Seattle came to play exhibition games each summer. The occasional visits of NBA players added glamour and excitement, and the fence was always packed with spectators. Everyone knew everyone else. It was family.

The principal beneficiaries of Kenny's labors have been the players. Some who fail to get picked up after college do eventually make it to the professional ranks. This happened with Anthony Mason, who played at the Cage for four years before he got his big break with the Knicks in 1991, and with Mario Elie, who spent summers after college at West 4th Street before he was signed by the Golden State Warriors in 1990.

The tournament does even more for those who don't make it to the big time. It gives them a chance to be seen and be appreciated outside their neighborhoods. In the final moments of the marvelous movie *Hoop Dreams* (1994), the high school hero, William, reflects on all the people who've asked him, "Will you still remember me when you are a big star in the NBA?" William then replies, "I should have asked them, 'Will you still remember me if I'm not?'"

The tournament's most glamorous years were the 1980s, and this was a high point in Kenny's life too. He was the center of everything. In addition to West 4th Street, he was running a popular winter league, which kept him involved all year. If you played serious basketball in New York City, you had to know Kenny. He was an important person to the city's best athletes.

At the same time, Kenny had two jobs and he was making good money at both. He drove his taxi during the day and worked at a print shop four nights a week. He took some money out of his tournaments. The taxi medallion that he owned increased in value every year. He owned his own apartment, which had doubled in value since he picked it up at the insider's price. Banks were sending him credit cards monthly, and he was not shy about using them, so he always had cash available. Every year he bought a new Cadillac. By the time he was thirty years old, Kenny had created an empire.

# chapter three

# Brownsville Arrives:
# Game One

**Sunday afternoon West 4th** Street plays three games, but Brownsville often gets the featured time slot at 4:00 P.M. Indeed, if any single team can be said to epitomize the toughness and diversity of the Cage, it is Brownsville. They have been coming here for over twenty years, and the coach, Charles "Bo" Keene, is one of the tournament's best-known characters. Today they play a new team in the league, Westchester Hoops, with Rock Bunce, a three-time slam dunk champion, and Virgil Smith, one of the league's standout guards in the early nineties.

Bo's team is to West 4th Street what the Detroit Pistons of the early 1990s were to the NBA. Detroit had great talent and they were physical. Tough guys Rick Mahorn and Bill Lambeer would clear the way for the Pistons' finesse players, Isiah Thomas and Kelly Tripucka. Brownsville has bruisers like Hassan Duncombe, Darryl Glenn, and Mo Les (his real name is Lester Barrows, though no one at the park ever uses it), along with its brilliant shooters, Wayne Freeman and Lloyd

Daniels. Bo is proud to have established himself as their leader.

Kenny is seated in his director's chair, relaxed and seemingly unconcerned with the activity going on around him. As long as things move smoothly, he will have little to say. Like everyone else, he hopes to enjoy a nice afternoon.

Rick Johnson, the number two man here today, is chatting with Antonio Brimmer, Nike's league representative. Joe Merriweather introduces Kenny to a parks department representative who is visiting. Relations with the city are delicate, and Kenny gives his guest six West 4th Street T-shirts.

Rosy Jackson is seated next to Kenny, leaning back and relaxed in his director's chair. He's wearing shorts, sneakers, and the latest West 4th Street T-shirt; he never dresses up. Rosy's official job as a tournament director is to keep track of uniforms and equipment, but he is probably Kenny's most consistently supportive friend. He is prudent and cautious, a man of few words. He has a good job, owns income-producing real estate, and owns his home in Yonkers. He, like the other directors, drives a Cadillac.

Rosy often acts as if he were Kenny's personal banker. He pulls money from his pocket to handle tournament expenses, like paying the staff, buying supplies, or settling with a referee when one of the teams comes without money. If he thinks a person wants what is best for Kenny and the league, he will do anything. He is impatient with people he thinks are freeloaders, or with men who don't work and then complain about being broke. Rosy is the opposite of talk; he is a guy who gets things done.

Most people are at the park because it is a nice summer afternoon and they want to watch a good basketball game. Rebekah arrives just before the game begins and says hello to Rick, Joe, and Rosy. Kenny, who remembers her from the previous weekend, greets her with a kiss on the cheek.

Moneybags does not make it today, so Isaiah Jackson will take over the scoreboard at midcourt. Generally Isaiah sweeps up and helps set up the tables and chairs for each game, but he can do most anything. He's a medical miracle. He has been one of the regular workers at Kenny's tournament for twenty-one years, but for the last fourteen years he has been living on dialysis. According to the odds, he should not have made it this long; clearly his days are numbered. Isaiah has a grown daughter, but he lives by himself in the Bronx (though he proudly points out that he was born in Brooklyn). He undergoes a three-hour blood transfusion every Tuesday, Thursday, and Saturday. This is a torturous existence. Isaiah has to watch what he eats, and his energy level is erratic. For years he was compensated for his work at the park with free food at McDonald's, or with nothing at all except some sneakers and T-shirts. Now he gets $10 a day. He is a quiet, gracious man.

Brownsville, where Bo Keene gets his players, is a forty-minute subway ride away from West 4th Street, but in many ways it might as well be in another country. The once-proud home of Jewish and Italian immigrants—the great Knickerbocker player and coach Red Holzman grew up there, as did composer Aaron Copland and comedian Danny Kaye—Brownsville now claims Mike Tyson as its most famous alumnus.

The emigration began in the 1950s. The Dodgers abandoned Brooklyn in 1957, and local breweries Rheingold and Schaefer shut down soon after. Over the last thirty years, Brownsville's population has declined by over one third and real estate values have plunged. With the exodus of a politically active and rising middle class, public and private services left too. Today few private-sector jobs exist, so by default, the city bureaucracy is a major employer of those who do work. Now the neighborhood is almost entirely black and Hispanic. Over 40 percent of residents are on public assistance, and 13 percent of the land is vacant. Drug lords and teenage gangs took over in the mideighties and Brownsville became a center of violent crime and crack dealers, rivaled only by nearby Bedford-Stuyvesant. Brownsville was more than bad—it was vicious and defiant. Nobody visited

Brownsville without good reason. The neighborhood was out of control.

Its sidewalks remain cracked and ragged, litter and junk are a monotonous and depressing eyesore, and good restaurants, so common throughout most of New York, have vanished. No major supermarket chain will serve this community of eighty-five thousand.

The great hope of the neighborhood lies in two homegrown institutions: the Christian Cultural Center (CCC) and the Brownsville Recreation Center (BRC). The CCC grew up in neighboring East New York and had an enormous impact on the community. It has over fifteen thousand members, and five thousand attend each of its two huge religious services on Sunday. The church has an athletic program, a prep school, and meetings every weeknight. During the 2002 season it entered a team in the West 4th Street tournament for the first time.

Equally important is the BRC, run by Greg Jackson, once a guard for the New York Knicks and the Phoenix Suns. Greg was another of those phenomenal college and playground players who mysteriously did not stick for long in the NBA. "It made no sense to me that Jocko didn't play longer in the NBA," Pete Edwards remarks today. "I'll tell you, he was a load; when he hit you, he hit you with power. And in those days he could jump out the building. He was also a very smart player. Makes no sense to me."

Youth programs are important because over one third of Brownsville's population is under eighteen years of age. This explains, in part, why gangs can run the community—in terms of numbers, they *are* the community. In order for a youth program to succeed, its leaders must be just as tough and determined as the gang leaders.

The centerpiece of the recreation center is basketball, Brownsville's game. Basketball connects Brownsville to Kenny Graham and to West 4th Street in the Village.

A handful of Brownsville alumni come here today, the most prominent of whom is Lloyd Daniels, a New York high school great who played for Brownsville at West 4th Street in the 1990s. Daniels would have played at UNLV for Jerry Tarkanian in 1987 had he not been caught buying drugs and been ensnarled in recruiting violations. Daniels got Tarkanian and the school in trouble (three years probation for UNLV by the NCAA), and his own college career was wrecked. After being disqualified from college basketball, Daniels got involved in a conflict that resulted in his being shot in the chest.

Daniels overcame these obstacles. Without college or an NBA deal, Lloyd played everywhere he could, including the U.S. Basketball League, where he became an assist leader, not a scoring leader. Some West 4th Street regulars claim he was the best passer ever to play at the park. Tarkanian remained faithful, and as the head coach for the San Antonio Spurs, he got Lloyd a tryout with the team in 1992. Daniels had a reasonable NBA career playing with five different teams over a five-year period, although he was never the superstar in the pros that he had been in high school and at the parks. At thirty-six, Lloyd still lives for basketball. He's playing with Trenton in the little-known International Basketball League. He rarely gets back to Brownsville or the park; Bo is proud of Lloyd.

Also here from Brownsville is Darryl Glenn, forty years old, the father of two, and a conscientious family man. He works two jobs, and along with Greg Jackson, he is the heart and soul of the Brownsville Recreation Center. He works at the BRC every week-night and on weekends. Five days a week he is the head custodian for the Bushwick District office of the board of education. Not too long ago he was the toughest defensive player on the toughest team in the tournament: the 1996 championship team from Brownsville.

If an award existed for the West 4th Street alumnus who gave the most back to his community, Glenn might win it every year. He sets a fine example, he counsels kids tirelessly, and his boss Greg Jackson says he runs the best youth clinic in the city every Saturday morning. He no longer has time for West 4th Street, but he played with Bo for over a decade, and Glenn never forgets a friend.

West 4th Street was also a home for Fly Williams, another eccentric playground hero of the 1970s. Fly was the third-highest scorer in the nation when he played for Austin Peay University in 1973–74, and a star, briefly, in the ABA. Fly looks great at fifty-three. He plays competitively on Fridays at the BRC with other retired professionals, including Greg Jackson and World B. Free.

"If the other guys who show up aren't that good, we just play one-on-one," he says. Fly is charming and he loves knowing that all eyes are on him. Like the others with him, he is showing his respect for Bo Keene, his Brownsville neighbor, who kept his team going for nearly twenty years.

The New Jersey Nets are hosting the Lakers for game three of their NBA final tonight at the Meadowlands, and to hype the series back home the ABC-TV affiliate from Los Angeles has sent a film crew to interview West 4th Street fans about the Lakers-Nets playoff game. Dee Foreman, who lives in Brownsville, is on the megaphone announcing the game, and he points Fly out to the crowd. "My main man Fly Williams is in the house," he bellows. "He's a legend out here, and if you've never seen him play, you've missed somethin'. That's a ballplayer right there. He could take his man after he tol' him exactly what he'd be doin'. Yeah, he'll score fifty points and walk off the court mad 'cause he didn't get the ball enough."

The big-time TV guys don't get the hint and they ignore Fly. Instead they rely on their own instincts and approach a surly regular with a baseball cap on backward who rudely pushes their mike away and growls, "I don't want to talk to no camera guys. Go 'way." Shocked by this reproach, the cameraman quickly backs off. Dee lightens the atmosphere and consoles the visitors: "Don't be offended," he announces. "Lots of these guys are on parole, so they don't want no cameras."

When it comes to basketball, Fly is a nonstop talking machine. He is full of opinions.

"The Nets are gettin' a steady diet of Shaq, and he's too much. Lakers will win it in four straight," he predicts confidently. (They did.) Is Byron Scott experienced enough to handle his team in an NBA final? "C'mon. A problem? Byron should be coach of the year. You know that. He won a championship with a bunch of kids."

Bo Keene's Brownsville team is slow getting to the park, so the game starts late, when Bo finally gets five guys. These are not his best five, and they are disorganized and seem to lack the defensive fire of past Brownsville teams. They haven't played together recently, and one of the starters, Mo Les, is thirty-nine years old and out of breath early. At the end of the first quarter, they are down 21–14. No one is playing well, and Dee gets on them. After a blown fast break he blasts, "If you guys could make a few layups, we'd have a good game here."

When a game is sloppy, Dee keeps chatting away, a diversionary tactic. "My name is Dee, and I'll be with you the rest of the afternoon. If you want schedules, come to the scorer's table. We got water. And we got fine women, married women, I must remind you. We hope you enjoy the game. Ladies, if you need seats, we got 'em right here in front." Dee picks up on the good play of one of Brownsville's young players, Rodney Stiles.

"Look at Rodney playin' out there. He grew up in Brownsville and we used to call him Shorty. Now he's grown up. Just look at him out there with the big dogs." Fly Williams has noticed Rodney's play. He says to the man standing next to him, "Bo could be in this game. He's got to spread the court more and isolate the young guy [Rodney]. He's a slasher. He'll get to the hoop."

From a year of having players hang from them, the basketball rims here are bent down badly. Nike bought two new rims for the park, but the city has to install them, and the city is in no rush to do this. Dee can't avoid noticing the problem.

"I know we got funny-lookin' rims out there. But we're goin' to have real rims at the end of the season—if we're lucky."

## Bo Keene

Bo Keene is a forbidding physical presence in the Cage. While everyone knows he was once a big man in "the street game," Bo will not volunteer any details. Nevertheless, if one asks around the BRC, this is what the men there have to say:

Bo came from an orderly, religious Brownsville family, and he was a good high school basketball player at Thomas Jefferson High School. Because he slacked off in school he had to go to summer school to complete his diploma. In September of 1974, he left home to attend tiny Ferrum Junior College in western Virginia, where he hoped to continue his basketball career. He left for Ferrum in the summer of 1974, but soon after he arrived at Ferrum, Corlett, the girl he was dating, delivered a baby daughter, Shadell. Bo knew that he had to take care of his daughter, so he left college in January and took a job in the stockroom at Bonwit Teller.

A few years later he met another woman, Joyce, whom he married in 1977. Hoping to improve his chances on the job market, Bo left Bonwit's to attend Kingsboro Community College and to work part-time. There, some friends told him how to qualify for public assistance to help support his wife and daughter. But welfare and part-time work did not bring in enough money, so around Christmastime in 1977 Bo and a couple of friends got into the stickup game, mostly on Long Island. The men were armed, they scared their victims half to death, and they took only cash. No one was ever hurt. Inevitably, Bo was picked up by the police, but at this point there was not sufficient evidence to prosecute, so he was let off. But Bo was now on the police's watch list, so he realized that he could not continue. He began to look for other ways to make some money, but he was not yet ready for the straight life.

As a tough guy who was not a user, Bo was quickly spotted by a local drug dealer and offered a job working security. The dealer's name was Sha-Sha, and for the next three years Bo was paid $700 a week to protect key locations. To make detection more difficult, dealers never used their real names, nor did they use the real names of the people they worked with. Bo's job was to make sure no other dealer moved in on Sha-Sha's territory, and to warn him if he was being watched. Sha-Sha had half a dozen guys doing the same thing

Bo was doing in different parts of Brooklyn, and during this phase of his life, Bo was always armed.

Financially, these were good times for Bo. He collected welfare and he was learning a trade that he had a knack for. People say that Bo came to love Sha-Sha, as did most of the other runners and dealers who worked for him. When Bo's brother died, Sha-Sha bought Bo an expensive suit and new shoes so he would look right at the funeral. But their business relationship deteriorated when it became evident that Sha-Sha was acquiring a serious coke habit himself. Bo felt he could no longer trust him. The way the story is told, in an emotionally charged confrontation, Bo told Sha-Sha that he was leaving him. He put his .45 semi on the ground at the dealer's feet and walked away.

It was the winter of 1980 and Bo didn't have a job. But he had built a reputation in the Brooklyn drug community, so another supplier, known as Cookie, asked Bo if he wanted to work with him. Bo agreed, but after six months Bo realized that once again something was going wrong. Bo was getting his coke from a man called Ray, who was also one of Cookie's street workers. But while Bo would take seven or eight days to unload his supply, Ray was selling the same quantity of drugs in two or three days. At first Bo assumed he needed more experience and more contacts, but then one of his drug users told him his partner was cutting his coke. When his customers figured this out, they only came to Bo as a last resort.

Once again Bo was out on his own. Not surprisingly, Bo was able to get set up in business again, but this time there would be no more partners; Bo would run his own operation on the streets. Bo started with $200 to $300 in cocaine on consignment. He learned the mechanics of checking the cocaine's quality and putting it together for sale. One of the street survival rules is to starve yourself for the first few months so that you have emergency money. You never want to be desperate for a sale or panic when the cops make business impossible. People say Bo starved himself for those first months, and after that, he always had cash.

Over the years he developed his own street names. In one neighbor-hood in Brownsville he was known as Son. In another area he was Leader One. In East New York he was Juice. "When Bo started out on his own he had only himself, his .38, and the nearby Dumpster where he kept his stuff," according to one old friend. "After that, he had to live by his wits. And Bo was good at it."

Bo had as many as fifty people working for him at the peak of his business, and he often picked up men who were on the level but were locked out of straight society. One such worker was a poor, older man named Billy, whom Bo met around Christmastime. Bo has always been very sentimental about Christmas, and he knew that as an ex-convict, Billy was going to have a hard time ever getting a decent job. So Bo offered him money to be a security man for him—the same job Bo himself had been offered years before. Bo's new employee was faithful to the task. Bo paid him well, and Billy worked for Bo until he died.

By the mid-1980s Bo had become a big man in Brownsville. People say his daily handle was more than $25,000, a huge amount of cash. He worked only five days a week, just like a corporate executive. He was often lavish in rewarding those who worked for him, as well as those who played on his basketball teams. They flew on all-expenses-paid vacations to California, Florida, and the Bahamas. Bo was never stingy with money, which may be one reason why no one ever ratted on him or tried to turn him in.

Bo never got over his special soft spot for kids at Christmas. During the Christmas season of 1988, his standing in his housing project reached legendary proportions. One December afternoon he got his drug runners to assemble all the kids in the Noble Drew Ali projects in the central courtyard. The same guys were carrying base-ball bats to keep grown-ups away from the kids. Then, standing on the roof of one of the buildings, Bo dumped $18,000 in singles from four huge garbage bags down into the housing project. The kids could collect all they wanted. There was so much money flying around that Bo had to get his guys to round up bundles that totaled

$200 to $300 of unclaimed money. Then Bo and his buddies took the kids shopping on Belmont Street in Brownsville. "It was wild," one guy told me. "Three days after the event, we were hearing about it from guys who were in jail up in Albany. Word traveled that fast. No one will forget Bo for that stunt."

Unfortunately the track Bo was on was too fast for his wife, Joyce, who left in 1994. Bo was away too much and Joyce was never sure where he was. When he was home he was constantly on the phone. When she left, Bo was very upset. At the same time, he began to see other dealers getting locked up or shot. "There are plenty of guys richer than Bo," one BRC regular said, "but they are locked up for twenty years, so I don't know if they'll ever get to spend their money." Along with a New York City police crackdown on drugs, the Black Muslims were also fed up with the drug culture running the neighborhood, and they pressured Bo and people like him. Bo came close to getting locked up himself. His men were being followed and New York City detectives were quizzing family members. The net was tightening. Bo felt the heat, and as abruptly as he began his business, he quit. The weapons disappeared and Bo got off the streets for good.

Few things are tougher for a man than to be cut down financially in middle age. Misfortunes like this can lead to depression and violent, unsettled lives. One recent evening Bo was having a pregame drink at the private club in Madison Square Garden when a good-looking black girl in a low-cut blouse breezed in and noisily began ordering an expensive fruit drink. For an instant her eye caught Bo's. Bo shook his head and said quietly to the guy he was with, "In my street days she would be over here right now. She's a player. . . . Yeah, there are many times when I miss my money."

## The Game

For Bo's team the second quarter is worse than the first, so at the half Brownsville is down 41–28. But off the court, good things are happening. Brownsville's regulars are showing up. Keith Stroud and

Basketball Bob Washington, both of whom played on Brownsville's championship team, have arrived and are ready to play. Most important is the arrival of Greg Springfield, a lanky six-foot-seven forward who was a star here back in the late 1980s with Segarra's Five. His hair is flecked with gray, but he can still play. By the beginning of the second half Brownsville has ten men ready to run.

Bo has a good understanding of how to rotate his players in and out of the game. When Springfield arrives, Bo puts him in and keeps him on the court. Greg blocks shots, grabs rebounds at both ends, makes his tip-ins, and has a settling effect on the other players. He doesn't need the ball all the time to be effective. He draws fouls and makes his foul shots. He doesn't say anything, but the rest of the team wants to fit into his game. Brownsville's defense tightens up, and with two minutes left in the third quarter it has become a 10-point game. Then Springfield scores on a fast break, and Rodney steals the in-bounds pass and gets the ball back to Springfield, who stuffs it. The quarter ends with Brownsville down 51–49; they have held Westchester to 8 points in the period.

Dee is revved up. "Welcome to West 4th Street," he shouts. "Westchester came out here with a lot of energy, but this is a forty-eight-minute game. Brownsville with some defense has come back. I tell you, these guys play to the end. Greg Springfield is makin' the difference. He's makin' great decisions and he's changin' the game."

Between periods Bo takes one of his younger players, who has been lax on defense, off to the side. Bo holds the man's arm, puts his mouth inches from his ear, and in a snarling, ferocious whisper he says, "You actin' like you the underdog. You're *never* the underdog. You got six fouls to give, so use 'em. Show 'em how you feel."

Brownsville takes control in the last period, though Westchester has collected itself and is scoring again. But Westchester misses some key foul shots in the last three minutes. Brownsville is substituting freely, keeping fresh legs on the court, and the outcome is no longer in doubt. Keith Stroud, who is usually in the game at crunch time, is fully dressed in his street clothes with five minutes left. He knows he will not be needed. Brownsville wins 70–63. The horn sounds ending the game, and Dee announces, "It's a wrap." Bo is unhappy that so many of his players came late, and he says he has recruited three or four more good players for next week. The game was not a brilliant victory, but it was a good start.

When the West 4th Street tournament ends at nightfall, Kenny will still be here, making sure all the trash is swept up, the banners are taken down, and the chairs and furniture are put away. He will quietly hand out ten-dollar bills to eight or ten people who helped. The money he gives them comes from the entry fees he has received. If the money runs out, Kenny will not be able to pay these people, but they will come just the same. Given the effect money has on people, this is remarkable. Institutions can be abruptly abandoned when the cash stops coming. But everyone understands Kenny's way, and they trust him. As he explains it, "When I have the money, I give it to people who are here day in and day out. If I don't have the money, they will just have to understand."

# chapter four

# Father's Day at West 4th Street

**Iron Mike has always** argued that no games should be held at West 4th Street on Father's Day. Since Mike is the guy who puts up the American flag and has more than a dozen grandchildren, one might want to say that he is an exception to the rule. Everyone knows the cliché about black fatherhood. But at West 4th Street he is not the exception. Bo Keene doesn't want to play today, and Mark Figueroa, whose Nike One team is scheduled to play after the Brownsville game, starts bitching at Kenny as soon as he walks into the Cage.

"Kenny," he pleads, "this is the third year in a row you've scheduled me on Father's Day. I always lose on this weekend. You know that. Junie is doin' a barbecue in Brownsville today. He does it every year. Three of my guys are with him. I'm lucky if I get five guys here. I may have to pick up a guy hangin' on the fence just to have a team. No more, man."

Kenny backpedals. "Look, Fig, I completely forgot. I won't do it again."

Iron Mike is not here today, and some of the regulars on the staff are also missing. The crowd behind the scorer's table is about half its normal size.

As Fig continues to protest, Kenny responds as best he can. "I realize this is a tough day for many teams, Fig. I tried to schedule the CCC Eagles for today. They are a new team so I figured they'd do whatever I told them. But those CCC guys won't play any games on Sunday. Not one all year. It's not easy, man."

Kenny honors Father's Day by bringing his father, Amos, and his brother, Dennis, to the park. They get director's chairs. They come to watch the Brownsville game, but they will stay to see the start of the Nike One game at 6:00 P.M.

Kenny has always been close to his family, which includes eight siblings. His mother, Arlene, and father, Amos, are still living. His oldest brother, Joe (fifty-two), lives in Albany, and Kenny has two younger brothers, Dennis and Barry. His oldest sister, Phyllis, is a high school track coach, and he has two younger sisters, Darlene and Robin, plus twin baby sisters, Pamela and Paula. They have good jobs and they own property. Kenny's father, now seventy-seven, spent his life as a guard at a branch of the Bank of New York in Brooklyn, and his mother had a staff job in the public school system, also in Brooklyn. Kenny sees his family regularly.

As the second oldest, he always had some sense of responsibility for his younger brothers and sisters. "My older brother was a rebellious type," Kenny recalls. "All he cared about was fighting the system. He got involved with the Black Muslims. Because I was always working and always had money, I often helped out. For example, when my wife's mother moved to North Carolina and bought her first house, I loaned her five thousand dollars."

Kenny has two children of his own, Eric and Melinda. He separated from his wife in 1983 when she decided to move to North Carolina. They were legally divorced in 1990, and he has never remarried. By selling his taxi medallion in 1986, he was able to give his wife enough money to make a down payment on a house in Charlotte and to buy a car. Kenny's son, Eric, lives in Philadelphia. Kenny's daughter and her three children live in North Carolina. This past Christmas he flew down to Charlotte for the day just to see them. "We have a tremendous relationship," he says. "I talk to my daughter most every week."

Bill Parker is at the park with his son, Smush, who has been flying all over the country working out for NBA teams. Smush has played in the Cage all his life, and he is one of those rare playground players with little college experience who has the intelligence and talent to play in the NBA.

He just got back from the NBA rookie camp in Chicago, after which Jerry West invited him to Memphis for a private look. He has gone to Atlanta to try out for the Hawks, where Rodney Parker, his adviser and lifelong supporter, feels he has a good chance to play. These constant tryouts have kept Smush off the hard asphalt of West 4th Street this summer. He appears here only as a visiting dignitary. When he plays in the city, he plays indoors at the Nike Pro City at Hunter College or at the clinic at John Jay College.

The segregation of pros from the playground game has become more pronounced. It was not always this way, but with the huge money at stake, the potential pros play it safe. Even the best high school stars are told to avoid street ball and the parks. The surface is too cruel, and the risk of injury is too high.

It has rained off and on today, so the games are running late. Brownsville is playing Ashanti Tribe, and unlike last week, Bo Keene has ten guys ready to run at tip-off time. The old guys are here early: Keith Stroud (thirty-three), Lamont Long (forty-two), Bobby Washington (thirty-four), and Mo Les (thirty-nine).

Stroud's attitude is typical. "I haven't played for six years and I'm way out of shape," he explains. "I got three jobs and I'm busy. I been playin' here since I was fifteen and I got nothin' to prove. We won a championship here. My provin' days are over. I'm here for one reason." He pauses and points to Bo. "That man right there. He wants me, I'll be here. You'll see. Five or six games I'll be back in shape."

Brownsville's young legs (still in their early twenties) are Rodney Stiles, Keith Jackson (Smoke), John Williamson (Dice), and Rich Henry. This is a good team, but Bo will have his work cut out for him just keeping them together. They get Brownsville off to a good start, leading 22–14 at the end of the first quarter. The older guys can't seem to get good shots, but Rich and Rodney are scoring at will. Rodney is quick, cagey, and agile. He can score before you realize he has the ball. Rich Henry is stronger and has more raw talent, but he can slow the offense down. He won't give up the dribble easily, and he takes his time getting the position and the shot he wants. "Rich Henry is a man on a mission," the announcer shouts after Rich blasts through two defenders to drop in a high-percentage bank shot from ten feet out.

At courtside Kenny is gabbing with friends, commenting on the game, the fans, the league's history. "Some o' these old guys been comin' out here so long I got pictures of 'em with Afros. I got a picture of Lamont out there; his hair was out to here. Now look at him. He ain't got no hair at all."

Kenny goes into a minirant on contemporary styles. "Look at that guy with the nappy hair an' a do-rag. What a mess. And he playin' in one pair o' anklets. You can't get no support that way. I used to play in three pair o' socks. Used to be, guys would go to the barbershop before they come down here so they look sharp. And I'll tell you what else. I seen these guys changin' an' most all of 'em ain't wearin' no jockstrap. How stupid can you be, man? You got to protect yourself." Kenny watches a tricky pass sail out of bounds. "You know somethin' else has changed?" he asks. "There's no longer any such thing as a fundamentally simple pass. Now a guy'll pass you the ball only if he looks good doin' it. Otherwise, he ain't givin' it up."

•••

With three minutes to go, Ashanti Tribe has narrowed the spread to 6 points. Brownsville has lost its concentration. Bo calls a time-out and gives all his players a short, withering lecture about intensity. They can't wait to get away from Bo—anything is better than Bo in your face—so they hustle back on the court. For the last three minutes the defense tightens up and Ashanti Tribe gets no more second shots. Brownsville steals an in-bounds pass. Rich Henry scores on a drive, and then Rodney knocks in three baskets in a row, the first on a twelve-foot jump shot, the next at the end of a lightning-fast give-and-go up the middle, and the third on a tip-in. In scoring 6 quick points, the ball was in his hands less than ten seconds. Lamont Long gets fouled and makes both shots. Rodney winds up with 30 points, Rich Henry adds 22, and Brownsville wins, 77–68.

Bo is never satisfied. "We got to stop squeakin' by and we got to get our big men here. We got a long way to go." Well, maybe; but he's off to a good start.

## Rodney Parker: Godfather of the Playgrounds

Rodney Parker is another twenty-five-year regular at the Cage. He has eight children of his own, but he has been the surrogate father, the formal and informal adviser, to hundreds of kids playing in New York City playgrounds. In the basketball world, he knows everybody. Rodney's current project is Smush Parker, but he has been involved with young players from New York's playgrounds since the 1950s. He likes to chat about the old days.

"Jack Molinas? Yeah, I knew Jack Molinas, and I was warning players way back then to stay away from him," he recalls. "I don't want other guys, especially hustlers and gamblers, running my kids. I tell them, once you sell yourself, you can't buy yourself back." Molinas was America's most famous game-dumper and point-shaver when he played for Columbia University and the Fort Wayne Pistons in the early 1950s. He was shot dead in his home in southern California in 1975, reportedly owing the mob $650,000. Jack was not a nice guy, but the business of spotting and exploiting young talent is full of guys who are not nice.

Rodney is well known among basketball's inner circle. He was a central character in Rick Telander's *Heaven Is a Playground* (1975), and he has been profiled twice in *Sports Illustrated*. He has a terrific instinct for spotting unpolished talent, so college coaches often call him. Many on the outside want to know what Rodney gets out of it. "Why do I do this?" he asks rhetorically. "I don't do it for money, because I don't get any money from colleges and I don't ask for money from my kids. I make my living with a ticket brokerage business. The reason I help kids is simple: I do it because I am able to do it.

"I've had parents of kids I am working with ask me what I get out of it. You know what I tell them? I say, 'I'm doing this because I want to help your son. I've got a reputation, I have contacts, and I will help if I can. Now if you want me to go away, I'll go away.'"

Rodney does have a financial connection with Smush. Rodney brought Smush to Billy Ceisler, Smush's agent, and Rodney expects to be compensated by Ceisler if Smush delivers.

When Rodney says college coaches often call him, he is not exaggerating. He first built his reputation with coaches of an earlier era, including Jerry Tarkanian, Al McGuire, Leonard Hamilton, and Billy Packer. One of his early successes was sending Fly Williams to Austin Peay in 1974. Rodney claims there are twenty-eight pros who have come out of Brooklyn, and he knows them all. A recent call from a college coach went like this:

The time is just after midnight and the call is from Phoenix. "Hello. Rodney? I need to talk to you. I've got all sorts of problems and I need some help. I've got a whole lot of bad grades. I'm losing players left and right. Now I don't want a Rodney Parker Special this time, I want a guy with grades. Give me a call. Here is my office number, and here is my cell phone number. Call anytime." Rodney chuckles over the "Rodney Parker Special." "I don't get many real good students. As a rule I wind up with the hard cases, kids who can't get help anywhere else."

The game has changed. "In the seventies the players were more basic; now they are more creative. And of course you will notice the high school players coming out now are big, developed kids. Kids who mature early, not scrappy little point guards. Did you see LeBron James on TV?" he asks. "I'll tell you what I saw," Rodney continues. "I saw a kid that couldn't shoot. He was eight for twenty-four. Of course he will learn to shoot better, but he's not there yet.

"That's why I like Smush so much. He was never big in high school. He was not big as a freshman and was never a high school star. He was skinny, and even now he is still growing. But that's one reason I like him; he's always getting better. He's got long arms, great hands, and great instincts."

Almost all of Smush's playing experience has come from playing in parks and going to summer camps and clinics. He is almost exclusively a product of street basketball. In this regard, he is not like most young NBA players, who have had a long history of big-time coaches and programs. With Rodney's guidance, Smush has sought out people who could help him, and he has listened to their advice. As far as parks and clinics go, he's been to every one, and he's played with the best.

Rodney's faith never flags. "I tell you, even in the NBA, he's going to be one of the great ones."

### Kenny in Rio

In two weeks, right after the Father's Day game, Kenny will be going back to Rio de Janeiro. The tournament is going well, and he is losing interest. The weather is hot now, and he wants to leave for a few weeks to cool off and then return for the all-star game. His trips to Rio are getting more frequent; New York is where he works and where all his responsibilities lie, but Rio is where he gets his energy.

In the 1950s Hollywood was making popular movies about escape vacations in Europe—*Roman Holiday, Three Coins in the Fountain,* and *Love in the Afternoon* come to mind. In a way, Kenny is recreating the thrill of a more romantic, carefree life in Rio half a century later.

The restless American living abroad is a long and honorable tradition. In the late nineteenth century the poet Walt Whitman found some of his earliest and most sympathetic readers in Europe, and during the last years of his life it was an open question whether he was more appreciated abroad or at home. Between the two world wars American writers Ernest Hemingway, F. Scott Fitzgerald, and Gertrude Stein found a more congenial environment in Paris, and poets Ezra Pound and T. S. Eliot discovered a needed respite in Europe from America's commercially driven culture.

The difference today is that American blacks find Europe far too expensive and more racially divided than America. Yet Brazil is culturally close to Europe—especially to Portugal and Italy. The country has a European feel, and integration is deeper and more natural in Brazil than in the United States or Europe. When English settlers came to America, they brought their wives with them, but the Portuguese settlers left their women at home and married the locals. Thus, interracial marriages and dating has long been part of the culture.

Rio's buildings are not as modern and spiffy as those in richer cities like Paris, Vancouver, or New York, but life is far less formal. Ten months of the year the weather is hot, and tour guide books will remind you that a couple of those months are "fry an egg on the sidewalk" hot. Everyone wears less clothing, and you see plenty of glow-in-the-dark pinks, greens, yellows, and turquoises. In the Ipanema and Copacabana sections of town, the center of social life is the beach. You can bum a smoke from a neighbor, read someone else's newspaper, or borrow suntan lotion—and then ask him or her to rub it on your back. Vendors of all ages will sell you chilled coconuts, beer, and sandwiches. On the city streets, you'll notice that most cars are nicked or dinged in a number of places. Honking a horn is not an offense, and passengers and drivers seldom buckle up. Kenny is as popular and well known in the Copacabana section as he is in New York. Everywhere Kenny goes, he meets people; his charm is universal.

Foreigners can meet with the locals at Mia Pataca, a popular beachfront restaurant in the Copacabana section. It is said that if you want to meet a girl, go to Copacabana beach. Once she is your girlfriend, you take her to Ipanema, just a few miles away. One morning Kenny was supposed to meet some guys from New York, and while he was waiting, a good-looking young Brazilian man walked in and gave him a big hug and a big hello. The man's name was Arnoldo, and he was a detective on the Rio police force. Kenny always brings stuff from the States to give away, and this time he had brought some NYPD hats and shirts, which are popular here. Arnoldo put on his new stuff immediately and chatted with Kenny for about an hour in English, describing local beach scandals, his job, and his hopes of coming to America to attend law school. Then he left to report for duty.

An hour later Kenny decided to go shopping downtown. As soon as he got outside the restaurant he was met by a huge, burly man with enough necklaces, rings, and assorted gold jewelry to make Cleopatra look naked. He gave Kenny a big hug and many vigorous back slaps. They spoke in Portuguese for about ten minutes, concluding with another powerful hug. An American friend who was with him asked who the guy was.

"Garush," Kenny replied.

"He seems like he's doing well," his friend remarked. "What does he do for a living?"

"He sells shirts and stuff like that on the beach."

Kenny's companion asked if selling shirts on the beach paid that well. Did Garush have any other job?

"Well," Kenny said, "he helps people get things done around the city from time to time. He can help you out with your problems.

"For example," Kenny continued, "two years ago I loaned a guy six hundred rais, and for months he kept dodging me. Eventually, it became obvious that he was not going to pay me back. I had been bringing Garush clothing from New York for years, and he would sell it on the beach. I never asked him to pay me anything for whatever I gave him. He heard me mention this guy, so he asked if he could help. He suggested that he go along with me next time I asked for the money.

"So the next day Garush and I call on him in a big retail clothing store where he worked. Garush was dressed the way you saw him today: silk shirt, wide-open collar, and lots of jewelry. We walked into the store and right away the guy spotted us and he looked like he was going to be sick. We went up to the counter, and Garush leaned over, smiled, and asked the guy when he intended to pay back my six hundred rais. His good friend Kenny, he explained, needed the money now.

"Without taking his eyes off Garush, the guy opened his cash register, withdrew six hundred rais, and handed it to me. Garush thanked him, and nobody said a word.

"Now I don't know what will happen to this guy when his boss finds out he stole six hundred rais," Kenny continues, "but I do know he would rather deal with his boss than he would with Garush."

Thus, in one morning in Rio, Kenny was embraced by a cop and a gangster. They all love him. Kenny likes his friends to feel safe in Rio, and as long as they are with him, they are. Traveling with four black Americans with shaved heads and leather jackets does not encourage hooligans and muggers.

Kenny's reputation allows him to sell West 4th Street shirts and bags at a handsome profit. People in Rio want Kenny's stuff because they want to be like Kenny. They want to be a part of his world. They know Kenny is an important person in New York because he is becoming an important person in Rio. He does that to people.

Recently he found an Italian national in Brazil named Franco who rents out apartments and runs cambios, the tiny money-changing shops that seem to be on every street corner. Because of Kenny's connections with visitors, Franco has hired him to rent his apartments to tourists, and Kenny makes a good living at it.

Kenny's other business venture in Rio is boat cruises for tourists. He knows hundreds of visitors who come to Rio, and many of them look him up when they arrive. He also knows lots of locals, so his cruises are convenient icebreakers for new arrivals. With these cruises, Kenny is selling his knowledge of Rio's clubs, beaches, people you ought to know, and people you should avoid. Kenny quickly helps you to understand Rio, so tourists from half a dozen countries will call him. He's already hosted over a dozen cruises, and he's always got one more planned.

When Kenny goes to Rio he's not just dodging work and cold weather. Rio is Kenny's opportunity to build his new empire. His apartment rentals and boat trips are not likely to make him rich, but they will keep him visible and involved in the street life of Copacabana. He's an adviser and big brother to some, a party animal to others, and a mysterious late-night operator to more. He is an insider and a man of his word in a shadowy world of deception and even danger.

Kenny is more relaxed in the dating life of Rio. The women he meets there are softer, younger, and perhaps less cynical than the old Brooklyn crowd, and they appreciate his generosity and up-front honesty. Generally, men who like Rio are attracted to the women.

To European and American tourists, as well as to hustling Brazilians, he has become a valuable man to know. "If I came up with a decent amount of money, I would move to Brazil now," he said recently. "If I could set up shop in Brazil, I'd sell my limousine and get out of there. But that is a pipe dream right now, because it would take a significant amount of money to do that."

Kenny never regrets his decision not to develop a big limo business in New York, rather than just drive for himself, even though times for him have changed. "Back in the 1980s I had everything. I had a cab, two jobs, two basketball leagues," he recalls. "Why take on more stress? Why should I give up something that is keeping me viable to put a whole lot of stress on myself so I can say I got a whole lot of money? Money is nice to have, but peace of mind is more important.

"I can put an ad in the paper in New York and get a job tomorrow working for somebody and making a thousand dollars a week. But why at this point in my life do I want to be committed to somebody when I've got freedom? That's not what I want."

A young woman who has seen Kenny operate in Rio observes, "Most people are content just to watch basketball or to vacation in Rio. Not Kenny. When he loves something, he has to be part of it."

# chapter five

# Brownsville in Greenwich Village

**It is Sunday morning** at the Noble Drew Ali Plaza at the intersection of Mother Gaston Boulevard and New Lots Avenue in Brownsville. At 8:30 A.M., Bo Keene is up, shuffling about his apartment, making breakfast and taking calls on his cell phone. His thirteen-year-old son Maurice and his younger son Antoine are still asleep. Bo's older son is big and strong, and he likes boxing. Antoine is a crack baby Bo and Lauren adopted as an infant. He's quieter than his older brother, but he is an honor-roll student, a life saved from oblivion.

At 4:30 that afternoon, Brownsville will be playing at West 4th Street. For Bo, this is game day. Bo's return to West 4th Street is going well. His team won its first two games, and it should win again today. He's assembled a good group of players. Kenny has accommodated him by scheduling most of his games on weekends, when none of his players will have conflicts with work. Weekends draw the most old-timers to the park, so Brownsville should have an appreciative crowd.

What's more, the Village is a nice place to visit on an early summer afternoon.

The carefree street life of the Village contrasts sharply with the feeling of confinement one gets from Bo's housing project. A twelve-foot-high fence with barbed wire now encircles the five-building Noble Drew Ali Plaza, once a sought-after apartment complex, and there is only one iron gate through which everyone must come and go. Squatters who have not paid rent in years occupy many of the units. Their apartments are run-down and neglected. A guard is at the iron gate, and a visitor must identify himself and the person he is visiting before he can enter.

It is hard to understand the stultifying atmosphere of this part of Brownsville without living here. It has no movie theaters, no supermarkets, no restaurants, no malls, no national brand clothing stores, no McDonald's, no Starbucks, no street vendors, no new buildings, no fresh paint on old buildings, no pretty girls laughing and jumping rope, no boys playing stickball, no parks or grassy fields, no streams or shady groves, no pools, no police officers, no Good Humor trucks, no tourists, no visitors, and few churches. Nothing here is beautiful or suggests growth and life. Here you are reminded that the final end of chaos is not wild activity, but a lifeless stillness. These residents must sustain themselves in a dusty and decaying wasteland.

Ironically, the clean, new cars parked on the streets are the only signs of prosperity and beauty. Because so few people here can afford a car, you can park on almost any street. If you own a new car, the entire neighborhood sees it. Bo drives a four-door Lexus. Others drive recent models of Cadillac, Mercedes-Benz, Honda, Acura, Audi, and Infiniti. Keith Stroud, who left Brownsville in the mid-1980s, now drives a new Lincoln Navigator—$49,000 list, $61,000 with all the extras. The most beautiful objects of the community, its cars, are the means of escape, the way out.

Run-down areas quickly become abandoned in the most complete sense of the word. They are abandoned by their natural residents, visitors, development, and the surrounding communities. No one wants to live with hopelessness.

The contrast between urban poverty and rural, agricultural poverty is instructive. The poor farmer may live in a run-down shack and dress in rags, but his human contribution to his land is positive. With minimal attention, grass will grow and flowers will bloom. But in a steel-and-asphalt world, man's building has replaced nature's form of renewal. As may be expected, man's buildings decay, his paint peels, and his trash litters the streets. Whatever is natural has been paved over. Man has smothered nature's regenerative power, so without constant reinvestment, he is left with cracking concrete and rusting iron. Money is the sunshine of big cities, for only money can buy regular trash collection, fresh paint, and new buildings to replace the old.

Where hope, regeneration, and order are absent, power fills the void. Satan, as he is described in John Milton's *Paradise Lost,* believed it was better to rule in Hell than to serve in Heaven. Among the damned, the self is realized through power. That's what it means to be in Hell. Heaven is a place of compassion and peace. Hell is a place of retribution and suffering. The powerful people in a tough neighborhood can lord it over others. Asserting one's dominance provides a relief from suffering. The prison culture, where cigarettes are currency, seeps into the ghetto culture and becomes a part of project life. A little money goes a long way. Bo claims that since 1998 the violence and drug traffic has quieted down, but still, drugs are easy to buy and teenagers carry guns.

One place of vitality and cheer is the Brownsville Recreation Center, located diagonally across the street from the gate and the guardhouse. For many men in Brownsville, the BRC is the true center of town.

At 10:00 A.M. the Funsport Fireball Pro League will begin the first of five games that will keep the gym busy all day. It is a men's tournament, drawing most of its players from Brownsville and nearby East New York. Ricky Rivers, who runs the tournament, will be taking a team of his best players to West 4th Street that afternoon to take on Bo's team.

Half a dozen players and assorted old guys arrive before 9:00 A.M. to hang out and drink coffee. The air-conditioned BRC lobby has a large, comfortable leather sofa, and around its walls are seven tropical fish tanks, a birdcage with two live birds, and a lizard cage. The murals on the walls portray famous African Americans. Early in the morning the place is quiet and relaxing. Fly Williams is doing most of the talking, but his principal audience seems to be a sixteen-year-old high school boy, who is there to get into the men's game later that morning. Like most Brownsville kids, he idolizes Fly.

Fly is now a responsible citizen, managing a successful summer basketball program for kids in Brownsville, and he has recently prevailed on Nike to support a wintertime Fly Williams Youth Basketball Program in the BRC. But Fly's life is far from exemplary. For a long time he seemed to be the prototypical misfit: a brilliant athlete who could not deal with straight society, the kind of black screw-up the media loves to glamorize. Fly left college after a year, and he lasted just one year (1974–75) with the Spirits of St. Louis in the ABA. He became involved in drugs. Fly once tried to rob his own coach, James Ryans, only to wind up with a shotgun wound in the chest and a prison sentence for his efforts. He has been incarcerated twice.

Clark Elie, point guard of the great Harlem USA teams in West 4th Street's early days, saw Fly at his best and at his worst.

"I remember one Sunday afternoon game at the park when Fly arrived straight from one of his all-night parties. He looked terrible and he started off a little shaky in his play. Then suddenly he called time-out, walked over to the side of the court, and threw up all over the place. It was awful. It must have taken five minutes to clean his mess up. Then he came back into the game and finished with forty points. I don't know how he did it."

This morning Fly is full of fatherly advice for the young boy. "You got to pull yo' weight in school, ma' man," Fly begins. "I heard about that jive report card you gave yo' mama. Maybe you can fool her but you can't fool me. I hear you ain't even goin' ta' classes. I tell you right now, you ain't doin' nothin' without no education."

This good-looking young man was, in fact, planning to drop out of high school. When he does this, he will become one more playground memory, a talented player with no education, no prospects, and no organized basketball experience.

Fly rambles on. He comments on current events, such as the upcoming trial of Jayson Williams, the former New Jersey Net player being tried for manslaughter. Because Fly has spent time in jail, he considers himself an expert on the legal system. "Jayson's goin' ta' get it, man. Since 9/11 they ain't playin' 'round no more. I heard in Brooklyn court, they had a hundred trials, and a hundred dudes is in jail."

Turning his attention to the permanent members of this BRC coffee klatch, Fly recalls the hard times of his youth. "I see these kids today walkin' 'round in a new pair o' Nikes every month. Where they get the money for that? They got way too much stuff, and they's always lookin' at themselves. Man, I remember playin' in shoes with leather soles 'cause that's all we had. And we didn't get no new ones until the next year. When the soles wore out, we put cardboard in 'em to fill up the hole. In the winter we'd go to school and just hope it didn't rain or snow. Kids today get off too easy. And they don't show no respect."

He asks one of his buddies, "You ever get spanked with a strap? 'Course you did. So'd I. I remember a lady on our block—I think she was nothin' mo'n a crossing guard—but she spanked her boy so much she invented a spankin' machine! It was driven by a belt with a motor and you'd get strapped in there with your bare bottom stickin' out and wack-it-a, wack-it-a, that leather strap could spank you forever. It'd never get tired."

Fly Williams can go on like this for hours.

•●•

Just as the first game at the BRC is getting started, Bo arrives. He is wearing three-quarter-length dungaree shorts, sneakers, a basketball shirt, and a cloth fisherman's cap. He watches the game for a while, talks to friends, and then goes into the exercise room and turns on the treadmill. He walks rapidly for forty minutes and talks about his team.

Bo knows he has too many older players. "When I was in the streets, five or ten years ago, I could move around. I could see things. Freedom to run the streets is a big advantage. It allows you to search for talent. I would go to every corner of the city to find a player who could help my team. But I'm not out there as much." Bo pauses for a moment. "I used to hang out at clubs and parties. I knew Stephon Marbury and all those guys. Quality ball players want to hang around quality people, celebrities. I'm out of that now. I can't be arrogant. I can't be no tough guy no more, and I don't know no thugs with pensions. I realize that everywhere in life, even on my basketball team, you've got to gamble and take a chance with people. Somebody did it for me, and I'll do it for somebody else. Buddy Keaton knew me since I was thirteen, and he took a chance."

Bo's challenge this year is to assemble and hold together a team capable of competing for the championship. He has lost one big man, Greg Springfield. "His wife sent a message to us that she did not want Greg out in the streets. He's already playin' in one tournament in Jersey, and that's enough."

On the other hand, Bo has picked up a longtime Brownsville six-foot-eleven-inch shot blocker, Shane Drisdom, who will be with the team today, joining John Harris, a six-foot-seven-inch center who starred in the 1980s with another great Brooklyn team, the Homeboys. Both men are close to forty and past their prime. Bo talks about Shane as if he were still in high school. "Too often Shane plays to the level of competition of those around him," Bo says today. "It winds up bringing down his overall game. I don't think he knows his full potential."

John Harris is an imperturbable post-up player who never seems to lose his concentration—whether he is dunking over a defender or being brutally hacked. He is an old-fashioned center who is used to getting banged around, and fifteen years ago he was a successful professional playing in Belgium. Now Harris is a schoolteacher. Though John's overall game is tough and physical, his jump shot is so gentle it seems out of character for a man so strong. His eyes glare intensely at the rim as his arms reach up over his head. Quickly his wrist and fingers flick the ball out of his huge hand with such a soft, floating backspin that one can't imagine the ball doing anything but settling quietly into the net.

Bo wants to enlist another power forward, Jamal Faulkner, who lives close to the BRC in Brownsville. Faulkner was a high school star at Christ the King, and, after a so-so college career, he played briefly overseas. Jamal has yet to make it to his first game with Bo. This is a constant annoyance with pickup teams like this. Players don't show up, or worse, they join another team. Bo does not baby-sit his players, and he does not nervously call on game day. "I don't chase 'em. It's a courtesy thing. The loyalty has to be there," he says.

When Bo has finished with the treadmill, he goes over to the weight machines, doing a number of reps with the lighter weights. He loves coaching and talking about it. After being a rapper, every street kid's dream, Bo would like to be a basketball coach somewhere. "Coaching to me ain't getting five guys together and watchin' 'em win. A good coach can take a team that's not that good and advance. That's coachin'. During a game I see things on the court and I bring it to my players' attention. I emphasize fundamentals. I'll say, 'Why's you takin' a jump shot when you can walk your man down?' Players got to know that when I'm correctin' 'em, I'm not attacking their manhood. On my team, if Bo's not on top o' you, you is in trouble, because it means Bo don't care.

"We should never ease up. I tell my players, it ain't your fault if this other team's no good. You still got to put 'em away. The longer bums hang in with skilled players, the more you givin' 'em confidence.

The good teams we try to upset. Keep 'em off balance so they don't know what to expect. Brownsville used to be good at that; by the time the other team snapped out of it and got their rhythm, it would be too late."

Like most good coaches, Bo stresses defense, and West 4th Street rules prohibit zone defense or double-teaming a man without the ball. "We play help-out defense. There's gonna be no one-on-one clear-out against Brownsville. Somebody tries that on us, we send two men at 'em right away." Bo's coaching idol is the late Gil Reynolds. "He was the John Wooden of the ghetto," Bo recalls. "He used to have these 'skull' practices to keep you crashin' the boards. He'd play three-on-three or four-on-four, winner's out, half-court games, but you never had to take the ball back after a missed shot. So everyone went for the ball and just put it back up. That keeps you poundin' the boards."

Bo always rides the referees, and sometimes he overdoes it. "I know I work the refs pretty good too; I think I know how to get to 'em. You can't just shout. I'll say, 'Nate, two hundred people know you made a mistake. Now you owe us one.' But I try not to come on too strong. I can't win no games when it's seven against five."

Bo enjoys being in charge of a dozen other men for one hour a week in a setting where achievement can be measured. Beneath his insistence on the disciplined execution of basketball fundamentals is a personal cry for orderliness in life itself. In his anger with players who take bad shots or don't get back on defense, those who would bring his team to defeat, one can sense his own fear of the chaos of street life. He knows failure's deadening consequences. If your team is good, you get respect; if it's not, you don't. As Brownsville's leader Bo is prominent, always a force to be dealt with. This is his team, and he will not be misunderstood, he will not be ignored.

That may be the main reason Bo prefers West 4th Street. In the Cage, Brownsville and Bo Keene can be recognized for the best of what they are by people who have been ignoring them for years. It is no mere coincidence that one of the finest American novels written by a black man (Ralph Ellison) is called *The Invisible Man* (1952). No whites go to Brooklyn to watch basketball, and few travel up to Harlem for the Rucker games. Few fashionable Upper East Siders know when there is a game at Hunter College, and the crowd at the Hoops in the Sun tournament at Orchard Beach is predominantly Hispanic. Remaining prominent at West 4th Street helps Bo offset life in the parks department bureaucracy. West 4th Street brings him back to a more glamorous aspect of street life.

Today Brownsville is the featured game. The crowd at the Cage is a bit smaller than usual at tip-off time, but it builds steadily. Party promoters, who appear here frequently during the summer, are passing out invitations to a midnight cruise around the city on July 13 and "Operation Get Down," a hip-hop benefit at the B. B. King Blues Club on 42nd Street in Times Square.

Bo has timed his departure from Brownsville for the Cage so that he will arrive just a few minutes before game time. Rodney Stiles, who lives in the Noble Drew Ali projects, rides in with him. Because Bo is late, he has to risk an illegal park on West 3rd Street. Shane Drisdom and John Harris arrive on time.

With Kenny visiting in Rio, Rick Johnson and Arizona Pearson are running the game. Joe Merriweather is perched in his director's chair, alert to everything. He is dressed in neatly pressed slacks and a starched dress shirt; he could just as well be in church. Tournament director Rosy Jackson is slouched in his director's chair, dressed in his usual shorts, sneakers, a huge wide-brimmed straw hat, and heavy dark glasses. He is taking great pleasure in needling Joe about one of his park duties.

"Joe," Rosy begins, "for four weeks you have been tellin' us that you will get the parks department to put up our new rims. You always tellin' us 'this week,' but 'this week' never comes." Joe barely nods. Perhaps Rosy will drop the subject. "Now, Joe," Rosy continues, certain that he is getting under Joe's skin, "you know we already paid these people fifteen hundred dollars to play here, and we owe 'em more. Now shouldn't they provide us with some of the services they've promised?"

Joe nods and, looking straight ahead, mumbles, "I'll take care of it." Joe would happily pay someone at the parks department to hang the new rims, but the parks department worker would probably take his money and then do nothing about the rims. As it turns out, Joe will have to endure the same needling the following week.

Vanessa Charles has not shown up, so the announcer Dee Foreman is keeping the books, and Butter, the other announcer, will call the game. Dee is chatting with Rebekah, who came here early. At Dee's request she has brought them both ice-cream cones. After three weeks, she's mixing in easily. Because one of the refs fails to show, Arizona Pearson will fill in. Moneybags, the mysterious scorekeeper, is missing, so Isaiah Jackson will be at the midcourt blackboard with his chalk and a rag. As the season wears on and the heat rises, absences become more common.

Fireball gets most of its players from Brownsville, so Butter introduces the game as the Battle of Brownsville. Bo's team should win, but by the end of the first quarter they lead by only two points. Their shooting has been bad, and their defense is streaky. Bo keeps shouting, "Force everything to the middle," but Shane is not blocking any shots when players come to the middle. Fireball's guards, Donn Chung and Karl Sanders (Butter calls him the Crossing Guard because of his good crossover dribbling move), are getting good shots from ten feet or they are getting in for layups. Rich Henry has 10 points for Brownsville, but when he dominates the scoring this early in the game, the other players can get accustomed to standing around watching. Brownsville is lucky to end the period ahead by 2.

The second period is awful, and Bo is shouting constantly. Rich Henry scores no points in the period, and Rodney Stiles, who is playing small forward, is missing easy shots and not following up.

Meanwhile Fireball's two guards score consistently, ending the half with 31 of their team's 54 points. Chung (Shaw University) and Sanders (St. Francis) are among the top guards in the city; this team can't be taken casually. Brownsville is down by 4, and it is violating one of Bo's cardinal coaching rules: Don't let a weaker team hang around too long.

Midway through the third quarter, Brownsville is down 67–57 and Bo takes time-out. He gives his team hell and puts John Harris into the game alongside Shane. The two big men make a difference. Point guard Vinny Matos makes two foul shots, John Harris cleans up a missed layup, and a rejection by Shane leads to another successful fast break. John Williamson scores twice: first after Shane steals a pass in the lane and sends him down the court for an uncontested layup, and then with a driving layup on the next possession. Rich Henry scores on a clear-out. The quarter ends with the score tied at 73–all.

Fireball is gaining even more confidence. Coach Rivers reminds his players that they have played more quality minutes than Brownsville. Their team is younger and quicker. They tighten up their defense and don't blow any easy shots. With three minutes left, Fireball has pulled ahead 89–84.

Once again Bo calls time-out and lashes out at his team, demanding tougher defense, better shot selection. Constantly coming from behind and relying on short spurts is a dangerous strategy. Brownsville makes its run, blocking shots and stealing passes. Fireball counters by denying Brownsville any easy shots; they use up all their remaining fouls, sending everyone to the line.

Fireball's strategy works; it is turning the game around. Rich Henry is fouled on a drive and misses both foul shots. Shane is hit on a put-back, and misses his foul shots. Even John Harris misses two in a row. Vinny Matos is hit on a drive and he misses one of two. That is seven straight missed foul shots at a time when Brownsville is dominating its opponents at both ends of the court. They are still down 92–85. Just when the game seems to be slipping out of reach, Rich Henry hits a three-pointer and John Harris scores on a pretty fadeaway jump shot along the baseline. It's 92–90 with one minute remaining.

Fireball's Donn Chung misses a jumper, and Williamson leads the fast break back the other way. His game-tying layup is deflected, but Shane gets the deflection on the weak side. He soars high up over the rim and then—unbelievably—slams the ball into the back of the rim, staring in amazement as the ball sails harmlessly back toward midcourt. Butter groans aloud into the megaphone. Bo is moaning, shaking his head.

At the other end, Chung is fouled and makes one foul shot. Fireball leads 93–90. With no more time-outs remaining, Harris gets the ball down low but misses a five-foot jumper. Brownsville steals the ball again and, with fifteen seconds left, Rich Henry misses a three-point shot. Shane swats the rebound back to Henry for the last three-pointer, one that could tie the game. It too is wide, and Fireball's Bill Onje clears the last rebound; the game is over.

Brownsville has its first loss, a game they did not expect to lose. They play again in four days, on Thursday, against Greg Brunson's Macy's team, and then again on Sunday. To remain one of the tournament's elite teams, Brownsville can't afford to lose again. Not like this.

# chapter six

# The Comeback

**It is a beautiful** June 30, with a cloudless blue sky, the temperature in the midseventies, a light breeze. For Brownsville, this will be the last game before the midseason all-star break. The Gay Pride Parade is moving down Fifth Avenue, and the kids have come to the Village for its carnival atmosphere. Playground basketball is only one choice of the free entertainment that is naturally part of New York's street life.

The women's game is first this afternoon, so about twenty women have come to watch. Half a dozen are wearing tight white tops—high neck, scoop neck, sleeveless, gently torn, or tailored. The slacks are low-cut hip-huggers. One woman, probably in her midthirties, arrives in a tiny tiger-striped bikini top. "Hell of a shirt you've got there," one of the young guys says to her. He sets her up in a director's chair and continues his rap.

About this time, the regular fans start to file in. Sherman arrives and shakes a dozen hands. His friend Robert Blue is dressed in a complete Los Angeles Lakers uniform (Shaquille O'Neal's shirt, number 34) with a matching purple bandanna around his head. As usual, Joe Merriweather arrives dressed neatly in off-white; his shirt has a modified Nehru collar. He slides into his personal director's chair. Rosy Jackson is sitting on the wall of the fence at the back of the park. He's reading the *Post*. When Moneybags enters the park, he also shakes a dozen hands. He sits in a shady corner and lights up. He'll be at the scoreboard at midcourt for the men's games.

Robert Jackson, the tournament's unofficial medic, is here early. Jackson is a certified personal trainer, and he is qualified in CPR and first aid. Five days a week Jackson is a sanitation worker in Brooklyn, and he will proudly remind you that he hauls away eleven to twelve tons of garbage every day. That, he points out, is real work, and that's what keeps him in shape. He is over fifty years old and competes against men his age in the half-mile and the one-mile run. He says he can run a mile in under five minutes. At Howard University he was a varsity swimmer.

Iron Mike Montague, the security man, is carrying the scorer's table and a couple of chairs. Mike has set up more games at the park than anyone. He puts up the American flag first, above everything else on the inside fence facing the street. Mike has been coming to the Cage for over forty years, and he used to play here regularly. He claims he was better at football, which he played for twenty years as a fullback with the semipro Yorkville Rams. He got his nickname from the Knicks player Mike Riordan, who during the late 1960s came off the bench to intimidate the other team's top scorers.

Mike lives in Harlem with his wife of forty years, and he makes a good living as a butcher on the Upper East Side. He is unapologetically middle class and a conventional family man, but he likes to spend a few hours at the park with the boys on the weekends.

Mike, like Kenny, is able to keep things peaceful. On one occasion many years ago, when a drunken regular named Walter was threatening one of the other regulars with a carpet cutter, Mike ambled over, looked at the two men sternly, and then quickly and silently placed his hand on an inconspicuous leather case under his T-shirt on his right hip. The case contained an army knife with a heavy black handle and a glistening, twelve-inch, gently curved steel blade. Walter saw it too. "Walter," Mike said quietly, "sit down. If there is any cutting to be done around here, I'm gonna do it." Order restored.

## Game Time

In the Cage's two games, all four teams have a winning record. Brownsville will play Khari Edwards's Pick & Roll in the second game, and the Youngsters play the Arc Angels at 4:30 P.M. The Youngsters are just that, and last week they upset Nike One, the defending champions. This summer the Youngsters have with them two standout high school players, Gary Irvin, a blazing fast guard from Paul Robeson High School (he has delayed college for a year by prepping to improve his grades), and Lenny Cooke, a McDonald's All-American forward who starred at Northern Regional High School in Old Tappan, New Jersey.

Unlike Irvin, who made the decision to prep for a good college program, Cooke has put an equally promising career in great jeopardy. He received much flattering, but ultimately misleading, attention from the New York press, and he chose to believe it. The *New York Times* discovered him. Having done nothing to prepare himself for college's academic aspects, he entered the NBA draft this year and signed with an agent. When you sign with an agent, you lose your amateur standing, and your college career is over. Unfortunately, Cooke was not picked in the draft.

Today's game will prove to be another learning experience. The Youngsters are having trouble in this hard-played, close contest. As the game wears on, the bigger, older players gradually take control. Cooke finds that he cannot post up, because defenders easily drive him outside his range. When he does get the ball down low, he is double-teamed, and he loses the ball. On defense he gets called for holding because he can't control a stronger man. When he drives from the corner, he is forced behind the backboard, where the shot is almost impossible. "Welcome to the Cage," the announcer hollers, as one of his attempted layups is sent back toward midcourt.

In Lenny Cooke's long afternoon he winds up with 7 points. Gary Irvin does better with 15, but only 5 come in the second half. The Youngsters are upset, 82–79. Shawn Eastwick, the Arc Angels shooting guard, who has been playing in Europe for years and is comfortably over thirty, has 27 points to lead all scorers.

Brownsville, too, will have its hands full. Pick & Roll is a team of huge men, a few of whom look like they spend all day in the weight room. Pick & Roll's Jason Hoover is six foot six and 240 pounds. Ulysses Moran (Uly) is bigger. Hoover will be matched up against six-foot-eleven-inch Shane Drisdom, a good shot blocker, but not as strong physically. Pick & Roll has two more guys just as big, and they will play all three together much of the game.

Their point guard is Javone Moore, known in the park as Bam, a star at Canisius College in Buffalo, New York, where he was the all-time assist leader. A park veteran, he's five eleven, strong and quick, with every imaginable point guard skill. He can pass, score, and play solid defense. He is all business, and he will be matched up against the feisty Vinny Matos, Brownsville's court leader. The shooting guard playing with Moore is Chauncy Johnson, a great leaper with a deadly jump shot. Rich Henry, Brownsville's top scorer, is not here. The strains of keeping a team together are beginning to show.

Brownsville cannot get on track during most of the first half. Pick & Roll gets three uncontested breakaway layups on turnovers. Too often, no one helps out on the help-out defense. Bo keeps screaming, "I don't want no baseline. Everything middle. Send 'em to the middle. Box out. No baseline. No baseline." Hoover is scoring against Shane at will from the low post, and no one is shooting well for Brownsville. Rodney Stiles, who can be effective in a less physical game, is having the same problem that Lenny Cooke had earlier. He's getting pushed around and he can't get clear for shots. In his frustration with his team's poor play and some questionable calls by the referees, Keith Stroud starts riding the refs, and he is rewarded with a technical foul. Pick & Roll leads at the half, 35–29.

The second half looks like more of the same. With two minutes to go in the third period Brownsville is down 55–47. Bo Keene calls another time-out to get his team organized. He grabs John Harris by the arm as if he were going to introduce him to the other players for the first time. "I want you down low," he says to John. "And I want the rest of you to get the ball to him when he gets down low. That's all I want to see."

Point guard Vinny Matos finds a way to do just that. Harris gets the ball down low and is fouled. He makes one of two free throws. Matos steals the ball at the other end and pushes it up to John Williamson, who misses a corner jump shot, but Shane clears the rebound and the ball goes back to Harris in the post. John is fouled again, and this time he makes both his foul shots. The score is 55–50 with fifty-five seconds remaining in the period.

The crowd starts shaking the fence and cheering. They're getting involved. It's hard to be neutral about Brownsville. A middle-aged black man in a Panama hat is taunting them: "Go back to Brooklyn, you bums. Go back to the projects where you belong." Bo glares at him, but not for long. He's got work to do.

At the other end of the court Moore misses a fifteen-foot jump shot; then Williamson drives from the right corner to the basket, where he is fouled. He makes his foul shots. Matos steals the ball at the other end and comes down on the fast break with Williamson. Matos rewards his hustle with an alley-oop pass that Williamson slams. The crowd goes wild. This is the Brownsville team they came to see. Brownsville is down by one, 55–54. Hoover comes back with a layup as the buzzer sounds; the period ends with Pick & Roll in the lead, 57–54.

••

The fourth quarter is played with the kind of nonstop ferocity that has given the Cage at West 4th Street its reputation. This is what the fence crowd has come to see. The taunter in the Panama hat keeps riding Brownsville. Brownsville gets the ball to Williamson in the corner, who makes the score 57–56 with a driving layup. Mo Les scores three baskets from down low and Brownsville pulls ahead for the first time, 62–59. Pick & Roll turns the ball over twice at the offensive end of the court, but Brownsville can't convert. Bo is pleading with his team to make every possession count and to get the ball down low to Harris.

Hoover gets the ball in the post. He's fouled, but he misses his free throws. Because neither team has a consistent three-point shooter, both teams are going to the basket on every possession, so the paint area has become a dangerous place.

With three minutes left in the game, Mo Les is elbowed in the head and a fight nearly breaks out. The crowd is still, waiting. The refs move between the players and restore order. Rick Johnson scrambles down from his stepladder onto the court and starts talking to the players, the refs, and anyone who will listen. He doesn't want a brawl on a weekend when he is in charge. Mo is given a foul and a tech. Things quiet down. Older players like Mo know better than to fight, but they will not be pushed around.

With Brownsville still leading 62–61, Jason Hoover, who has grabbed twenty rebounds, fouls out. Harris makes one of two free-throw attempts. Chauncy Johnson, Pick & Roll's shooting guard, drives to the hoop, makes the layup, and is fouled. He hits the foul shot to put his team ahead, 64–63. Brownsville does not abandon Bo's grind-it-out-with-Harris strategy, and its patience is rewarded. John gets the ball in the low post and makes a soft jump hook to retake the lead, 65–64. Vinny Matos finds Stroud down low and he converts, putting Brownsville ahead 67–64 with forty-four seconds remaining.

Pick & Roll goes to Moore for a clear-out against Matos, but in backing up slowly to set up his drive he moves behind the three-point line. He is high in the air, shooting. He never did want the clear-out; he just wanted room for his jump shot. Moore hits the three-pointer to tie the score. A gutsy, brilliant move, and the crowd is shaking the fence. The sound is like a thousand nails falling on concrete from the sky. With fifteen seconds left Johnson steals an in-bounds pass and sends it over to Moore for the jumper that can win the game, but this time he misses. It's overtime.

Overtimes at West 4th Street are only three minutes long; by NBA standards this seems like sudden death. Bo has Keith Stroud, Shane, and John Harris playing with Matos and Williamson. These are the moments when every player in New York City wants to be on the court: crunch time at the Cage. The crowd on the fence is three deep, and perspiring bodies are pressed together, watching the show. The middle-aged man is still waving his Panama hat, yelling, "You lucky, Brownsville. You nothin' but lucky."

Both teams are playing an intensely physical game. Players are packed in the paint area, and turnovers are frequent. Rushing up the court, Vinny Matos starts an aggressive drive to the basket, but suddenly he leaps—still ten feet from the basket. He releases an unopposed, high-arching finger roll. Uly lunges, but he can't get to it. Nothing but net: 69–67.

Pick & Roll fails to score at its end, and on Brownsville's next possession Shane makes a beautiful pass to Keith Stroud, who has flashed to the basket from the weak side, leaving his defender behind. After another steal, Stroud chips in another breakaway layup to make the score 71–67 with one minute remaining. Pick & Roll comes back with a three-pointer, this time by Uly, to bring the score to 71–70.

Back at Brownsville's end, Shane gets the ball under the basket but he is stripped, probably fouled, enabling Pick & Roll to break away for what could be a game-winning shot. Matos and Williamson hold up their fast break, and Shane, who is furious at being stripped of the ball, flies down the court, gets into the lane, and violently rejects an open twelve-foot jump shot by Moore. The crowd goes berserk.

With thirty seconds left Matos hits a short jumper to put Browns-ville ahead 73–70. Right away Chauncy Johnson retaliates with a slam-dunk layup with nine seconds left, bringing his team to within 1 point. He and Moore, the Pick & Roll guards, have been carrying the offense in these last minutes. With little time left, Matos is inten-tionally fouled on the in-bounds pass, giving him a chance to put Brownsville up by 3. He misses both foul shots. The Brownsville crowd on the fence groans. The man in the Panama hat is ecstatic.

Pick & Roll gets the ball to Moore with three seconds left. He's their money player. Matos is all over him. Moore gets off a whirling jump shot from ten feet away. But it is wide to the right. No good.

In a brutally competitive game, an old-fashioned war at West 4th Street, Brownsville has survived a furious rush by an excellent team and won, 73–72. The brilliant Pick & Roll guards, Chauncy Johnson and Javone Moore, both of whom would later be selected for the league all-star team, combine for over 40 points. This may have been the best game at the park all year; this is the reason people come down here. Most important for Bo, Brownsville is back on track.

After the game Bo wants to talk about how his team can get better. "John Harris [20 points] saved us today. We need beef down here; these refs don't make it easy. This ain't no BRC, this is West 4th Street. You got to be big down here. Blockin' shots ain't enough, and I don't need no scrappy point guards getting pinned under the basket."

Most of the players dress slowly. They like to linger when they've won a big game. The regulars on the fence loved it, and the gentleman in the Panama hat is moaning. Bo's team has reestablished itself as one of the big draws at the park. "You want to see a good game?" I over-hear one shirtless young man on the fence say to another. "You come down here when Brownsville's playin'."

Brownsville will enter the all-star break with only one loss. It remains among West 4th Street's elite teams.

# chapter seven

# Smush Parker: Playground Prodigy

**Ever since Smush Parker** announced that he was putting his name in the NBA draft after only one year at Fordham (his freshman year was at a community college in Idaho), he has been the subject of endless talk at the park. He is a legitimate NBA draft candidate.

His mentor, Rodney Parker (no relation), says that Smush should be drafted by the twenty-fourth pick, which means the first round. The press likes his story too. Smush was featured in *ESPN Magazine,* where his picture was used to introduce an article on the top underclassmen coming out for the draft. MSG-TV did a five-minute feature on him, and *The New York Times,* the *New York Post,* and the *Daily News* contacted his agent, Billy Ceisler. They wrote about Smush often, and they reported on his tryout schedule. The press smelled a big summer success story in the making. Smush has had one-day workouts with twelve teams, and he has gone back to three of them (Indiana, Orlando, and Toronto) twice.

Smush Parker has a good head for basketball, and he has astounding athletic gifts.

Smush can fly, and men have always dreamed of flying.

Psychiatrists explain that dreams of flying are related to the desire to escape from a difficult predicament in one's life. Likewise, when someone escapes from a dangerous situation, he is said to have taken flight. If a man breaks out of jail, we say he flew the coop. Flying means freedom from earthly concerns; power with no obstacles; becoming, for a moment, untouchable.

For the last forty years, the astounding, full-speed leap of an athlete as he heads for the basket, ball in hand, slamming the ball down and from above the rim, has been the game's defining spectacle. Dunking has become basketball's supreme performance act. The dunking era is a fairly recent phenomenon, probably beginning in the late 1960s. Since then, everyone can dunk, so the fast break, which generally ends with a dunk, has become the game's supremely magical event. (Dick McGuire did not finish off any fast breaks with dunks when he played for the Knicks in the 1950s).

Smush Parker on a fast break is a wonder. Racing down the court with no one ahead to stop him, he picks up the ball just before the foul line, takes his last long stride, and launches himself above all those around him. He rises, his hips at the level of the players' heads at his side, his right arm extended forward, balancing the ball deftly on his upturned palm. He reaches the peak of his leap nearly ten feet from the basket, he appears almost eye-level with the rim, and we fear that he has jumped too soon. He will not get the ball to the basket. Is something amiss? Then, as he begins his descent, he lightly flips the ball up into the air with his fingertips. For Smush, the act is one of grace, not violence. He can no longer defy gravity, but the ball can, and does, for two stop-action seconds longer. The ball rises higher than it needs to, perhaps two feet above the rim. For an instant it is motionless. Then it accelerates downward—*swish*—sliding cleanly through the net. No rim. As the ball falls downward,

Smush's feet hit the ground. The ballet is over. Two points.

Of course, many of the guys at West 4th Street believe Smush won't make it. All agree that his main problem is his lack of experience. With one varsity year in high school, one year at Southern Idaho Community College, and one year at Fordham, he has not put in enough seasons of structured play. Some park regulars also think he is too full of himself and ungrateful for favors granted. Like many young stars, he has a temper, and these attitudes will catch up with him. Some say that at six foot four and 170 pounds he is not strong enough for the pros. One regular remarks, "He played with Nike One down here last summer, and they did win the championship. But he never dominated. Junie Sanders was better than Smush. Junie was always their go-to guy." Sanders may be the best playground player in the city right now; he's been around for years.

But the pros may be more patient than fans here realize. Every team has someone on the roster who may not be ready to play right away, but who shows real promise. Smush is adored by the high-school-age kids at the park, and he has defenders of all ages. This is their retort: "Junie may be better now, but Junie's too old. Plus, Nike's guys never wanted to give him the ball. They always favored Junie. Smush has promise and probably more raw talent than anyone down here. You've seen him play. You know he's good."

And so it goes. Late last week the draft finally happened.

Judgment day.

Smush was not picked.

Twenty-nine teams had two shots to take him, but they all declined. Smush's supporters at the park were shocked. Others were saying, "I told you so." The New York press was miffed, as reality had upset its big story. Being passed over was a huge disappointment for Smush.

Now the pressure is on, because few young players slip into the NBA this late. He needs a new plan.

Rodney Parker has one. "The kid is a great talent. You'll see. This may be the best thing that could happen to him. Now he can make his own deals, and he won't be tied up for three years, which is what happens when you're drafted."

For most regulars at the Cage, Smush is their guy. This court has been so much a part of his playing life that his rejection is a rejection of West 4th Street. The Cage helped older players like Mario Elie and Anthony Mason get into the NBA; now everyone wants to see it work with a youngster.

The Cage has always been a place to build up young players, to round out their game. The youngsters may be quick, but they are not strong. They can't handle the double-team. They can score, but they cannot defend. They turn the ball over too often.

Last Sunday Lenny Cooke and Gary Irvin began their West 4th Street education. As one of the veterans observed, "If you come here from high school, you better have a note from your mother." It appeared that Cooke and Irvin should have gotten that note.

Yet over time they will improve and they will be back. They have so much to prove, and so much is at stake. In the culture of the Cage, the veterans who challenge them become their instructors for the day. They are their marine drill sergeants. They train their minds as well as their bodies. You may be good, but you've got to get better.

When young stars confront seasoned veterans here, more than the final score is at stake. Bo Keene always keeps a fatherly eye on his young players. He explains, "You just can't put a good playground player out there against a guy who's played in college and played in Europe. Those older guys are at another level. This is where the young guys begin to learn."

For all these reasons, watching the young players at the park offers a special drama. It becomes a game inside the game. Of course, the same veterans who make these young players defend every possession want them to succeed—but on *their* terms, having learned *their* lessons with a code the veterans believe in.

•●•

Among the second-generation West 4th Street players—that is, the sons of West 4th Street players who are good enough to come back here—Smush occupies a special place. Sean Rooks, son of referee Roland Rooks, has been an NBA center for more than ten years. But Sean grew up in California and returned to the park only when he was an established star at the University of Arizona. Young Curt Sumpter, at Villanova, is the son of one of the Cage's most prolific scorers, but he didn't play frequently in the park. The same holds for Bobby Willis Jr., who followed in his father's footsteps by playing with Sid Jones's United Brooklyn.

But Smush grew up in the Cage. Bill Parker began coming to West 4th Street when he was twenty-two, single, a pal of Kenny's, and a pretty good player. He kept coming back every year, but he played less and less. He married in 1976 and settled in Tribeca, south of the Cage. When his first son, William, was born in 1981, he proudly brought his new baby to the park. Young Smush had his diapers changed at West 4th Street.

"The Cage at West 4th Street was his crib," his father says today. "He's spent his whole life at the park."

Young Smush played catch with his father here when he could barely walk, and while his father was watching the big game, the four-year-old Smush was throwing hook shots into the garbage can behind the scorer's table. He could dribble behind his back when he was five. During time-outs at the Cage he would run onto the court, get the ball from one of the refs, and take his shot. Whether he made it or not, the crowd would applaud.

He grew up playing at Carmine Street, the same park Tony Dapolito had the city build when the expansion of West 4th Street was blocked. "When he was a peewee, seven years old, he was already showing his moves," his father recalls. "He would fake one way, then go the other. As a little tyke he understood the full-court game."

In the summers he played in Arizona Pearson's West 4th Street youth league, and he played in many good YMCA and AAU leagues.

He has performed well in the annual slam dunk contests, and last year, as a point guard, he helped Nike One win its third championship.

Rodney Parker has seen to it that Smush has played everywhere in the city he could learn something. Smush got little from his high school and college coaches; he's learned almost everything he knows from the streets. Rodney's recollections run like this:

"As a high school player I got him into the Adidas-sponsored ABCD basketball camp run by Sonny Vacarro in Teaneck." Kobe went to that camp. So did Tracy McGrady. In Smush's year Kenny Satterfield was there. Every great player goes there, and Smush was there after three years of high school, before his senior year. And he played well.

"One summer he went to Paris with a bunch of high school McDonald's All-Americans. Clay Wade, a photographer in Washington, DC, ran the trip.

"He played in the Aim High camp in Queens, run by Kenny Smith, the ex-NBA player. He played with Pete Edwards, who runs the IS 8 high school tournament that runs all year. I remember that he played in a tournament called Utopia, and then at the Earl Manigault tournament uptown. He's played with Gary Charles and the Panthers on Long Island. All of these guys are good teachers.

"As he got older he played at West 4th Street with Sid Jones and later with Nike One, which took him to Hunter College. He played at McBurney Street Y and at 23rd Street on the pier. He played in Brooklyn at Kingston Park, and at Rucker in Harlem."

Rodney pauses for a moment, still thinking. "I'd say Smush has played basketball every day of his life. He's played in every good tournament and he's attended every good clinic in the city."

One problem Smush had living in an upscale Manhattan neighborhood was that the basketball competition was not good. So in the tenth grade he switched to Newtown High School in Queens. In high school he had one good year—good enough to be named Second

Team All-City, so some big schools were looking at him. The University of South Carolina, Illinois, Purdue, Oklahoma State, St. John's, and Oregon liked what they saw on the court. But his grades were terrible, so none of these schools made him an offer.

Bill Parker provided a stable, loving home for his son. Smush's mother died when he was eight, but Bill remarried and the family lives together in Newark. Bill is a twenty-eight-year veteran of Amtrak, working around Penn Station.

Young William got his curious nickname, Smush, when he was a little child. It was a term of endearment his mother used for his father around the house. Whereas big Smush kept his nickname at home, little Smush loved the name and took it with him into the streets.

Smush is a charming young man, but he is charming in the new way. He wants to be noticed. He is good-looking, a careful dresser, independent, and he has cultivated a manner that attracts an entourage. He projects a cultlike aloofness that worries some of the older men at the park.

Smush is almost a poster child for street fashion, always sporting the latest hairstyle, the right cap, and the hippest footwear. When he was a junior in high school, Nautica used him as a clothing line model. As a result, his picture was at every bus stop in New York City, plus every mall where Nautica had merchandise to sell. Nautica put up a five-story-high poster of Smush at Houston Street. He became a minor celebrity before he was out of high school. Girls have always chased after him—in high school, in college, and as a professional. He's been living on his own since he was seventeen, and he likes the city nightlife. If he ever makes big money, he may spend it quickly. After only one year of community college basketball in Idaho, Smush transferred to Bob Hill's program at Fordham in the fall of 2001, but that year was a problem too.

Coach Hill admitted that many of Smush's teammates were jealous, and the team morale was poor. So was their record: Fordham won only eight games all year. Their second point guard, Adrian

Walton, quit in the middle of the season because he wasn't getting enough playing time. Walton was a star at Bronx Regional High School, and he had been selected for the Atlantic Ten Conference All-Rookie Team the year before. Walton complained that not only was Smush getting too much time, but that he wasn't functioning as a point guard anyway. Smush was always looking for the shot. Hill got Walton to return, but the team chemistry remained bad.

Parker's own play was erratic. He averaged over 16 points per game, which included 30 points against Iona and 32 points against St. Joseph's of Philadelphia. He was selected for the Second Team All-Atlantic Ten. On the other hand, he had a number of games when he failed to reach double figures. The most obvious mark of his inconsistency was his season record of 125 assists and 122 turnovers. This is not good for a point guard.

Rodney Parker attended all of Fordham's home games, and he defends Smush's record there. In part he blames Coach Hill, in part he criticizes the basketball intelligence of the other Fordham players, and in part he recognizes that Smush has to grow up, to be less self-centered and more patient. Fordham may not have been the right school. "He's still young," he told me during halftime at one of Fordham's games. "He's only twenty, but he's better than everyone out there. By a lot."

Smush was not playing at the park this summer; all his time was committed to getting an NBA contract. Having attended a number of NBA rookie camps, he was now aiming for the NBA veterans' camps. His agent, Billy Ceisler, wanted to get Smush paid for coming to these camps, so the negotiations were very tricky, and time was running out.

The press was still fascinated by Smush's story. The *New York Post* ran a full-page article by Lenn Robbins entitled "Who Sabotaged Smush?" and it speculated publicly why the younger player had not been selected in the NBA draft. This got West 4th Street buzzing. Whether they had read the story or not, everyone at the park had an opinion. In the *Post* article Smush was quoted as saying, "I was black-balled. He [Coach Hill] wanted me to stay one more year. I didn't play his game." Ceisler had a conspiracy theory of his own. He was quoted as saying, "A GM [general manager] called me the morning of the draft and told me that my client was getting hosed."

Bob Hill responded that Smush's accusations were ludicrous. He had contacted a number of GMs on Smush's behalf, and he had put Smush on the phone with one GM who told him he was not going to be a first-round pick.

Rodney Parker assumed that while the reporter went along with the sabotage angle, it wasn't true, and all the story did was to stir up trouble. "Smush was stupid to say such a thing about his coach," Rodney said. "That's a psychological thing with him. It's ridiculous for him to say that. Smush sabotaged himself. The kid didn't do anything to earn first-round consideration."

Hill may not have gone out of his way to help Smush, and after all, Smush had not helped Hill much during a disappointing, losing season. Perhaps the coaches were worried about the same things that the park skeptics had noticed. Smush was missing classes, and he may not have been eligible for his junior year anyway.

Rodney is blind to none of Smush's weaknesses. "Smush does not need more excuses. He needs to produce, to have a good camp, and to have an NBA team take a real interest in him. He has a good chance now with Orlando. Doc Rivers will be good for Smush. Psychologically, Smush has a long way to go, but he has NBA talent, believe me." So as the teams at West 4th Street move toward playoff time, young Smush will be moving through NBA camps, hoping for that one good camp that will get him a shot at an NBA career.

He's put West 4th Street behind him. What's ahead is anyone's guess.

# chapter eight

# Bobby Willis Uptown

**Bobby Willis's story offers** an instructive comparison with Smush's. At the highest level of play, small differences in talent result in enormous differences in outcome. Bobby Willis is a great athlete, but he will never play in the NBA. He is going to find out just how far he can go this summer.

Willis and Smush both grew up in stable, well-to-do homes in the New York area. Both of their fathers played at West 4th Street. Like Smush, Willis is young (just two years out of Lehigh University) and he is obsessed by the game to the exclusion of almost everything else in his life. He wants to continue to play professionally, perhaps in Europe, perhaps in the NBA developmental league. Neither player reached his full potential in college.

Bobby Willis played in Portugal last winter, but his franchise has folded. Now he just hustles, hoping to improve his game and get a tryout somewhere. There are lots of Bobby Willises out there.

"This life is brutal," Willis says. "Guys like me will go anywhere to play where we think someone may notice us. We live very humbly. I live at home because I can't afford an apartment. After all, I have no income. And I really don't have an agent. At this level it is hard to get an effective agent. Mostly, we're all just scrambling, networking where we can."

At a practice session being held at John Jay College near the end of the summer, Willis revealed the life of an undrafted, unrepresented prospect. "A couple of weeks ago I was invited to a workout run by the Washington Wizards. While I was there I ran into a guy who had driven himself to Washington all the way from Houston. He had no more than twenty minutes' playing time on the floor, working out in front of an assistant coach of the Washington Wizards. He finished his workout, took a shower, got back in his car, and drove all the way back home. Nothing came of it. But that's what you do. I'd do the same thing."

The top aspiring NBA players in the city can be found at the Nike Pro City at Hunter College. For years a predecessor tournament was held at the City College Gym uptown; now Nike runs this pro league and Ray Diaz manages it for them. This tournament, along with the one at West 4th Street, is among the few leagues that Nike supports.

Nike is the most important basketball sponsor in the city. In addition to West 4th Street and the pro league at Hunter, Nike sponsors the year-round high school developmental program run by Pete Edwards, and two important summer high-school-age tournaments: an eighteen-team Swoosh League for boys and a Swoosh League for girls, each running from mid-June to mid-August.

Unlike West 4th Street, the court at Hunter College is indoors and regulation size. It is unfortunate that the games are not promoted more, because while the talent level is high, games draw a few hundred loyal regulars but little street traffic.

While the quality of play is closer to that of the NBA, the tournament is far smaller than West 4th Street, supporting only eight teams (there are twenty teams at West 4th Street), with only seventeen game days throughout the summer (West 4th Street will play on close to ninety days).

Tonight's game pits Nike One, coached by Mark Figueroa, against Omar Booth's Uptowners. Willis is playing with the Uptowners here. With a reduced number of teams and the enticement of an indoor, professional-size court, these teams are bigger and better than those that play downtown. Nike One is the best team at West 4th Street, and it has essentially the same personnel up here, with one important exception: It has added Tyrone Grant, a six-foot-nine-inch power forward from St. John's, now playing in Italy. Up here teams need more strength at the center position, so most good teams have a legitimate seven-footer; big men do not want to risk the chance of injuries at the Cage downtown.

The Uptowner's lineup tonight includes Jared Johnson, a six-foot-seven forward out of Manhattan College; J. C. Mathis, a six-foot-eight, 224-pound forward with two years at Virginia; Luke Walton, son of the great Bill Walton, a six-foot-eight-inch forward from the University of Arizona; Chris Jeffries, who averaged 17 points per game at Fresno State last year as a junior; and Bobby Willis, from Lehigh. This is a fast, young team that loves to run, and most of them want to make a career in basketball.

Can Bobby Willis make it at this level? These are all top-flight Division I players. If they are not NBA caliber, they are close. Willis rode the bench for a team that lost more games than it won in the Patriot League, a conference that has the dubious distinction of never having any team win a single game in the March NCAA sixty-four-team championships.

Willis endured a totally frustrating college career. He is a tragic example of what can happen when a player and a coaching style do not fit. At Lehigh, he was a promising sophomore and an even more promising junior. He is a six-foot-four left-handed shooting guard who is quick in the open court, passes well, and has a good three-point shot. He is adequate on defense. But he needs a running, open style of play. Sal Mentesana was the best-dressed coach in the Patriot League; nothing was ever out of place. His coaching style followed his dress code. Mentesana could never live with an on-the-fly, improvisational running game.

Because of his obvious talents, everyone expected Willis to blossom in his senior year. His picture was the central image in the three-foot poster used by the school to promote its basketball program. In the first game of his senior year, an exhibition game against a touring international team, Willis led Lehigh in scoring with 26 points. But for the rest of the season he seldom played more than eight minutes in any game. He became invisible as Coach Mentesana installed a slowed-down, more disciplined style of play that accommodated the majority of his players.

Unfortunately, the same fate struck Willis's classmate, six-foot-eleven center Sah-U-Ra Brown, who is now playing professionally for the Roanoke Dazzle, in the NBA developmental league. Brown, too, was a highly recruited player who was used sporadically at Lehigh. Like Willis, he was forced to spend most of his senior year on the bench, giving up his time to a promising sophomore, which Brown had once been himself. But big men are more valuable than shooting guards, so he got a second chance in the NBA developmental league.

Ed Lacayo was captain of that Lehigh team and a friend of both Coach Mentesana and Willis. "Bobby was really too quick and had too much skill for the rest of us at Lehigh," Lacayo explains. "I've played with him for a long time and I can tell you he has real talent." Lacayo, a muscular small forward, was himself a product of the Gauchos AAU team in the Bronx, so he knows firsthand what big-time high school basketball is like. "I like Coach Sal, but the clash was inevitable; Willis was not going to fit in." So Willis came to the Uptowners with something to prove.

Tonight at Hunter, Willis not only started, but he played well. He came out shooting, asserting himself right from the outset. He shot a dozen three-pointers and made seven of them. He followed up missed shots and made tip-ins. The Uptowners took the lead and held it throughout the first half; Willis's play was valuable. The Uptowners widened their lead to 11 points by the end of the third period, and Willis continued to score and play under control.

But in the fourth quarter Nike One's shooting guard, Junie Sanders, and Tyrone Grant, their big forward, began to take charge; Nike One squeaked out a 115–113 victory. Still, Willis led his team with 33 points. It was a solid achievement amid formidable competition.

Where does this leave Bobby Willis right now? Well, this is not a simple story of a mismatch in college suddenly being rectified at the professional level. Even in a run-and-gun game like the one played at Hunter College, the quality of the points scored and the interaction with the rest of the team are important. Willis showed that he can play at this level, but can he rise above it? Can he take the next step?

To get noticed at this level players have to play *very* well, and they must be able to score at crunch time. In this game, many of Willis's baskets could have been scored by others on his team. He took shots and made them, but if he had not taken the shots, someone else would have, and his team would probably have made about the same number of baskets with the same number of possessions. As the score indicates, the defense was not intense, so most times down the floor the team with the ball could get a reasonably good shot. Willis scored more because he felt he had to score more.

Now Willis has to show that he can make important shots at crunch time; he will have to score when the pressure on him is greater. His defense will be tested further. So will his passing and ball handling. Hopefully, he will be able to show his coach that he makes other players around him better. If he can't do all these things, he becomes a replaceable part. Just making baskets will never be enough.

Willis is an old-fashioned nice guy. His manner is sincere and earnest. Instead of blowing off school, he worked hard, got reasonable grades, and graduated from a good college on time. He is articulate, and his dress is inclined toward the traditional, almost Ivy League. He's not a leader by nature, and he will never have an entourage. His game is good, but not at a professional level.

On the other hand, Smush has speed and savvy that casual spectators might miss. The pro scouts spot it right away. Smush is still being flown around the country so that other NBA coaches and general managers can get a closer look at him. Willis will be happy with anything he can get. For both of them, this is an important summer.

# chapter nine

# The All-Star Break

**Early in July, West** 4th Street marks its midseason with an all-star game and a slam dunk contest. In the big game, the all-stars from the Eastern Division will play the West. A good deal will change by the time the finals begin because players come and go, leave losing teams, return from overseas looking for a game, or take off for pro camps.

The big surprise this year is that the defending champions, Nike One, are zero and four, dead last. They must win all their remaining games to make the playoffs. Fig's team is suffering from tournament fatigue; they're playing too many games in too many places, and it's getting old. For the first time ever, he's having problems with no-shows.

The power team in the Western division is the undefeated X-Men, coached by Dytanya Mixson. This team has played together since grade school in Bedford-Stuyvesant, and they won the championship here a few years ago. They are led by Long Island University star Mike Campbell and power forward Brian Elleby, known everywhere as

Hammer. In Reggie Roberson and Aaron Walker, the team has two of the best guards in the tournament.

Karriem Memminger's Shooting Stars, from Queens, have lost only one game. Karriem, who is just over thirty, has been hospitalized for most of the summer with an obscure nerve infection—not AIDS—which has debilitated his muscles and is draining his strength. While he is being treated at St. Vincent's Hospital, his team has been run by Lambert Shell. Like the X-Men, they play well together, and they could very well make it to the finals.

All Out, with only one loss, has two high-scoring guards, Chris Sandy and Sidney Smith, known as Magic. They may not have the rebounding to make it to the finals.

In the rival Eastern Division, B & B Foods is the only undefeated team, followed by Brownsville and the perennially powerful United Brooklyn, each of which has one loss. Sid Jones's United Brooklyn has the most talent in the tournament this year. Sid is particularly adept at attracting the top players: NBA all-star Chris Mullin used to play for Sid's pro league teams uptown. Sid's assistant this year is James Ryans, who is one of West 4th Street's most successful coaches, and a first-rate strategist and bench coach. He directed the Prime Time championship teams of the early 1990s (with Anthony Mason), and for the last five years he has been a full-time scout for the New York Knickerbockers, which gives him a good call on talent. United Brooklyn scored 119 points against a good Fireball team just before the all-star break.

Of the new teams in the tournament, the most successful is the Christian Cultural Center Eagles in Brooklyn. The CCC has a large, well-organized evangelistic church program and its team has brought dignity to the league, along with surprisingly good players, two of whom were picked for the all-star game. Brent McCullum, a small forward, played with Brownsville years ago, and he has been scoring 20 to 30 points a game with the Eagles. They have the strongest post-up player in the tournament, Claudius Johnson, six foot five,

240 pounds. Like the rest of the Eagles, Claudius attends his church's worship services regularly. What is most amazing about Claudius is not simply his strength, but his agility and leaping ability. Although he is built like a football player, he was a finalist in the slam dunk contest.

The best new player in the league is probably Obadiah Toppin, known as Snoop, a rangy six-foot-seven forward who will start his collegiate basketball life this fall at Globe Institute of Technology, one of three junior colleges in New York with a Division I basketball program. Obadiah is twenty-four, which leaves him with three years of college eligibility. After his first junior college year, he hopes to transfer to a top-flight four-year program, perhaps Manhattan or St. John's. His team, Lance's Crew, which is in the Western Division, is comprised of West 4th Street playground regulars, the guys who play pickup games at the park all day long.

Pulling off a big event like this easily strains the league's informal organizational structure. Kenny Graham was not here because he could not get connecting flights through Miami on his way back from Rio. He spent twenty-four sleepless hours in the airport arranging a flight, but only last-minute premium-priced tickets were available. He was needed for the big all-star event; after all, he was the man the sponsors wanted to see, and they would be here at the all-star game. They were investing in Kenny, not just a bunch of basketball players. But Kenny didn't have the $700 that the airline wanted for a last-minute purchase (with a reservation, flights generally cost around $250), and the buddy pass was already paid for. So he went back to Rio. Rick and Arizona would have to run the all-star game.

At tip-off time the crowd was enormous, pressing against the fence on Sixth Avenue five people deep. These were New York's best basketball fans, appreciative and orderly. As usual, no extra police were on the street for the event; West 4th Street basketball could take care of itself.

Mistic, the sponsor of the day's events, had set up two small carnival tents on West 3rd Street, and it had wisely brought about a dozen staff members to manage its activities. The staff passed out free cold soft drinks to players and fans, and made sure its banners were on the park fences. Mistic brought its own photographer and publicists and put up a $1,000 cash prize for the slam dunk contest winner. Part of the Mistic entourage included half a dozen good-looking girls in short-shorts and Mistic tank tops who acted as hostesses. The girls gave out souvenirs, shirts, and drinks. They mixed with the crowd, posed for pictures with middle-aged out-of-towners, and smiled a lot.

Mistic also brought its sponsorship check, which meant that the tournament would have enough money to operate for the remainder of the season. Kenny needed Mistic's money because the team's entry fees were exhausted. Shirts for the slam dunk contest were again provided by Ray Hands, a freelance clothing designer and longtime friend of Kenny, who had been doing this for twenty years.

The new Internet video partner, *Slam from the Street,* brought its cameras for the game as well. I-Hoops had sold the right to make DVDs and offer Internet-TV coverage of the games to this group, and Adam del Deo, a young Venice, California, sports impresario, came to the Cage himself to oversee his crew. Nike's Antonio Brimmer was there also.

Having all these people around did not make running things any easier.

Mistic took care of itself.

Official scorekeeper Vanessa Charles got each player to sign a media release form before he was allowed to sign his name in the scorebook. She accepted no whining and allowed no exceptions.

But Arizona Pearson mysteriously disappeared just as the game should have begun, and Rick spent most of his time outside the Cage dealing with Mistic's people and other sponsors. This meant that no one was physically present around the scorer's table to start the game. No one was in charge.

Everyone who had done anything at all for Kenny during the

season wanted his past services recognized today with special treat-ment. Thus, perhaps twenty good-size men were crowding into a space normally set aside for five or six. They jostled with one another around the scorer's table, grabbing places for themselves. Nobody could move freely, and as people pushed against the scorer and the timekeeper, everyone was getting curt and irritable.

Rebekah arrived a few minutes late and was looking flustered as she worked her way toward her usual spot near the scorer's table. After relating breathlessly how it took her five minutes just to push her five-foot-two-inch frame through layer after layer of restless and edgy fans, she explained what was bothering her.

"I brought my friend Julie with me. She lives in the Village and thought she would like the game and the slam dunk contest. As soon as our taxi pulled up, she started getting nervous, and I thought she might back out. The Cage is a mob of bodies out there and no one will give an inch to let you in. I think she was a little intimidated. She sent me ahead to get her a spot, but now I have to go back to get her." Rebekah then wiggled her way back through the crowd and out of the park to retrieve Julie.

The unchecked chaos of the scene had been too much. Julie's a small-town girl and her husband is from Tennessee. "I think this Brooklyn-in-New-York business was too much for her," Rebekah said, as she worked her way back. "She's going to settle for a less confronta-tional Greenwich Village experience—shopping at Urban Outfitters."

As it turned out, Julie's instincts were pretty good. As game time neared, people were still pushing and maneuvering. A few guys wanted a better seat to see the game, while others didn't care so much about seeing the game as being seen in the front rows. Others wanted to get a free soft drink or a spot next to the Mistic girls. Whatever the motive, it was every man for himself. In fifteen minutes the staff cronies finished off the Mistic drinks that were supposed to be kept cold for the players at halftime. Rosy tried to get more bottles brought in, but no one would give up his spot to go get them.

It was difficult to tell who was with the film crew, who was with the local press, who was with Mistic, and who was just crashing. The staff and the sponsors, Mistic and Nike, irritated one another or got into arguments. Proper introductions were never made. Guests from the parks department or TV stations were ignored or inadvertently insulted; photographers were pushed around; everyone seemed to be in everyone else's way.

As a rule, the commissioner sits in a high director's chair just behind the scorer's table. Kenny dictates everything from this position. He never moves. He prompts the announcer on the megaphone and starts events on time.

The announcer, Ron Creth, could have taken charge, but he became so irritated with people pressing in around him that he threw up his hands and walked out, handing the megaphone to Dee Foreman.

The game did not start until 6:35, when Joe Merriweather went to the scorer's table and insisted that it begin. Once things got started, the playing was good, with some impressive three-point shooting, flashy passing, great jams, and no rough stuff.

When the halftime slam dunk contest began, the proceedings again fell apart. The master of ceremonies talked too much, wasting precious daylight. The Mistic girls had politicked themselves into being the judges, replacing the usual park regulars, and they eliminated some of the best and most popular slammers, including finalists from last year. This produced groaning and discontent from the boisterous crowd around the fence. While decisions were being reversed, appealed, and re-reversed, it was getting darker by the minute.

The slam dunk contest winner was Karl Joseph, known as Air Jamaica because of his long dreadlocks and high-flying acrobatics. He won the contest last year, and he is a regular at the playground pickup games. In the past, contest winners have glided over small boys and sailed over rows of chairs. One year a player slammed a ball splashed with lighter fluid that was ignited an instant before he grabbed it—the ball was on fire as he jammed it through the net. A player disguised in a wig and a grandmother's housedress won the contest two years ago. Last year Joseph hit the ground after his final one-hand slam holding a cell phone to his ear.

Joseph's winning slam came somewhat as a surprise. For a while he seemed to be dribbling the ball aimlessly, about twelve feet from the basket, his back to the backboard. He bounced the ball hard backward through his legs. The ball bounced off the right side of the backboard. Joseph turned around, leaped high enough in the air to take the ball just as it came off the backboard, spun himself around 270 degrees, and with two hands slammed the ball through the rim.

A clear winner. His dreadlocked buddies from the park jumped up and down, high-fiving him in midair, and two of the Mistic girls gave him a hug. Not bad for five minutes' work, and he was $1,000 richer.

After the contest it took another ten minutes to remove the fans who had pushed their way in. The second half of the game did not begin until 7:40, and half the fans had lost interest and gone home. Running time was used in the last period in order to end the game before total darkness set in.

The West, the division with the X-Men, won 111–107. Obadiah Toppin put in the best performance, and he was high scorer for the winners with 21 points. Claudius Johnson, who also played for the West, had 16 points and dominated the boards.

The tournament's details reveal why it needs an active commissioner. The executives of companies sponsoring the tournament were disappointed; they expected more from West 4th Street management.

A glum group of directors met while the park was being swept up and the chairs were being put away. As a showcase event, it exemplified all the things that can go wrong. The next day Kenny called from Rio to confirm the stories staff members had reported. Clearly the tournament needed him around.

Part Two

·•·

PLAYOFF TIME

# chapter ten

# Midsummer Interlude:
# In Harlem, Greenwich Village,
# and Brownsville

**Half a century ago,** baseball was New York's favorite summer game. Basketball was a largely wintertime recreational activity for poor Jewish kids in Brownsville and Concy Island. In the summers the best players would leave the city to play in the Catskills. Summers in the early 1950s revolved around Yankee Stadium, the Polo Grounds, and Ebbets Field, which were neighborhood parks. The city's three most populous boroughs each had one. Admission was cheap and you could generally get a ticket. Games were played during the day. In those gentler times, a trolley ran by Ebbets Field, Idlewild Airport (now JFK) had just opened, and baseball teams traveled to away games in Pullman cars. New York's best players came from rural states like Kentucky, Georgia, Arkansas, and North Carolina, and they retained their country ways, even in the city. Roger Kahn celebrated this pastoral paradise in a beautiful book about the Brooklyn Dodgers in the 1950s, *The Boys of Summer* (1972).

All this has changed. New York is no longer pastoral. Almost all of its playgrounds are paved, and the surface of the city and the life itself has become harder. Basketball is played all year long, and the summer leagues of New York City's playgrounds have become woven tightly into the fabric of neighborhood life. Professional baseball is something you watch on TV at night; basketball has replaced baseball as New York's summer game.

Tournaments are everywhere. The Dykeman tournament is uptown in Washington Heights. The Big Dogs of Harlem, a weekend Rucker tournament, and the Entertainers Classic (sponsored by Reebok) are all in Harlem. Gun Hill Road (sponsored by Game Over), the Forest Projects, and Hoops in the Sun (sponsored by Adidas) are in the Bronx. Tillary Park, Kingston, and the Brownsville Housing Projects tournaments are held in Brooklyn.

These tournaments, and many more like them, are major local events. Thousands of neighbors and passersby have taken these basketball tournaments into their lives. Some become rabid fans; others remain casual observers. From toddlers in diapers and crippled women in electric wheelchairs, to flashy young dudes in shades with their stylish ladies in tank tops, summer basketball attracts them all.

If you watch neighborhood sports in New York, you watch basketball. Golf and tennis are too distant from and elite for the city. Swimming is a recreation, never a spectator sport. The good Yankees games are sold out, and the Mets have been awful. Minor league baseball is just getting started, and at the neighborhood level, there are too few playgrounds with baseball diamonds. When you do find ball fields, they are generally in large parks removed from local neighborhoods, so few people watch.

This summer three major neighborhood events illustrate just how important basketball has become to inner-city life. They are all different, but they are all enormously popular.

## Rucker Park

Possibly the biggest basketball event of the summer takes place not at West 4th Street, but up at Holcombe Rucker Park at 155th Street and

Frederick Douglass Boulevard in Harlem. Rucker is a first-class outdoor basketball facility. It has outdoor lighting with permanent and temporary seating for over 1,200 people. Security is always tight. The court is located across the street from a large housing project built over what was once the historic Polo Grounds. The older residents of the area will remind you that this site was the home to the New York Giants baseball team, as well as the home of Babe Ruth and the New York Yankees before Yankee Stadium was built across the river in the Bronx. Rucker Park has hosted most of New York's finest amateur and professional players since 1946, and its featured tournament now is the Entertainers Classic, organized by local entrepreneur Greg Marius.

The Entertainers play Monday through Thursday evenings, and the league is dedicated to the proposition that playground basketball should be a central, but not the only, feature in a major entertainment package that includes music, commentary, and hype. The game announcer is physically on the court, roaming about, waving his arms, pointing here and there, all the while carrying a cordless microphone as he talks up the game. He is not on the sidelines or part of the audience; he is one of the performers, and he never lets you forget it.

This is not to say that the players at Rucker are not first-rate, because they are. Unlike the Hunter College league, these players are presented as performers in a colorfully staged event. Thus, the games have an exhibition-like aura, with lots of running, slamming, alley-ooping, and behind-the-back passing, rather than patient half-court play-making or hard-nosed defense. They are a showcase for individual athleticism.

The games are a mix of World Wrestling Entertainment and the Harlem Globetrotters. Unlike West 4th Street, this is an NBA-affiliated tournament, so NBA players can play here. The similarities between the old Globetrotters and the Entertainers are striking. Both emphasize the most visible basketball skills, and both have a simple story line repeated in each game. The Rucker story line presents tough-talking, dangerous, street desperadoes who meet for the big park showdown. The players' pregame babble for the Madison Square Garden television cameras is like what you hear from professional wrestlers before their matches: scripted boasts and empty bravado.

Fifty years ago, the Harlem Globetrotters featured their players' great natural ability, but they mixed in good-humored basketball tricks and continuous clowning. Everyone knew that the loveable, talented Globetrotters would win. Goose Tatum and Meadowlark Lemon, the Globetrotters' comical centers, always made you laugh. Though the rap in-your-face lyrics of the Entertainers project fearsomeness rather than the laughter of the old vaudeville clowning, both are showbiz caricatures of black culture. In both cases, the goal is to simplify the black stereotype to broaden the audience.

Rucker Park's speaker system is powerful, and a moment's silence is rare. Commentary is loud, and continuous music blasts away during teams' time-outs, while a comedian often performs at center court during halftime. Announcers like Al Cash, Duke Tango, and Boobie Smooth the Politician are themselves media personalities at Rucker. Almost no one uses his given name, at least not for long. Baron Davis immediately became Too Easy. Cuttino Mobley was transformed into Gets Buckets. Players are known as the Franchise, the Problem Child, the Prosecutor, Lethal Injection, the Unknown, and Matrix. Teams have theatrical names like the Eye of the Tiger, Murder Inc., and Terror Squad. Highlights of big tournament games are broadcast on MSG Network television each week; this is the city's most publicized tournament.

At 6:00 P.M. on Thursday, July 18, Rucker Park was packed, and it had been packed for an hour. New York City police barricades were three deep, extending far into the street to keep pedestrians away from the park and its gates. Three mounted police officers patrolled the sidewalk, but their horses were being upset by the blare of the sound system inside the park. Perhaps fifty law enforcement officials and rescue squad workers were visible. The park itself was jammed with at least fifteen hundred spectators—more than its official capacity. About five hundred were outside the barricades, peeking in through the open gates to get a glimpse of one rim, where they could still see dunks taking place.

This was no ordinary day at the park.

Kobe Bryant was playing today.

Kobe's arrival had been widely touted. Ed Lover, movie actor and disc jockey for Power 105, one of New York's leading hip-hop stations, had been announcing that Kobe was *not* coming for much of the previous week. When Kobe did arrive, the tournament promoters asserted that he had predicted that he would break Rucker Park's all-time tournament scoring record of 74 points, set in the 1970s by Joe Hammond, a famous Harlem park player, now fifty-two years old. (Kobe had said no such thing, but this kind of talk is part of the hype.) Kobe did, however, oblige the hype-meisters by bringing his own entourage of Men in Black to keep his fans at a respectful distance.

Kobe obliged by posing for photographs with Joe Hammond and other league dignitaries. He may be the best player in the game today, so his status-bestowing qualities are real. He is not, however, a ghetto product, nor does he have much in common with his Harlem fans. His father, a professional basketball player, was well off, and Kobe grew up in Italy (he speaks Italian well) and Lower Merion Township, a wealthy Philadelphia suburb. No one could be more unlike the typical ghetto homeboy. He's adapted easily to being a media giant. Kobe in LA is not *like* Hollywood, he *is* Hollywood.

Kobe played well, but he scored fewer than 20 points. He had nothing to prove here. Nor was he the only professional player at the park. Jerome Williams, Baron Davis, Shawn Marion and Stephon Marbury, Jermaine O'Neal, and Moochie Norris all played well. Brownsville's center Shane Drisdom was the center for Murder Inc., the team Kobe joined for the evening. Shane loved it. Rain ended the game in the middle of the fourth quarter. No one cared who was winning. It was everything it set out to be, a good show.

## Old-Timers Week in Brownsville

In the basketball world an underlying competitiveness has always existed between Harlem and Brooklyn. Fly Williams recalls that shortly after he finished high school, he tried to get on a team in the Rucker tournament. For two straight summers, no team would take him. "It was hard to get on teams up there in those days," Fly recalls. "They only wanted guys from Harlem or the Bronx. They didn't want anybody from Brooklyn, especially a skinny kid like me. But I finally got a spot. I'll tell you, I had a lot to prove. In my first game I scored sixty points." Brooklynites love to hear stories like this.

Brownsville is rebuilding its civic pride. Greg Jackson, the director of the Brownsville Recreation Center, has created the most festive event of the summer for his community, Brownsville Old-Timers Week, a tradition that has been carried out in some form for more than thirty years. Friday is the Dorothy L. Rice Memorial Reunion Night, and it offers free food to more than three thousand residents, along with a concert in the city playground adjoining the BRC.

The dinner could have cost a fortune, but Greg has done a great job of raising funds from private and public sources. His nearly successful run for the all-Democratic borough council last year served as a brushback pitch for local politicians; he made it clear that if you do not put money back into the community, you could lose your job. Brooklyn is a one-party town, but the party still has internal rivalries.

Food was given out for three straight hours on Friday night. The line was seldom less than twenty yards long. The food was first-class: crab, lobster, chicken, fries, salads, and dessert. Keith Stroud was in charge of keeping the line moving and orderly. Sid Jones, James Ryans, Dee Foreman, and dozens of other West 4th Street players were there. It was a major reunion event. Locals, most of them women, got to the playground early with their lawn chairs to get a good seat for the feature show, a Marvelettes concert that began around 9:00 P.M. The program began about 4:00 P.M. and lasted until 1:00 A.M. There were barricades and a handful of cops around, but they had little to do.

The parade was held on Saturday morning. During the afternoon, the kids rode ponies (on a lead line) and went to an organizational rally for the Pop Warner football league, which was to begin the following week. The men played handball and softball. People sold home-cooked food on Hegeman Avenue.

Basketball was Saturday's central spectator event. In the gym, three basketball games were played before a packed house. The first game decided the sixteen-and-under champion of the BRC Summer League, and the second game did the same for ages sixteen to eighteen.

Between games, Darryl Glenn, who runs the youth basketball program, held a final one-on-one event for the peewees. It was quite a show. Shooting at a toy plastic basket adjusted low enough so the boys could dunk, two tiny kids went head-to-head for five minutes. Both boys could dribble through their legs and behind their backs, both had mastered good crossover moves and a clean drive to the basket with a running dunk. How old were these talented tykes? One mother who had her own children with her guessed eight or nine. Her husband thought they could be as young as seven. When the matchup was over, Darryl announced their ages: The winner was five; the little boy who lost was three.

The featured Legends game did have a number of legends, but the team that Brownsville played against, a touring Christian evangelical squad led by ex-Laker Adrian Branch, was too young and too athletic for men in their late forties. Nevertheless, watching the old-timers was a treat. Fly Williams has retained some quick moves to the basket and his shooting is excellent. World B. Free, who works out regularly at the BRC, is as powerful as ever. Free was an early practitioner of the long three-pointer, and he put a few long ones away to show the younger people what it was like. Ron Moore, a six-foot-eleven center drafted by

Detroit in 1987, started at center for the Brownsville Legends. The point guard was Teddy Augustus, the varsity men's coach at Bishop Loughlin High School.

For the halftime show Jackson had recruited Bruce Crevier, the world's premier basketball trickster. Bruce spun balls on his fingers, and he transferred the spinning ball from his finger to the fingers of kids selected from the crowd. He dribbled two balls at the same time, between his legs and behind his back. He juggled three basketballs, then two basketballs and an apple. He rode a unicycle, and he replicated his *Guinness Book of World Records* stunt—spinning twenty-one basketballs at once, which he manages with a candelabra-like contraption that he holds. Seeing a middle-aged white man perform tricks invented by the Harlem Globetrotters may seem out of character, but the audience loved him.

Greg Jackson may be the most important man in Brownsville today; if there were a mayor, he would be it. He has brought money into the community, he has forced the politicians to get involved, and he has shown that he is a masterful organizer. He is upbeat and constantly optimistic. He keeps in touch with Brownsville natives like Willie Randolph, now the manager of the Mets, and Earl "The Pearl" Monroe now spends Saturdays at the BRC helping with the youth basketball games. Every year the program at the BRC gets better, but Greg is modest about his role. His explanation is always the same: "We've been blessed."

Greg does have an unrelenting belief in his community. Though it sounds trivial to most American suburbanites, when Home Depot opens a store close to the community, it is a great step forward. Home Depot brings the tools and materials necessary to rebuild a neighborhood that desperately needs them, and it brings jobs.

Similarly, Jackson is encouraged that there is a new Red Lobster restaurant nearby. Again, most Americans cannot imagine what it is like to live in a community with no restaurants. Red Lobster is not the 21 Club, or any of the other trendy restaurants in Manhattan, but it is an important step in making Brownsville more like the rest of America.

In Brownsville, basketball is the unifying community activity for much of its civic life. Indeed, sports have been the only way for many inner-city communities to feel they have anything to contribute to America. People like Greg Jackson understand that basketball can't be the end of the line; sports must lead to something else, but basketball is the place to start. One of the men at the Legends exhibition game was wearing a T-shirt that said: BROWNSVILLE HAS PRODUCED MORE BLACK PROFESSIONAL ATHLETES THAN ANY PLACE ELSE IN THE WORLD . . . PLUS FIVE BOXING WORLD CHAMPIONS. Brownsville pride begins with its athletes.

## Nike's BattleGrounds

"Ball or Fall. Winner Take All."

"Your rep is no longer valid. Only your skills will save you."

These are the messages of Nike's big posters and the programs for tonight's one-on-one tournament. It is the central event in the company's promotion of its new BattleGrounds line of footwear and clothing.

Tonight street ball addicts will find out who is the king of one-on-one basketball in New York City.

Nike has spent the last month promoting this final showdown. They began with the top thirty players in New York City. The first elimination round took place in New Jersey, and the second round on the retired aircraft carrier *Intrepid,* docked along the Hudson River in New York Harbor. Nike constructed a half-court basketball facility enclosed in a West 4th Street–like cage, with professional lighting for night contests. It had already been disassembled and moved twice.

Nike also purchased billboard rights on a large building on the northeast corner of Sixth Avenue and Houston Street, facing the Houston Street Playground and Sixth Avenue. This location, where many of the West 4th Street women's games are played, is two blocks down from the Cage at West 4th Street. Normally, Nike would fill this billboard space with a huge picture of Michael Jordan or Tiger Woods. Next month a new face will be overlooking the Houston Street playground. The three-story-high image will be the man who wins the Nike BattleGrounds One-on-One Basketball Championship.

The finals are being held here Thursday night, August 1, with John Salley, a Canarsie High School star before he made it with the Detroit Pistons, acting as master of ceremonies. The top eight players will play three rounds of single-elimination one-on-one to determine the winner. In addition to the billboard and some gear, the best man will collect a $5,000 cash prize.

The crowd was a few thousand, all that the park could hold. The gates opened just before 7:00 P.M., but when Kenny and the West 4th Street crowd arrived at 6:30 the line was more than two blocks long. Everyone went through metal detectors at the gate and was frisked. Temporary stands had been erected with a dozen Rent-A-Johns. No refreshments were served, but the evening was free.

It was a serious basketball crowd, and they understood the intricacies of what they were watching. For those of you who have never seen one-on-one played at a highly competitive level, it is a physical game. John Salley announced the games and encouraged the refs to tolerate a good deal of shoving and fouling. Games had an eight-minute limit, but the game would end whenever the first player reached 22 points, with each basket counting as 2 points. Long shots counted for 3 points, and foul shots were 1 point.

The key to winning one-on-one basketball is to have a good inside post-up game along with a good three-point shot. If a player can only do one of these things, he is unlikely to win consistently, because he will have to play against all kinds of competition. These games are tiring because there are no time-outs, and neither man can let up on offense or defense. Players need endurance as well as skill.

•••

Twenty-five-year-old Kevin Houston is one of those brilliant Brooklyn players who did not play in college, although it is said the Denver Nuggets invited him to try out. He is a muscular six-foot-four-inch shooting guard. Mike Campbell is a rangy six foot six, and he plays everywhere in the city with the X-Men. At Long Island University, Brooklyn, he played with his buddy Charles Jones and the controversial high school phenom Richie Parker. Last winter Campbell played professionally in Italy. Of the eight finalists here, six of them play at West 4th Street, and three of those, Darren Phillip, B. J. McFarlan, and John Strickland, are with United Brooklyn.

Houston played a much bigger John Strickland in the first round, and Houston's 19–18 win was an upset. Throughout the game the crowd rooted for Houston, perhaps because it didn't like Strickland's pushing-and-shoving post-up offense. Strickland's game can be subtle and skillful, but tonight he went along with the playground rules, which are tolerant of fouls and body contact.

Kenny was annoyed by what he saw; he resented the way Nike and Salley were highlighting rough play. "They put a couple of black men in a cage and encourage them to act like animals. Certain players intimidate the refs and get all the calls. What kind of message does that send? I'd like to run a one-on-one tournament at West 4th Street with real referees and present a game that would highlight the players' skills."

For his second round, Houston met another big man, B. J. McFarlan, who is six foot six and 230 pounds. By controlling McFarlan down low and making his own three-point shots when he needed them, Houston won 22–16 and advanced to the finals.

Mike Campbell, who grew up in the Jackie Robinson projects in Brooklyn, shocked a bigger, stronger Darren Phillip in the first round by dropping seven straight three-point shots. Phillip, who led the nation in rebounding while he was at Fairfield, could not believe Campbell could continue to make shots from farther and farther away. So he did not chase him on the perimeter, and Campbell's shooting produced a 23–12 win. Next Campbell defeated a quick and skillful Cameron Benison 22–16, relying on his three-point shooting.

Thus the final matchup featured two skilled players, both from Brooklyn. Both had relied on quick layups and jump shots. The West 4th Street staff had assembled to watch the last rounds. They were all rooting for Mike Campbell.

Campbell got off to another amazing beginning, making his first two three-pointers and hitting six of his first seven attempts. It looked like a runaway, until he began to tire. Suddenly, he just ran out of gas. After three straight misses, it became clear that his 14–6 lead was in danger. All the pushing and shoving against stronger men that he'd had to endure to get to the finals had worn him down. He was not getting off the ground on his shots, and his three-pointers were not falling. Meanwhile Houston kept grinding out layups and medium-range jump shots. Campbell seemed to have lost the energy to attempt a drive.

However, as the contest wore on, Houston started to miss his shots as well. With two minutes left, both players were exhausted. Now Campbell's early lead was looming larger; it looked like the clock would settle the game. No one could get to 22 points.

With less than one minute remaining, Houston had pulled to within 2 points of Campbell, 19–17. Campbell missed another jumper, so Houston got the ball back. He was determined to drive for a layup, but Campbell summoned up whatever strength he had left to keep Houston away from the basket. After a positioning battle that took almost two minutes, Campbell deflected Houston's post-up jumper. With eight seconds left Campbell got the ball and did something smart. He abandoned his jump shot and drove hard for the basket. He was fouled.

The rules for the game stipulate that each player has ten seconds to take his foul shot, but the game is played on running time. Campbell realized that with only eight seconds left, if he didn't take his foul shot, the game clock would run out and he would win. This is what he did, and that is how the game ended. An exhausted Campbell defeated an equally fatigued Kevin Houston, 19–17. Two great players, invisible at the media level, had achieved a feat their grandchildren would hear about. They were the best one-on-one players in New York City. A week later a five-story-high poster of Mike Campbell went up overlooking Houston Street and Sixth Avenue.

Mike Campbell played in four different tournaments this summer. He is a polite, articulate young man who leads a sensible, unsensational life. After his victory in the Nike one-on-one championship, Salley interviewed him at center court and then asked what he would do with the $5,000 prize money. "Pay some bills," Campbell replied.

"Shucks, man," Salley responded, "you can do somethin' better'n that. You'll always have bills to pay." But Campbell didn't change his answer.

This is one of the differences between NBA players and guys who play on New York's playgrounds. Playground stars must pay their bills and deal with real-life issues every day; the rules of life can't be brushed aside. Still, like all great performers, they are dedicated to making themselves better. New York City has hundreds of them.

# chapter eleven

# The Season Continues:
# Brownsville Gets into Trouble

**Kenny will return from** Rio next week, but in the meantime, the season is grinding toward the playoffs. Rick Johnson has taken over as de facto commissioner, while Arizona Pearson is spending his time with the kids. Rick is at the Cage every day, getting games started on time, making sure the garbage is picked up, and resolving disputes. Kenny has been missing for over a month, but routine and habit are marvelous stabilizers. The players behave themselves and the staff knows what to do.

On the court, the premier tournament teams are asserting themselves. The top three teams appear to be United Brooklyn, the X-Men, and the Shooting Stars.

Sid Jones is getting his top players together and the team is mauling its opponents. In its last two games United Brooklyn beat Fireball 116–68 and Chaz Hoops 101–67. Although they lost one game in the regular season, which knocked them back to second place behind B & B Foods, they are the league's most talented team.

The X-Men are undefeated and are recording lopsided wins. In their last game they led 72–47 midway through the third period. They lack a big center, but Brian Elleby is one of the league's top rebounders, and Mike Campbell, who won the Nike one-on-one championship, may be the most dangerous scorer in the tournament. Guards Reggie Roberson and Aaron Walker are as good on defense as they are on offense. Artie Lawyer, a lean forward who has been playing at the park for over a decade, is Coach Dytanya Mixson's sixth man. He is good enough to start with almost any other team.

Lambert Shell's Shooting Stars have been playing games with only five and six men, but their victories too have been impressive. They won their last two games 105–81 and 118–89. Two brilliant guards, Antawn Dobie and Laron Mapp, have been their leading scorers, and Shell is their post-up player. When Shell was at the University of Bridgeport he was voted the best Division II player in the country (1992), and he scored 3,000 points and grabbed more than 1,500 rebounds in three years. This achievement got his jersey placed in the Basketball Hall of Fame in Springfield, Massachusetts. At six foot five inches and 260 pounds, he is 40 pounds overweight, but he is still effective in the Cage.

The big surprise this year is Nike One, which lost its fifth game. Mark Figueroa told Rick that he wouldn't be playing any more this year. With one win and five losses they had no chance for the playoffs, so their four-year dominance of West 4th Street has ended.

The Brownsville game against B & B Foods, the first game after the all-star break, should determine the fourth-best team in the tournament. B & B Foods, from Brooklyn, is undefeated. Yet they have never beaten Brownsville. Bo can't wait. "If we knock off an undefeated team, it will be good for all of us. And I'll tell you, this is a game we can win. I can only do so much by hollering from the sidelines. The desire has to come from everyone." Rebuilding his team has been difficult, and Bo becomes frustrated when his team plays badly.

B & B is not undefeated by accident. The team has no natural center, but it does have ten guys six foot to six foot five who are very good. They have playground regulars like their point guard, nicknamed Shorty Brooklyn, but their scoring comes from Dickie Lloyd and Seth Marshall. As a lefty who can play away from the basket and post up, Lloyd is difficult to guard. Seth Marshall is a six-foot-four-inch, 225-pound shooting guard who starred at Fresno State and has made it to NBA tryout camps. Nike uses him in occasional promotions and advertisements. Both of these guys can score 30 points on any given day. This afternoon Brownsville is missing its center, John Harris.

The first quarter was faster and looser than most Brownsville games, as both teams were shooting quickly and getting good looks at the basket. Shane blocked three shots, deterred half a dozen others, and grabbed five defensive rebounds. All-stars Lloyd and Marshall matched Brownsville basket for basket to keep the score close, but Brownsville was off to a very good start.

Yet as the first period came to a close, mental errors began to hurt Brownsville on defense, and they missed a few easy shots. Perhaps they needed John Harris, their calm and reliable go-to guy in the post. Vinny Matos could not get control of the offense, which became random, opportunistic. After a missed shot or a muffed defensive assignment, the players did not press harder; they bickered with one another. Veterans like Keith Stroud, Shane, and Matos, who should have been moderating influences, added to the confusion by complaining about every call and yelling at one another. Shane stopped blocking shots. At the end of the first period, Matos and Stroud were slapped with technical fouls. Bo began screaming at the refs and at Rick, who was seated in the commissioner's chair. "Where did you get these guys," Bo yelled at Rick, "Toys 'R' Us?" As the quarter ended, B & B had pulled ahead 28–27.

The official who slapped these early technical fouls on Brownsville was Mel Chettum, a veteran of the ABA, CBA, USBL, Division I college, and countless city leagues. Mel is one of the few white referees who works regularly at West 4th Street. He is a civilian working with the New Jersey State Police (he is licensed to carry a gun), a fact seldom talked about but never forgotten. The staff and the coaches respect him. One of them told me, "He calls the game close, but he is fair. We'd like to get him down here more than we do." James Kelly, the timekeeper, who never misses a game, added, "These early techs are no surprise. Mel averages one tech per first period in every game. He wants to make sure players understand he will be calling the game close and he won't take any crap."

Bo was losing his temper, yelling constantly at Chettum. Perhaps if Kenny had been here he would have talked to Bo and tried to nip the problem early. But Bo is a hard man to confront. Rick's attitude was that if Bo wanted to destroy his own team, let him. Bo should know better.

For whatever reason, Bo continued riding Mel Chettum. Shane was embarrassed by Bo's behavior, so his own play became lackadaisical. Keith Stroud then reacted by abusing Shane for his lack of hustle. Shane and Stroud were getting on each other's nerves.

Throughout the second period, B & B got a number of easy shots, including half a dozen three-on-two and two-on-one fast breaks. Brownsville got no breakaways. Further, their half-court offense was frustrated by an artfully executed near-zone defense. Inside the Cage it is the job of smart point guards to call this to the attention of the referees. The savvy guard will freeze his dribble, point to the illegal defender when he is most flagrantly out of position guarding no one, and shout "zone" at the ref, letting everyone in the park see what is going on. But Brownsville's guards didn't do anything about B & B's tactic.

Brownsville stayed in the game because it controlled the ball for most of the time and because B & B was shooting badly. With just average shooting, Brownsville should have been 10 points ahead. Shane was blocking shots again and playing well at both ends of the court. At the half they still trailed by only one point, 48–47, but they should have been comfortably ahead.

In many basketball games the first five minutes of the third quarter can determine a game's outcome. During this time it is difficult to regenerate the adrenaline rush of the opening tip-off, yet the urgency of the final minutes remains far away. Third-quarter losses suggest a lackadaisical mentality. Anyone can lose in the final minutes of the fourth quarter—luck often determines an outcome with a few seconds left, and any team can have a bad day and get blown out.

For Brownsville the third quarter was a total meltdown, and by actual measure it may have been the longest period of the season. Bo blamed every turnover and every missed shot on the referees, and his frustrated players picked up his animosity. Ron Creth did his best to help. "Stop cryin' and play ball," he shouted into his megaphone. Ron then turned to Vanessa and remarked, "When Bo was playin' he never did this stuff. He concentrated on playing."

With B & B pulling away, 62–52, Keith Stroud exploded at referee Mel Chettum over a call. Since this was his second technical, he was ejected from the game. Then Shane started hollering and he was slapped with a technical foul. Players from both teams started shoving one another. Seth Marshall leaned against the fence, amused by it all. Players were all over the court. Rick hustled out to calm down the coaches and talk with the officials. Bo was ejected from the park (he went peacefully) and Stroud followed him, but it took twenty minutes to clear the playing area. The quarter ended with B & B comfortably ahead, 77–66.

The fourth quarter ended in the same farcical mood. With twenty seconds remaining and B & B leading 88–76, Shane cleared a rebound and started dribbling slowly down court, mercifully running out the clock. But Bo, who had been exiled to the street, shouted to Shane, "You're not supposed to be dribbling, Shane." Shane looked at Bo in amazement and took him at his word. He stopped dribbling, letting the ball roll freely wherever it would. He then called time-out, ignoring the cries of his stunned teammates. He shuffled toward the basket, passing under the backboard to the scorer's table. As he bent over to pick up his athletic bag, he said quietly to James Kelly, "I've had enough. What a mess. I'm outta here."

The referees got the next call right for sure. "It's a wrap," Mel said as he picked up the ball. "Time to go home."

## Finishing Out the Season

Bo kept trying. For the last game of the year, he brought back Hassan Duncombe, his great post-up player from his 1996 championship team. Hassan had played evenly against Anthony Mason in the deciding play-off game back then, and his stubborn defense, along with more than a dozen rebounds, had given Brownsville the win and the championship. Hassan, whose class of Penn was 1991, was always an imposing presence under the basket, but he was bigger than ever, six foot seven and over 300 pounds. During the winter he had been hospitalized with a blood clot that the doctors feared might be moving toward his heart, so he had been on blood thinners and other drugs for more than six months. Though he was out of shape, on a small court like West 4th Street he could be a fearsome presence under the basket. Hassan still had a gentle touch and a powerful drop-step move to the basket. Defensively he was simply unmovable.

Unfortunately, for the final game of the year Brownsville drew Sid Jones's United Brooklyn. Today Sid had four men in the lineup who had qualified for the Nike one-on-one championships: Darren Phillip (Fairfield), forward Tariq Kirksay (Iona), shooting guard Duane Woodward (Boston College), and point guard John Thomas (St. Francis). The game was a blowout.

In the first period, only John Harris was playing well for Brownsville. He scored 7 of his team's 13 first-quarter points, but they trailed 21–13. In the low post, Phillip was so overmatched by the bigger and stronger Duncombe that he found himself smiling at his own inability to drive Hassan back even an inch. Phillip was scoreless in the first period. But Hassan could play only for brief stretches without rest. Taking his game to the corners, Phillip scored a respectable 7 points in the second period, mostly with jump shots.

Brownsville fell asleep in the first five minutes of the third quarter, so United Brooklyn rolled up a 20-point lead. After that run, the game was effectively over. United Brooklyn won in a runaway 91–65. The playoffs would begin the following week.

# chapter twelve

# Kenny's Back

**Tyler, the bartender in** the tavern where Kenny hangs out around 42nd Street, is happy to see him back. For guys who feel hemmed in by life, Kenny Graham is like a prince in a fairy tale. He's always confident and cheerful. He has a good word for everybody, so everybody has a good word for Kenny.

Tyler, on the other hand, is one of those middle-aged guys who can't understand why life hasn't rewarded him more richly. He was recently forced to vacate his East 20th Street apartment near Gramercy Park to move into a smaller first-floor one-bedroom in Alphabet City on the Lower East Side. New York City rents can kill a guy like Tyler, for whom money is tight.

Kenny has always moved amid an aura of adventure and mystery. He is a man's man in a man's world dominated by strong personalities, not by business cards and institutional relationships. Kenny is confident, not because he is untouchable, but because he has been in so many tough situations that he knows there is nothing he can't work himself out of. The ladies like Kenny, but there is nothing of the play-boy about him. Like Uncle Remus's wily character Brer Fox, he knows when to lay low.

He enters a room confidently but slowly. As he approaches, the first thing one notices are his eyes. They are quick and alert, a puzzling contrast to his lazy, lumbering walk. His eyes are those of a man who lives on the streets, who for his own survival has to take in everything—background noises, idiosyncratic gestures, evasions of any type. He comprehends you and everything around you.

Then there are his hands. Huge, warm, powerful. He envelops a person with his handshake. A person is "in his hands," whether he expected it or not.

Now Kenny is back from Rio to see his West 4th Street tournament through the last weeks of the season. His dress is always sharp; tonight he's wearing a huge leather West 4th Street jacket. The boys at the bar take all this in, and tonight they want to hear about Rio.

"Since I have a permanent residence in Rio, I've gotten a Brazilian social security number," Kenny begins. "The next time I go down I may hook up with Snoop Dog, the rap star. He and his guys are coming down to Rio to make a video, and they may want me to make their arrangements. If they tell me what they need, I can get it for them. I'd like to be paid a fee, maybe fifteen hundred dollars, and I would take care of everything."

Snoop Dog? Now the boys behind the Budweisers are interested. Kenny knows Snoop Dog? One of them asks, "And hey, what does it cost to live down there?"

Kenny makes it all seem easy. "Living in Rio has become inexpensive for me. Guys used to pay forty dollars a night for a place to stay. I'm renting a one-bedroom apartment for one hundred eighty dollars a month. [Tyler was paying $1,900 a month.] This is cheap for me, and I can rent it out to tourists and pick up some extra money while I am up here.

"I can live in Rio on about fifteen hundred to two thousand dollars a month. I can't live in New York on that kind of money. Recently I went to Rio with seventeen hundred dollars in my pocket. I stayed there for a month and came home with eight hundred dollars. It's hard to beat something like that. Of course being in New York allows me to do things for my daughter when I have extra money. That's why I'm still here. But there could come a time when I say, 'I'm outta here.'"

In addition to hobnobbing with some well-connected people, Kenny has befriended a seventy-five-year-old retired railroad engineer from Pittsburgh named Floyd Wilford, who has been going to Rio for years. Floyd loads up on Viagra to re-create the days of his youth. For the woman, this re-creation can represent considerable labor, and even risk. On one occasion, Floyd prepared for his evening on the town by taking four Viagras at once—the normal dosage is one half of one pill—and he promptly passed out. His woman friend had to call the police for first aid to make sure Floyd stayed alive.

"I got Floyd a place for under two hundred dollars a month," Kenny says cheerfully. "When I'm not around, he spends too much money. I think I'm good for him in that way."

Tyler groans audibly when he hears that one can live on Copacabana beach for that kind of money. Kenny rolls on. "You've got to understand, in Rio five hundred dollars a month, which I should be able to earn, is phenomenal money. Remember how my life works down there. I sleep until I feel like waking up, I go to Mia Pataca for brunch and talk with the boys for a couple of hours, and we watch the girls go by. I do my errands. Then I go home for a power nap. I get up around ten P.M. and go out for the night. What's not to like?

"I'd like to get Mike Williams to come down to Rio. He looks tired. Rio would be a nice vacation for him. Maybe Ron Creth could come too."

Tyler interjects, "Can you take me around down there?"

"Sure, sure," Kenny answers, "anytime." Kenny means it; he takes care of all his friends, though Kenny suspects Tyler will never go.

Kenny turns again to Tyler. "I can fix you up with a nice place. I get a ten percent commission, and I have seven guys who have given me their apartments to rent. You'll have a choice of places to stay."

One of the boys, who has been idly peeling the paper label off his beer bottle, wants to know who goes to Rio. Any Americans?

"Rio is getting a lot more tourists from the United States, and the Italians are always there," Kenny answers. "A whole lot of blacks are coming down. More and more guys are coming down with money, too.

"My window of opportunity is very good. I think I may run a Super Bowl party in Rio for Kappa Alpha Psi, a big fraternity of black college men. They do functions all over the world, and they could bring forty to seventy guys down for the Super Bowl.

"Right now I don't want to be here; I want to be in Rio. But keep in mind I went down there planning to stay for ten days, and I wound up staying over a month. I arrived with eighteen hundred dollars and I came home with fourteen hundred. I made good money there, and I was able to send some money back here to pay for the car. Rio is at another level for me.

"After my last boat trip everyone had such a good time they were chanting in the vans coming back, 'Ken-ney, Ken-ney, Ken-ney.' I'll tell you, it was mind-boggling."

What's next?

"Apartment rentals are still the most stable income I have. But I may do more parties too. I still want to have a masquerade party for New Year's Eve. I had a costume party where the girl and guy with the best costume got a hundred rais. Everyone liked that. I've had bathing suit rides, where everyone had to come in a bathing suit. That was fun too. Now I've got a good DJ with good equipment. These parties are getting better and better." His life in New York is more complicated. "Ideally, I would like to live half the year in Rio and half the year in New York," he continues. "Especially if I am still involved in the tournament. There's no sense being in Rio in the summer. My grandkids are here, and my family is here. I try to get to North Carolina every couple of months to see my daughter and her kids. She's a good girl, but it is difficult bringing up three young children. So I stay in touch."

Americans outside of big cities may have a difficult time understanding the challenges of New York City life for people of ordinary means—people like Tyler behind the bar, Jocko in Brownsville, or Kenny with his limo. The high tax burden and cost of living encourages a tax-free underground economy. Fortunately, Manhattan's tourist trade produces a predominantly cash-based service economy, so the two are a perfect fit.

Service businesses and small proprietorships flourish here. All-night diners, Chinese laundries, car washes, newsstands, barber shops, delivery vans, delicatessens, construction subcontractors, waitresses, babysitters, and the city's countless street vendors are in cash businesses. They seldom take credit cards, and they don't report all their income. If they did, they couldn't survive. Even the Fulton Fish Market, the largest in the city, is a cash business. Kenny and his limo are part of this world, and it is not a marginal group.

In addition to legitimate residents like Kenny, thousands more are here illegally or aren't staying. They have come to make money, which they send home. They may not pay any taxes, and if the Internal Revenue Service comes looking for them, they simply get on the next plane and never return.

If a person reports everything to the IRS, he will need a huge income to live moderately well. Consider a couple reporting an income of $100,000 per year, which is far above the average. After their standard deduction of $14,200, their taxable income becomes $85,800. On this, they will pay $18,675 in federal taxes, an additional $5,000 to the State of New York, and $2,900 more to the city. Social Security and Medicare will absorb $6,700, and if they are like most families, they will have to make a contribution to their company's medical insurance plan, probably another $2,000. The sales tax of 8.5 percent takes out another $2,000. The couple will lose another $5,000, 5 percent of their gross, for an IRA retirement plan. Thus, their annual take-home pay will be $57,725.

If they have a car—which is parked on the street all year round—the insurance, maintenance, and yearly payments could run another $6,000 a year, not counting gas and tolls. Rent and utilities, including a cell phone and cable TV, could run another $30,000. In the end, their income for everything else, which includes essentials like food and clothing, along with some walking-around money, has dropped to $418 per week. This is for two people with no children. This is what two people get for $100,000 a year; reduce this income by half and a person can't really make it. That's why so many New Yorkers have roommates, and nobody keeps a car.

There are two ways to beat the city's tax bite. Greg Jackson and Darryl Glenn have one solution: They work two jobs, which are full-time and on the books. If they cut corners on either job, who could blame them? They are probably working six days a week, and they work sixteen-hour days. If they like their jobs, they may be away from home even longer. On the other hand, hundreds of thousands of others choose to be self-employed in a cash economy. To an outsider these lives may seem unnatural, even devious. But this is the way a huge number of New Yorkers live.

In New York, Kenny can have a good week or a bad one. He experiences periods of low energy, for which he takes a prescribed medication, so he can't always work a twelve-hour shift. "Monday to Wednesday is a struggle, but the rest of the week can be good. I'm still driving late. One Sunday I drove until four thirty A.M.," he reports.

Cruising with a limousine around New York is not a simple job. One has to hustle, and the business climate is shaky. Mayor Bloomberg is raising billions of dollars by hiking property taxes, and that cuts into disposable income. It's illegal to smoke in bars. The stock market decline and the tragedy of 9/11 have taken the starch out of the city. Apartment vacancy rates are rising, so apartments are easier to rent. With restaurants less crowded, car services are willing to work for less. Kenny used to have steady work from US Air, delivering packages and taking passengers into the city or to nearby airports where they needed to make connections. But US Air went bankrupt, so they can't afford Kenny any longer.

The mayor is cracking down on limousines that cruise the streets for fares. Legally, only a yellow medallion cab can pick up a passenger south of 96th Street in Manhattan. The black cars, like those run by Car Mel or Tel Aviv, can respond only to telephone inquiries. Since everyone knew there were too few cabs in New York, Mayor Guiliani didn't aggressively enforce the cruising laws, and a kind of unofficial compromise was the de facto rule of the street. Limo drivers were discouraged from soliciting fares, but doormen at hotels and clubs would put passengers in limos, and they let the driver and the passengers agree on a fare. But now the Taxi and Limousine Commission has undercover agents operating in midtown, so drivers take a risk in picking up riders. If a driver gets caught he can lose his license on the spot, the car will be towed, and he will have to pay a $250 fine.

So how has Kenny been able to make a living driving around the city all these years? Fortunately, he has a number of regulars and referrals. Once in a while he will get lucky, as he did recently, driving around players from the Oakland Athletics baseball team for three nights on the town. They're fun, and they pay. His expertise on New York City nightlife is a valuable asset. He knows the best clubs and restaurants south of Houston Street on the Lower East Side, below Alphabet City, and he knows the gay bars and the hot clubs in the old meat-packing district. He knows Harlem and Brooklyn, too. His advice alone may be worth the fare.

Kenny's limo is a bona fide stretch—it's about thirty feet long. The interior is set up like a nightclub lounge, with two types of overhead night-lights and a TV. The bar is always stocked with cold beer, wine, liquor, Coke, and three kinds of candy. It comfortably handles eight people.

On a recent evening he had theater business until around midnight, when he went down to Lafayette Street. There Kenny caught a crowd finishing dinner at Indochine and he took them home. Often a regular customer will call. If nothing is cooking, he may go to Times Square, near the ESPN Zone, or perhaps a hotel doorman will hook him up with a fare.

Late in the night Kenny will work the clubs downtown. Weekdays can be slow, but people are still out. On a recent Monday night, he recalled, he took two guys who had just picked up two girls. "The guys seemed pretty drunk to me, and the girls were one hundred percent gold diggers. Man, they were awful. As soon as they got in the backseat they started going into my liquor. Anyway, they wanted me to find another club for them. So I took them to Lot 61 in Chelsea between Tenth and Eleventh Avenues." (Zagat describes Lot 61 as "a nexus for people too beautiful for their own good . . . all attitude all the time.") Although Kenny knows these places, he does not frequent them himself. "Some of the New York Jets were partying there," he continued. "I figured they would like that."

Occasionally, he will get work around Privilege (a strip joint supposedly owned by the Mafia, where guys are looking to continue their partying), or go home. Kenny may buy himself a snack before calling it quits, and perhaps get into bed about 5:30 A.M. This is a hard life to sustain, and Rio is clearly a welcome break.

At the Cage no one hears any of this. Kenny's private life stays private. As far as the folks at the park are concerned, Kenny never has a bad day.

# chapter thirteen

# Playoff Time: The Early Rounds

**Kenny is back in** charge. Rick Johnson did well in his absence, so Kenny lets him run the game from the commissioner's chair. After twenty years at the park, it has become clear that Kenny and Rick work well together. Rick is always there, which gives Kenny a chance to escape once in a while. A congenial crowd of regulars has formed over the hot summer months, and they all show up at playoff time. Anything can happen in a West 4th Street playoff game.

**Day One: Upset**

In the opening round of the playoffs, B & B, which won its division, drew the number six seed Power Kingdom. Doug Herring, a great West 4th Street veteran, brings a team down from Schenectady, New York, every year. This game was close all the way, and as the third period wore on, Herring's gang began to believe it could win. The third period ended with Power Kingdom trailing by one point, 62–61.

With three minutes remaining in the game, Power Kingdom pulled ahead for the first time, 75–71. Kenny and Rosy were sitting together. He leaned over to Rosy and said, "Power Kingdom is playing like they have nothing to lose. B & B is in trouble."

With Ed Hinson, Power Kingdom's top scorer, and Dickie Lloyd swapping baskets in the final minutes of the last period, Power Kingdom took the lead, 84–81, with seconds left. Lloyd brought the ball up the court for B & B and pulled up for a last desperate attempt to tie the score with a long three-pointer. Only two seconds remained. Lloyd missed the shot but, unbelievably, he was fouled. He then coolly made all three free-throw attempts to send the game into overtime.

It was close to 8:00 P.M., and the sky was getting dark. The crowd was so noisy it was hard for the players to hear what the referees were saying. Kenny feared that the game could get out of hand, so he left his chair and stood under the basket in front of the scorer's table with the megaphone. He knew he had to control the last three minutes. The refs would tell Kenny what the call was, and Kenny would tell the players.

With fourteen seconds remaining Hinson hit a long jump shot to put Power Kingdom ahead, 94–92. Lloyd drove to the basket and was fouled. If he could convert both these shots, the game would be tied again. But luck was no longer with him and he missed them both. Herring had cleared over twenty rebounds, Hinson finished with 34 points, and the number one team was out.

### Day Two: Dominance

Unfortunately for the Christian Community Center Eagles, they were matched against Sid Jones's United Brooklyn for their first play-off appearance. Merely making the playoffs is an achievement for a new team, and this game set an attendance record. Of the five hundred or so people in the Cage and hanging on the fences, at least three hundred were from the CCC. Wives, family, and friends all came down to West 4th Street, and over half the spectators were women, including three of Kenny's sisters: Darlene, Pam, and Robin. The

Kenny Graham with the megaphone on a hot August afternoon

Rosy Jackson (left) and Wight Martindale Jr. (right)
wait for the big game to get under way.

Photo © 2004 Eve Josephson

Iron Mike Montague, thirty years in the Cage

Photo by Rebekah Berry

Fans of all ages are treated well
at West 4th Street.

Smush Parker during his season at Fordham University

**Merry Christmas**

Bill Motley
Harlem USA Champs

Bill Motley's (far right) Christmas card, from the late 1980s. This Harlem USA team dominated West 4th Street for more than a decade. Front and center is captain Clark Elie. His brother Mario is directly behind him.

Perennial scorekeeper "Moneybags" records a basket on his scoreboard at midcourt. Behind him are the park's handball courts.

Magic Johnson gives an informal clinic to the West 4th Street champions at Venice Beach.

"Air Jamaica," West 4th Street's slam dunk champion
soars far above the rim for an acrobatic slam.

Tony Sherman, director of the West 4th Street pickup games

Kenny Graham renews an old acquaintance
on the beach at Copacabana.

Bo Keene of Brownsville getting dressed for a day in the office—here,
the weight room at the Metropolitan Pool in Greenpoint, Brooklyn

Greg Jackson goes to work.

Dee Foreman calls a game with the battery-operated bullhorn on a hot Sunday in July. Vanessa Charles, the scorer, is seated behind the scorer's table; James Kelly (right) holds the official clock as the time runs down on the period.

Photo by Rebekah Berry

Rick Johnson (left) and Kenny Graham (right) discuss how the final playoff game will be managed.

Photo by Wight Martindale Jr.

Darryl Glenn at the BRC

crowd cheered wildly when the Eagles scored and never moaned when the team made a mistake.

Sid brought along James Ryans to help him coach, and he assembled perhaps his best team of the season. Six players in Sid's lineup had made the Nike one-on-one playoffs: B. J. McFarlan, John Thomas, Tariq Kirksay, Lamarr Parker, Jason Wallace, and Duane Woodward. Sid had three other solid players he could use: Bobby Willis, Will Samuels, and Shawn Simpson (Murder Inc.). Sid even brought along backup center Ken Bantam, a star in the league in the late 1980s. Bantam made the afternoon a family affair, bringing his wife and young daughter with him.

Eight United Brooklyn players scored in the double figures, and Shawn Simpson led with 19 points. In a wide-open game, United Brooklyn won 119–90.

## Day Three: Smush Makes His Bid

Raul Marti has been in the tournament for nearly ten years, and for the past few years his team, All Out, has been led by guards Chris Sandy and Sidney Smith. Smush Parker came to the park ready to join Sandy and Smith against the Arc Angels. They have played together in other tournaments, and his presence had the crowd buzzing. Smush took warm-up drills with the team, alternating lazy finger rolls with emphatic slam dunks.

Smush had put in a strong performance at the Memphis Grizzlies rookie camp earlier that week, and he expected to be invited to the Orlando Magic veteran's camp in a few days. But Kenny beckoned Raul over to the scorer's table, where he quietly pointed out that Smush had not played for Raul during the season.

"Here's the scorebook, Raul. Show me any game this year when Smush played for you."

"He's always been part of our team, Kenny. You know that. He's one of the boys."

"Raul," Kenny responded, "I love Smush like a son. I was with his father the day he was born. I would love to see him play here today. But we've got rules. The opposing coach is going to challenge him the minute the game begins. If he's not in the book, he can't play in the playoffs."

Smush himself asked Kenny to let him play. "Smush," Kenny replied, "I can't do it. Sid called me last night to ask if Anthony Mason could play with him in the playoffs, but I had to say no. It's not fair to the other teams."

Smush stormed back to his friend and adviser, Rodney Parker. "This is my park," he complained to Rodney. "Look at that T-shirt [he pointed to this year's slam dunk contest shirt, with his picture on it]. My name is even on West 4th Street T-shirts. How is it I can't play here?"

Rodney smiled and said, "Smush, I know Kenny just like you do. If Kobe Bryant himself came down here, Kenny wouldn't let him play. Kenny is a no-nonsense guy, and he's going to stick by his rules. They work. You know, this tournament will be going on here twenty years after most of these guys have passed."

So there was no Smush in the playoff lineup.

As it turned out, All Out did not need Smush. Nakiea Miller, an excellent forward at Iona, joined Smith and Chris Sandy to put on a three-point shooting exhibition. Miller hit five three-point shots, Magic made seven, and Sandy connected on eight three-pointers. It was a blowout: 98–73.

## Day Four: The Good Get Better

Lambert Shell's Shooting Stars have been crushing teams for the last month. In their first playoff game, they easily defeated the fifth seeded Chaz Hoops, 109-95. Forward Sha-ronn Brown scored 27, and Antawn Dobie got 28. Dobie is a five-foot-ten superstar guard from Long Island University, where he was all-conference in both his junior and senior years. He finished his last year averaging 36 points per game, including a single-game high of 53 points.

Doug Herring's Power Kingdom had upset B & B in the first round, but in this case lightning struck only once. Lambert Shell's guys showed what playoff-intensity defense can achieve; Power Kingdom was held to 54 points, while the Shooting Stars racked up 93. Dobie led with 23 points, but four men scored close to 20. As the tournament headed into the final rounds, the strong were getting stronger.

## Brownsville's Last Gasp

Because of their tailspin at the season's end, Brownsville had to play the top-seeded X-Men in the first round of the playoffs. The park was packed. The toughest team from Brownsville was taking on the toughest team from Bedford-Stuyvesant. Brownsville was the Brooklyn power team a decade ago, while the X-Men have that reputation today. This was not going to be a ballet.

A problem for both teams was that the game was being played on a weekday after work, so each team had only five players when the game began. Stragglers would arrive late, but Bo never had more than eight, and Hassan Duncombe and Rodney Stiles never arrived at all.

Without Vinny Matos, who had quit the team, Brownsville lost much of its outside shooting, so they would have to rely more on John Harris in the post. The X-Men would immediately collapse on him, forcing Harris either to pass the ball back out or take a quick jump hook. If Harris looked like he might get a good shot, he would be hacked. Brownsville missed a dozen free throws in the period, but it still led, 25–20.

Brownsville's best athlete, Rich Henry, was covering Mike Campbell. Fans here love to watch a good matchup. By the end of the half Henry had only 3 points (all foul shots) while Mike Campbell scored only 5 points, none in the second period. It was a quiet but intense defensive battle.

John Williamson matched up against the X-Men's best defender, Aaron Walker, but both men frequently got clear for open jump shots.

Williamson was Brownsville's most consistent shooter from the field, finishing the half with 17 points. For a time, Brownsville was up by 13 points. It looked like an upset was coming.

Then Aaron Walker began to hit some key three-pointers, which loosened up the Brownsville defense. Walker finished the half with 13 points. The X-Men hacked away at Brownsville's post-up players, and Brownsville cooperated by hitting only 50 percent from the line. Brownsville's hard work getting clear was not producing points. After a well-played first half, Brownsville was up by two, 49–47.

Once again, the early minutes of the third period loomed large. Hammer opened up for the X-Men with a three-pointer. Benny Timmons, a dangerous streak shooter, added another. Bo Keene called time-out to rally his team before the game got out of hand. He urged Shane to be more active in the middle on defense so Bo's guards could play Timmons tighter without worrying about getting beaten on his drives.

It didn't work. Timmons hit two more three-pointers in a row and Campbell converted a free throw, as the X-Men stormed out to a 63–55 lead. Brownsville's best shooters, Williamson and Henry, were not getting open. Brownsville was still in the game, but it would have to toughen up on defense. There was no time to lose.

At this delicate moment, Keith Stroud became so frustrated with Shane's defensive play that he took a swing at him. Fights do occasionally break out at West 4th Street, but it's rare to see a fight between two players on the same team. Shane and Stroud had to be separated, and both were ejected and assessed technical fouls. Everyone on the Brownsville team was pushing someone, and soon they started pushing the X-Men. The X-Men pushed back. The court was a melee of shoving, shouting players. Hammer, who had played on Brownsville's championship team in 1996, was chest-to-chest with Bo Keene. Kenny and Rick were on the court separating people and getting everyone who was not playing off the court. It took ten minutes to restore order so the game could continue.

When it did, Timmons hit another three-pointer; he had peeled off 15 straight points on five consecutive three-pointers. When the period was mercifully ended, the X-Men were ahead 78–65. Brownsville collected only 16 points in the last period, finally losing 105–81.

After the game Stroud and Shane got into another shoving match at the back of the park and had to be broken up by Kenny, Iron Mike, Bo Keene, and a few others. Bo was unable to control these two players. Rick was annoyed with Bo for again letting things get out of hand. Rosy Jackson, resigned and downcast, concluded, "We just can't have this anymore."

# chapter fourteen

# The Semifinals

### Game One: Hustle

**United Brooklyn's only challenge** before the finals was going to come from Lambert Shell's Shooting Stars. Sid's two previous playoff games had been runaways. The only unexpected absence today would be John Thomas (Mookie), the team's point guard. Darren Phillip, his top rebounder, would be backed up by Ken Bantam, so Sid would have strong rebounders to support his shooters: Duane Woodward, Tariq Kirksay, and B. J. McFarlan.

The Shooting Stars had no legitimate center, but the team had skillfully blended youth and age into their lineup. The old guys were the power down low. They had good young guards: Antawn Dobie (LIU), Shariff Fordham (St. John's), and Laron Mapp (South Carolina State), along with forward Sha-ronn Brown. Except for Karriem himself, who was at St. Vincent's Hospital, everyone showed up. Karriem had been there over a month, and his health continued to deteriorate.

Sid Jones may be the best-liked coach at West 4th Street, but today this did not work to his advantage. Shell's team knew they were underdogs, so it was now or never. These attitudes dominated the first quarter of play. United Brooklyn's Darren Phillip did not want to chase Lambert Shell out on the perimeter, so Shell quickly hit two three-pointers. The Shooting Stars guards, Mapp and Dobie, hit four more with little opposition. While United Brooklyn was waiting for Shell's gang to cool off, they fell further behind. By the end of the first period United Brooklyn had made no three-point shots. Clearly they had underestimated their opponents, and they trailed 31–17. The gap was narrowed to 51–40 at the half, but the most talented team in the tournament was in trouble.

United Brooklyn began the third period well. Darren Phillip began to control the offensive backboards, so he was regularly fouled. He made most of his foul shots, scoring 12 points in the period. But without their regular point guard, no one was taking charge of the offense. They gave up some easy baskets. With seven minutes remaining in the third period and United Brooklyn down 63–50, James Ryans arrived. Ryans is a tough bench coach and he knew the team needed a wake-up call. He immediately forced his players to press the Shooting Stars all over the court. The sudden pressure from United Brooklyn unnerved the Stars, and their jump shots got longer and longer. The press created turnovers that resulted in uncontested layups. The Shooting Stars' lead was cut to 80–74 as the third quarter ended.

Throughout the early part of the fourth quarter, defense was intense at both ends of the court. With six minutes left, the Shooting Stars were holding a narrow lead, 86–83. They had to figure out how to control Phillip's post-up game, which was wearing down an older Lambert Shell. Shell himself came up with the solution. Instead of fouling Phillip when he got the ball, Shell fronted him whenever he could and worked on denying him the ball. When Phillip did get the ball in the post, the Stars sent guards in after him. This constant double-teaming forced Phillip to pass back out to the corners.

In the last minutes of any close game at the Cage, you'd better be prepared to shoot foul shots, because every shot will be contested. As the game entered its final minutes, United Brooklyn became sloppy, and in the last six minutes the team made less than half of its free throws. That took away its post-up game and slashing drives to the basket. So United Brooklyn had to take more jump shots, and aggressive defense forced these shots farther from the basket.

United Brooklyn made its final run with three minutes remaining when Duane Woodward tied the score at 93 with a three-pointer and then added two free throws after he was hacked in the lane. This put United Brooklyn ahead for the first time, 95–93. Shell immediately retaliated with a three-pointer of his own, retaking the lead, 96–95. With less than two minutes left, the Shooting Stars' Corey Underwood tipped in an errant jumper to make the score 98–95. Sha-ronn Brown was fouled and he made both free throws; Woodward was fouled but made only one. Dobie drove the lane for 2 points and the Stars were ahead 102–96.

United Brooklyn was exhausted, but they continued the all-court press. Darkness helped. The fans on the fence could barely read the chalk scoreboard. After a Shooting Stars turnover, Tariq Kirksay was fouled on a successful jump shot and he made the free throw, so with fifty-four seconds remaining, the Shooting Stars lead was cut to 102–99. The Stars made a free throw on their next possession, but Woodward, who was on a rampage, made a driving layup to bring United Brooklyn to within one point, 102–101. Then with twenty-six seconds left, the fouling began. United Brooklyn fouled the Stars to get the ball back, and the Shooting Stars fouled United Brooklyn to prevent a clean shot attempt. The Shooting Stars took more free throws and they made more. With a few seconds left, the Shooting Stars had moved ahead 106–103. A last-second three-point attempt by Woodward failed (he scored 12 points in the period). Lambert Shell's gang had pulled off a stunning upset.

The players were exhausted, but no one wanted to go home. Large groups of fans hung around the court, talking basketball, shaking hands, happy to be there. Basketball doesn't get any better, not here, not anywhere. Carefree and content, Kenny, Rosy, and Joe had sat together for the entire game. With no flare-ups, it was all basketball. The scoring was balanced: Each team had five players in double figures. Shell led his team with 21 and Phillip had 22. Even the big matchup was close. For playground fanatics, this was basketball heaven.

## Game Two: Power

Hammer is proud of his name. Everyone uses it.

Its meaning is clear; you know exactly what kind of man you are dealing with.

He did not make up the name himself; it is a mark of distinction bestowed on Brian Elleby by his peers.

Over the twenty-five years of tournament play, only two men at West 4th Street have been given the name of Hammer, so he follows in the tradition of the original Hammer, Marvin Stevenson (now fifty-four), a great player for the Harlem USA teams that dominated the league in the early 1980s.

Hammer personifies his team, the X-Men. He is driven by uncontrollable restless energy. After an emotional and physically exhausting game of banging into people and running up and down the court for forty minutes (Hammer is seldom on the sidelines), he will unwind by shadowboxing or wrestling with teammates on the sidewalk. In seconds he has his teammate immobilized in a paralyzing reverse headlock. After holding this position perhaps a bit longer than his victim would like, he releases him with a great chuckle. What should he do next? Even in his midthirties Hammer can't stay still. One shudders to imagine the reign of terror he must have exercised over his junior high school teachers.

Like most of his teammates, Hammer grew up in Bedford-Stuyvesant and played at Boys and Girls High School. He started out at West 4th Street with Brownsville, where he was part of the 1996 championship team. For years, out of loyalty to Bo Keene, he would not play for the X-Men against Bo in the West 4th Street league. This year he relented. Now he plays in all the other tournaments the X-Men enter, winter and summer: BRC, Fireball, Eight Ball, Tillary Park, Gun Hill, and Rucker.

Hammer thinks the world of Dytanya. "The X-Men are more than a team," he tells me. "We're like a family; we help each other. When my sister Ann Marie died, the whole team came to her funeral. Dytanya has been there for me many times; he's helped me out family-wise. He's not just a coach. He's also a smart man. You know he graduated from the Police Academy. He's young [thirty-three] like us too."

In today's semifinal round the X-Men's opponent will be All Out, the fourth seed in the division, with Chris Sandy and Sidney Smith.

Often West 4th Street games fall into a familiar symphonic structure. The first quarter has the feel of an overture, when players check one another out and explore for strengths and weaknesses. This would be a period of introduction, not resolution. Hammer immediately posted up, called for the ball, slammed into power forward Raheem Jones, made his shots, and drew fouls. The crowd would see more of this.

For All Out, Sidney Smith and Chris Sandy began to work their wonders. They dropped a few three-pointers and drove to the basket to keep the defense honest. Mike Campbell hit a couple of jumpers for the X-Men. He moved the ball quickly and looked for teammates cutting or posting up, but he remained on the margin of play, a helpful fifth man. The first period was almost relaxing, recreational. All Out closed the period leading 26–25.

The second quarter developed what the crowd had seen in the first period. The soloists became more assertive and pronounced and the original themes were developed further. Raheem Jones picked up his third personal foul as Hammer took his jump shot into his chest at every opportunity. Smith and Sandy combined for five three-pointers (the entire team of X-Men had only three), and between them scored

28 points in the first half. Campbell finished the period with 13 points, but All Out closed the first half still in the lead, 47–43.

In a Shakespearean tragedy, the third act is the time when a critical action is taken that makes the play's outcome inevitable. In *Hamlet,* this is the act in which Hamlet refuses to kill the usurping king because the king was praying. Never again would Hamlet have the opportunity to control events. In the third act of *Othello,* Desdemona's handkerchief is stolen and Iago plants it so that Othello becomes convinced that his wife has been unfaithful. At this moment, Desdemona's fate is sealed.

In the first three minutes of the third period, Mike Campbell hit three quick three-pointers and the X-Men grabbed the lead, 52–51. Now Campbell called for the ball and played like a big guard rather than a small forward. He was too tall for Sandy to cover in the post, and Sandy was not getting help. When Campbell started from the corner, he was quick enough to get to the baseline on his way to the hoop. All Out's big man, Raheem Jones, picked up his fifth foul stopping Campbell's drive, so he had to sit out.

In addition, the X-Men seemed to be getting most of the close calls, which encouraged Hammer and Whyett Benn, another strong rebounder, to keep banging away down low. They dominated the boards, holding All Out to one shot on each possession. The third quarter ended with the X-Men leading, 67–59. Campbell had 15 points; the entire All Out team had only 12.

In a symphony, the tone of the final movement is stately and triumphant, with the early themes resolved. In the last act of a Shakespearean tragedy, the victors prevail and the bodies of the vanquished are carried away. Basketball is always a tragedy for someone. In a blowout the tempo is largo, perhaps funereal. In a close game the last act is frantic, vigorous, often macabre. This was All Out, fighting desperately.

Guards Sandy, Smith, and Roger Kellman started hitting their jump shots again. Raheem Jones was back in the game, and on a drive from the corner he put All Out back into the lead, 73–71. The players were glistening with sweat; their shirts were stuck to the contours of their bodies.

The X-Men's small guards, Aaron Walker and Reggie Roberson, were challenging Kellman and Smith defensively by clearing out against them, driving to the basket, forcing them to exhaust themselves on defense. With 1:40 left in the game, All Out missed two straight layups. The relentless running and pounding had worn them down. After the second miss, the outlet pass went to Campbell, who streaked down the court for an uncontested layup, putting the X-Men ahead 80–76.

When the in-bounds pass went to Sidney Smith on the sideline, Campbell and Walker immediately trapped him against the fence, stripping the ball, producing another uncontested layup. Now the score was 82–76. All Out had no more miracles left. Smith finished with 26 points, Sandy got 20, and Mike Campbell led all scorers with 36. Hammer's gang won 86–79.

The X-Men would play for the championship on Saturday against the Shooting Stars.

# chapter fifteen

# The Finalists

**Who plays in a** West 4th Street championship game?

Not big stars. Not high school wiz kids. Not hip-hop playground tricksters.

The teams that survive have good players, but they are players who have not been coddled into believing that the world owes them a living. Superstars no longer play on tiny concrete courts. Here, players respect their coaches. The tournament at West 4th Street is a nine-to-five, blue-collar, lunch-bucket, barbershop, middle-class collection of athletes who like the game and who like one another.

If Norman Rockwell lived in New York City today, he would be painting these scenes at West 4th Street:

A big power forward, dripping wet, high-fiving an adoring little kid who is looking up in awe, wearing an oversized NBA jersey;

A stunned defensive player, wide-eyed in disbelief, as a stern female referee hits him with a blocking foul;

The ever-observant Butter, with the megaphone in his hand, slyly checking out the good-looking girl in the tank top leaning against the fence.

The teams playing for the West 4th Street tournament championship have each played together for over a decade, and both are overachievers. The X-Men defeated a flashier team: All Out. The Shooting Stars beat a more talented team: United Brooklyn. Geographically, the matchup is between Brooklyn and Queens.

These same two teams met for the championship in 1999, with the X-Men taking the title.

Karriem Memminger has been coaching the Shooting Stars for six years, and he is a product of Far Rockaway High School in Queens. Many of his players are older than he, but his savvy and enthusiasm have allowed him to work with players of all ages. Karriem is a distant relative of Kenny Graham, and he is also the nephew of Dean Memminger, who played in college for Marquette, followed by eight years with the New York Knickerbockers and the Atlanta Hawks (1971–77). Memminger's team will play in at least one tournament during the winter and as many as three tournaments during the summer. He keeps his players busy. Karriem makes a good living at Jamaica Hospital, where he has worked for ten years.

Since he is still hospitalized, his team plans to visit him after this final game. Karriem's illness, which causes severe inflammation of his muscles, has kept him at St. Vincent's for eight weeks. (When he finally was discharged on September 12 he was a feeble 105 pounds. Recuperation kept him out of work for seven months, and a year later he was still on steroids and other medication to build himself up. It was a brutal ordeal.)

Lambert Shell grew up in the Boulevard housing projects in East New York (Brooklyn), but he attended August Martin High School in Jamaica, Queens. He does not consider his housing-projects upbringing a disaster. "I had my mother and my stepfather, and college guys who would come back and visit," he recalls. "It was a good life. Of course you always had big kids pushing around little kids. We'd be playing on the court, and when the big kids came and wanted to play, they'd just throw us off. If we complained, they'd throw our ball into the street and punch us some, but it wasn't real bad. Then when we got big, we'd do the same thing. You know, it's just growing up."

He is near the end of a successful athletic career. He led Bridgeport to the Division II finals in his junior and senior years, losing in the finals to Northern Alabama (1991), and then to Virginia Union (1992). As a senior, Shell played so well he won the tournament's Most Valuable Player Award even though his team lost. Division II had some good players back then. Manute Bol, Mario Elie, and Charles Oakley all played Division II basketball in the late 1980s and early 1990s.

Shell was selected as the Eastern Collegiate Athletic Conference Rookie of the Year as a freshman, and he was then named Player of the Year for the next three years. He was a three-time Division II All-American, and some people claim he may have been the best Division II player ever. During Lambert's stay at Bridgeport, the team won 103 games and lost only 31. Although Shell got a tryout with the Utah Jazz, he did not stick, so he went to Sweden for one year, after which he spent five years in the Philippines, finally leaving in 1998.

Lambert Shell hardly resembles the typical librarian, but that's what he is, in an unusual way. He works at the Laurelton branch of the Queens Public Library, where an ingenious New York State Juvenile Justice grant pays his salary. The Queens Borough library system, by the way, is no bush-league operation. Although the New York Public Library on Fifth Avenue and 42nd Street and the imposing Brooklyn Public Library at Grand Army Plaza are better known, the Queens system is more active. Queens Borough libraries circulate more books than any of the other boroughs, and it claims to be the most active library system in the country. Queens has sixty-three branches that contain more than 17 million items, and it operates on an annual budget of $70 million.

Laurelton is a predominantly African-American community, and its library had been vandalized three or four times before Lambert arrived. Older residents were afraid to go there because the black kids hanging around the front door in their baggy pants and do-rags frightened them. The library building is not particularly imposing—one floor and only 7,500 square feet, constructed in 1953 but recently remodeled. Almost the entire library is dedicated to the interests of children, who from 3:00 P.M. until closing completely dominate the library. On an average day there will be more than a hundred kids doing their homework, reading magazines, or just hanging out. "This is their library," Lambert says. "We want them to be comfortable here, but we want them to behave as well."

Although Laurelton is a reasonably well-to-do community, where the single-family houses have driveways and resale prices are in the $250,000 to $350,000 range, a huge number of the children here are with foster parents (Lambert thinks the number is close to 20 percent). Often both parents are working, so supervision can be a problem. Foster parents receive regular payments from the state to help meet the expenses of raising the child, and if the child is not formally adopted, within six months to two years the child will move to another home.

The younger elementary and middle school kids, all of whom must wear uniforms, appear to be well disciplined and concerned with their workbooks, but three-quarters of the kids are girls. The older teenage boys, who arrive at the library closer to 5:00 P.M., do not wear uniforms, they seldom bring books, and many of them make no pretense of studying. Nevertheless, the library is quiet; its orderly but crowded bookshelves suggest a thoughtful environment, and Lambert is always around keeping an eye on the kids, asking questions and telling stories. "We give kids their own library card in the first grade," Lambert continues. "That's very significant for a kid that age. It's the only personal identification young children have, and they are proud to take books out with it."

Lambert came here because the library staff got the bright idea that rather than hiring more security people to keep the kids under control, they should apply for a grant that would fund a youth program. The kids could still come to the library, but find supervised activities to their liking. So ever since December of 2001 Lambert has been greeting kids every day after school, offering them physical and mental recreation opportunities with tutoring, counseling, a chess club, and a cybertraining program that now has more than three dozen laptop computers.

"Even the timid regulars are back," Shell notes. "They tell me circulation is up thirty percent."

Shell's life is hardly filled with luxuries. He has one young child and his wife works. Lambert enjoys his job. "My happiness," he says, "has always come from seeing other people happy."

Of course it's not that simple. Lambert's concern for other people's children is moving, but even he realizes that he cannot be giving to others all the time. Someday he will have to do more for himself, make more money, get back to a more competitive, masculine life. He thinks in terms of sports and coaching, but he would also make a great factory supervisor or a plant manager in industry. Unfortunately New York has little industry to speak of; producing things is not central to its business and cultural environment. New York moves things and finances them; it is less likely to make them. The story of Lambert Shell is far from over.

Of all the West 4th Street coaches, Dytanya Mixson may be most like Kenny Graham. He is emotional, a risk taker, and a leader. His team is a big part of his life, and his players are loyal to him. A few years ago he left a secure job on the New York City police force to start his own construction company in Bedford-Stuyvesant. Police department politics wore him out. At the moment he's keeping busy, but being a construction subcontractor is a tough business. Getting paid can be just as difficult as getting work. While the future of his business is still uncertain, he is working long hours and hustling for more jobs, trying to keep his tiny staff occupied. He can never meet before 8:00 P.M. because that's when his workday ends.

Most of his work is refurbishing and remodeling existing houses and buildings, and he owns three residential buildings himself. Dytanya left Boys and Girls High School in Bedford-Stuyvesant and has been supporting himself since he was seventeen years old. He began work as a messenger and got his General Educational Development (GED) diploma. He quickly moved to a temp agency that found him an office job at the New York City Board of Education. They liked him there, but he could not gain full-time status until he turned eighteen.

He passed the Police Academy exam in 1994 and worked as a police officer until 2001, when he resigned to start his present business. Dytanya was married in 1997 and he has two children, but last year he was divorced.

"I guess one reason I got divorced was basketball," he says half seriously. "I spent a lot of time and money on basketball. You know, it is expensive to keep teams in a bunch of tournaments. Each summer I lay out over five thousand dollars for entry fees and other stuff. I never pay my players, and I don't give them sneakers or jackets. I don't take money from players either. I ask them to pay the referee fees, but that's it. The only other thing I give them is advice. This team has become my first love. It's been like raising a child. It's hard to let them go."

Dytanya raised his team from its basketball infancy to a West 4th Street championship. Back in 1990, when he was twenty years old, he started coaching in a local midget league for thirteen- to fifteen-year-olds. He kept the group together in the junior division, ages fifteen to seventeen, and continued with them as seniors, ages seventeen to nineteen. Every summer they played in tournaments all over Brooklyn, and some of the players were good enough to play on the varsity at Boys and Girls High School. Five of his players went on to Sullivan County Community College, located one hundred miles northwest of the city in the Catskills.

The heart of the team is Brian Elleby. He is a superb outside shooter, an aggressive defensive player, a good passer, and a consistent rebounder. His weakness is his size. At barely six foot four and 235 pounds, he is too small for a big-time power forward, but that is his natural position.

Like many of his teammates, Hammer grew up in Bedford-Stuyvesant, played for Boys and Girls High School, and went on to Sullivan. He still plays as many as five days a week during the summer. In the winter he cuts back to just two days a week, on weekends.

"I have a lot of energy inside me, a lot of frustrations," he says. "I have to let it out. That's why I play a lot, and that explains why I play the way I do. I like the bump-and-grind style of play. That's one reason I like West 4th Street. There is nowhere to hide. You got to play ball."

Hammer is not sure how he could live without basketball. "I am a competitive person," he explains. "Basketball gives me an emotional and physical outlet. I've always loved the game. When I was a boy in the Kingsborough projects, I used to start practicing at six A.M. I can remember people calling at me out of their windows to stop bouncing the ball. I was waking them up.

"Basketball has kept me out of trouble; I was busy playing. Basketball forces you to better yourself, and to focus. You know, basketball is a mind game too. Guys are always trying to talk you out of your game. You learn to be strong in your mind, and this can take you far."

Dytanya speaks of him with great respect.

"Hammer is a strong man, and his life has not been easy. In a way he's a mama's boy, so when his mother died in 1994, that hurt him. He took it very hard." Today Hammer is swamped by responsibilities. He has two sons, Bryant, nine, and Javon, who is eight. They live with their mother in Brooklyn, and Hammer spends a great deal of his free time with them. In addition to dealing with divorce, family tragedy has further complicated his life.

A few years ago his sister died, and she left five children behind. Hammer took on two of her daughters as a foster parent. His fiancée,

Christina, has a fourteen-year-old daughter of her own. So Hammer cares for three children at home in Queens, as well as his own boys in Brooklyn. This is a heavy responsibility for any thirty-year-old man. He has been working with the New York City Human Resources Administration for eight years.

Dytanya would like to help out Hammer more than he does now. "Hammer works weekends as a bouncer to make extra money. If I can get my business going a little bit better, I'd like to get him working with me. He's a good man."

All of the players in this final game are good men; but only one team will be the champion.

# chapter sixteen

# The Finals

**Saturday**

The weather for the last day of the season was uncertain: sunny one moment and overcast the next. By 2:30 P.M. the temperature was over 100 degrees, but dark clouds were forming in the east. In late August the city often experiences intense heat followed by brief, drenching showers. The championship game between the X-Men and the Shooting Stars was scheduled to begin at 3:30 P.M., and an hour before game time most of the good spots along the fence on Sixth Avenue were claimed, with battered deck chairs, cheap metal folding chairs, and plastic milk crates leaning against the fence, holding positions for spectators who got to the park early.

Kenny would be returning to Rio three days after the season concluded. Throughout the week, Rio was all he wanted to talk about. In the three weeks Kenny had been back in New York, he had come to the park every day. By 2:50 P.M. the once-brilliant sun was covered by the dark clouds, and minutes later the heavens opened. Kenny, Rick, and a few others scampered over to Burger King across the street for cover. Kenny's cell phone immediately began ringing. He answered the first two calls without a greeting: "The game is on. We will begin at four thirty. See you then." He hung up to take the next call.

In twenty minutes the rain had stopped, the sun was blazing, and Kenny's workers had taken over the court. Stacks of old newspapers miraculously appeared and the entire surface was blanketed with newsprint. The paper soaked up the water so the sun could do its job more quickly. Iron Mike, Nathanial Green, known at the park as Bean, Bobby Jackson, Isaiah, and Moneybags were spreading the papers out, and after a few minutes, sweeping them up again. Brooms were borrowed from local merchants. The puddles disappeared and the sun dried the remaining dampness in half an hour.

Kenny announced the final game. As the teams completed their warm-up drills he told the crowd about them, and he introduced the referees. They, too, are important. "The law firm today will be Martin Braxton and Nate Bradwell," he said. "If you have an issue, take it up with them."

The key matchup opposed the teams' leaders, Lambert Shell and Brian Elleby. They are friends off the court, but when they meet at West 4th Street, it is a battle. Says Shell, "No matter how tired he gets, Hammer keeps coming after you. It is punishing. We hate to play against each other because our games are so similar."

Tip-off took place a little before 5:00 P.M.

The Shooting Stars spread the court on offense to allow their guards, Antawn Dobie and Shariff Fordham, to cut to the basket or pull up for ten-foot jumpers. The X-Men blocked up the middle, deflecting passes. They understand this small court well, so they used a sagging defense, close to an illegal zone. They forced the Shooting Stars into an offense of long jump shots with no rebounds. It worked, because the Shooting Stars were missing everything.

Meanwhile, the X-Men probed for mismatches. Forward Mike

Campbell posted up against guard Shariff Fordham, who could not control him. Campbell scored 5 quick points. Hammer pulled Shell away from the basket and hit a three-pointer. In the first two minutes the X-Men grabbed an 8–0 lead.

When the Shooting Stars got in close, they were fouled and sent to the line, but they could not make foul shots. Hammer pulled Shell outside and hit another three-pointer to make the score a stunning 18–1. By the time Shell made his team's first field goal, a three-pointer, the score was 20–6. Playing with confidence on offense and defense, the X-Men could do no wrong. Benny Timmons poured it on with three straight three-pointers. The first quarter came to an end with the score a lopsided 35–17. Timmons and Hammer had 10 points apiece (outscoring the entire team of the Shooting Stars).

The Stars' shooting improved in the second period, so they wound up playing the X-Men even, but they could not stop the other team from scoring. Hammer was getting clear shots at the basket from the outside. The X-Men added a third guard, Artie Lawyer, to play with Reggie Roberson and Aaron Walker. Dytanya loves to use Artie at key moments. "He's probably the smartest player I have ever coached," he says. "When he's out there, it's like having a coach on the court. He's great with our younger guys."

The sky grew suddenly darker, and with two minutes left in the second period the rain came down hard. Kenny called the game and sent the players home with the X-Men leading, 50–33; play was set to resume at 1:00 P.M. on Sunday.

## Rain Delay

Since the rain was unrelenting, there was nothing to do but find a dry spot and wait. While Kenny was heading back to Burger King on West 3rd Street, he saw a crowd forming across the street. The crowd was noisy, moving slowly down the sidewalk, and it was clear that a fight had broken out. Sherman and a guy from the handball courts were swinging away at each other, grabbing, and tearing shirts. The crowd of thirty-odd people were watching intently, oohing and aahing with each blow.

For Kenny the fight was not amusing; it meant trouble. He and Iron Mike headed toward the crowd moving slowly down West 3rd Street. Together they talked to the fighters, urging them to break it up. At the same time Kenny went for Sherman, whom he had known for twenty years. He bear-hugged Sherman from behind around the chest and pulled him back, away from the grip of his opponent. Kenny never flaunts his own strength, but he is as tough as anyone at West 4th Street. Iron Mike enveloped the other fighter, speaking calmly while immobilizing his arms and pulling him away from Sherman. There were no knives, no weapons. Soon the fight was over. The shouting and threats continued, but Kenny kept talking, calming, reasoning, using his talking time to allow the fighters to cool off. Hopefully, no one would lose face. Each man, surrounded by his followers, agreed to go his separate way. The rain kept falling, so Kenny and Mike were soaking wet when they walked into Burger King. They put on dry shirts and settled down.

"I'm disappointed in Sherman," Kenny began. "He should know better. The city could shut us down over an incident like this. There are plenty of white people who would like to see us out of this neighborhood for good. The sight of black men fighting will do it. It doesn't matter if they are part of the league or not. They could all be handball players. For the city, it wouldn't be a money decision either. They'd just deny us our permit. That could be the end of basketball down here. It would certainly be the end of me."

The staff couldn't go home until the rain stopped because they had to put away the chairs and tables. They also had to clean up the mess that the fans and players made. Kenny decided to give everyone a summer-end bonus. As a rule the people who come every day would get a twenty-dollar bill, a handshake, and a slap on the back after the last game of the season. But since Nike and Mistic kicked in money,

Kenny could give meaningful bonuses. Kenny asked Rosy to go to his car to retrieve the envelopes with the cash for the staff.

Kenny gave away $4,000 to ten guys; the range was $250 to $500. The recipients did not know that Kenny had not actually received all the money he was due from sponsors, so he did not have the money he was giving out. Rosy was advancing it to him. Each man had been paid $10 per day whenever he helped out, and each staff person was wearing shirts and sneakers that Kenny provided. Joe and Rosy suggested that he give away less money, but Kenny didn't want to disappoint his crew. "Why should I skimp on these guys? Just so I can keep another few thousand?" he asked. "What good would that do me?"

## Sunday

It was another August scorcher, with the temperature in the high nineties before noon, and the blacktopped court was even hotter. The high for today would be 102 degrees, and the city is always humid in August. The staff arrived early, partly to set up, but mostly to be around one another. This was the final day of the season, the last chance they would have to hang out and talk. Shortly after noon Iron Mike and Moneybags hung up the Nike and Mistic signs. The American flag was on top, as usual.

A citywide handball tournament was going on next to the Cage, so two crowds of sports fans were here.

Mike Williams came out, just as he did on opening day. Mike had played here, coached here, run the tournament, and worked as a referee. He remembers the Cage in its glory days in the late 1970s and early 1980s when professional scouts were at every big game, and he recalled Kenny's early enthusiasm and commitment to the tournament. "Kenny is a great leader, and he is much more of a risk taker than I am. Together, Kenny and I spent an ungodly number of hours just sitting out here. I recall that at the end of the day, he would pick himself up and go to work at a print shop where he was working nights. I was always amazed at his energy."

Joe Merriweather was here too. He missed yesterday's game because, as a devout Seventh-Day Adventist, he would not come to the park on Saturday, which is his holy day. Joe smiled at the good fortune that had allowed him to see the final game of the year. He leaned over and whispered to Rosy confidentially, "Yesterday I prayed for rain."

The game resumed with the last two minutes of the first half remaining. Laron Mapp hit a jumper for the Shooting Stars, but Shell was still bottled up in the post. The half ended with the X-Men comfortably ahead, 51–36. Shell led the Stars with 10 points, four of them foul shots, but the Shooting Stars' guards were not on track. Timmons had 12 points and Campbell had 11 for the X-Men; their scoring was balanced, and they had hit eight three-pointers.

The third period, like the second, was even. It appeared that the 17-point hole the Shooting Stars dug for themselves in the first period had become too deep. Hammer was winning his matchup with Shell. He and Roberson each collected 10 points in the period, and the quarter ended with the score 75–60.

Late in the fourth quarter, with only three minutes remaining, the Shooting Stars made their final run. Dobie stole the ball twice and converted the last one into a 3-point play when he was fouled. Dobie's 5-point spurt brought the score to 86–79. The X-Men failed to score on their possession, and Lambert Shell got off a post-up shot without being hacked, making the score 86–81 with 2:24 left to play. The X-Men called time-out.

In the final two minutes the defensive play of Walker and Roberson saved the game for the X-Men. Walker challenged Dobie's hot hand by pressing him all over the court, contesting every cut, every dribble, and every move that he made. Dobie broke free for a layup to draw his team within three, 88–85, but he was working hard. Unfortunately, his teammates became momentarily hypnotized by his brilliance, so they forgot to get back on defense after his basket. As it turned out, this momentary lapse decided the game.

Hammer took the in-bounds pass at midcourt and streaked down the court for an open layup to reestablish his team's 5-point lead, 90–85. It was Hammer's thirtieth point of the game. Less than one minute remained. The Shooting Stars got the ball to Dobie on the in-bounds pass, but this time Walker stole his dribble and flipped the ball to Reggie Roberson for another breakaway layup. Hammer's basket and Walker's steal wrapped up the game. The X-Men won, 96–85.

This was the second time Shell's team had lost to the X-Men in the finals. When the game was over, Shell could only shake his head. "We didn't have enough left. *Our* championship game was against Sid. That was a great win for us, but it drained us. We just couldn't do it again." He paused. "Hey, these guys are good."

After the game Kenny presided over the awards ceremony. He stood in center court with his megaphone and shook the hand of each player on both teams. Being congratulated by Kenny is a distinction. The winning team members each received a leather jacket, a warm-up suit, a bag, footwear, and a Nike watch. The losers got most of the same stuff, but not the leather jacket.

The Sportsmanship Trophy was awarded to Lambert Shell, who led his team to the finals, and Mike Campbell, who had a spectacular summer, was named Most Valuable Player. Sidney Smith was selected the Outstanding Player in the tournament. These are trophies that matter.

No one was in a rush to leave. Kenny shook hands all around, lingering at the park until everything was put away and the last players went home. He thanked Joe for seeing him through another year; he slapped Rosy on the shoulder, said good-bye to everyone, and headed down Sixth Avenue for his limo.

# chapter seventeen

# Smush Parker and
# Mike Campbell: Where Next?

**Mike Campbell**

**Since the West 4th** Street championship game was over by 3:00 P.M. on Sunday, a handful of die-hard fans from the Cage drove up to Orchard Beach in the Bronx to watch the final game of the Hoops in the Sun tournament run by Rufino "Pops" Cruz. When they arrived, they were amazed to see Mike Campbell warming up with the GDC Studios team. His teammates here included Duane Woodward, who played with Sid Jones at West 4th Street, and Amal McCaskill, a six-foot-eleven center with the San Antonio Spurs.

Since Mike had been playing with the X-Men downtown an hour before, he was asked about playing in two championship games in one afternoon. He smiled and said, "Just call me the Iron Man. Like Lance Armstrong." Mike was going to play two championship games in a row, and he not only knew who Lance Armstrong was (the world's greatest long-distance bicycle racer), but he knew a good deal about him.

Mike's team won the final game here, 62–58, giving him his third championship trophy of the summer and two in one day. His team had also won at the Nike Pro-Classic, where he was voted the Most Valuable Player, just as he was at West 4th Street. Mike played in a fourth tournament at Kingston Park in Brooklyn, but his team lost in the final game to finish second. Add three championships, two MVP awards, and his victory at the Nike one-on-one championship with its huge billboard of Mike in the Village, and you have a brilliant summer of basketball. It is reasonable to claim that Mike Campbell is the best player (not in the NBA) playing in New York City.

Yet Mike still doesn't have a job playing professional basketball. The previous winter he played with the Rida Scarfati team in the Italian league, but he will not be invited back. Why?

One reason is that basketball worldwide is becoming more competitive. One sees this in the NBA. Three of the top seven NBA picks this year were non-American. In 2002 Sacramento got to the finals with three Europeans in the lineup at crunch time. In 2003 the two best players on the Dallas Mavericks were Canadian Steve Nash and German Dirk Nowitzki. The World Champion San Antonio Spurs are led by Tim Duncan, from St. Croix, and Tony Parker, a French point guard. This has become an old story.

As Europe develops better players locally, they have less need for imported Americans. Recognizing this trend, the league in which Scarfati plays has reduced the number of Americans permitted on each team from five to three. Scarfati has already signed a friend of Campbell's, Randolph Childress, who starred at Wake Forest and spent some time in the NBA. Only two spots are left, and they will go to big men.

Athletes like Mike Campbell are the game's great purists. They play for hours every day of the week, and the best of them think only of their game. They are amateurs in the most fundamental and most joyful sense of the word. The word amateur is derived from the Latin *amare,* "to love." They play because they love the game. No dedicated pianist, actress, gymnast, or golfing professional works any harder. "Playing all day every day is normal," Campbell remarks. "I'm always trying to improve my game, or at least to stay sharp." How long has he been on this regimen? "How long? Why, ever since . . . ever since . . . just forever, I guess. I don't take vacations. I play every day. I've always played every day."

Mike is well known in local basketball circles. After transferring from Westchester Community College, he became a standout at Long Island University from 1997 to 1999, where he averaged 17 points per game. Along with a neighborhood buddy, Charles Jones—who transferred to LIU from Rutgers—they led LIU into the NCAA tournament his first year and into the NIT his second. Many of Mike's admirers think he made the wrong choice of schools, that he should have joined a bigger program. He realizes that he may have not made the best career choice. "Charles and I were convinced we could have a big impact on the LIU program, so we went there together," Mike recalls.

Mike Campbell is single, he has no children, and he completed his undergraduate degree at LIU. He's not a churchgoer, but he respects those who are. "Everybody's religious in his way," he says. His coaches in college loved him. "Mike is a great guy," says Greg Fox, the director of sports information at LIU. "He was very reliable. You never had to worry about him. He was a complete player too. People forget that he led us in rebounding for two years." In city playground leagues he's become an assist leader.

Mike's admirers are not sure why he is not playing professionally. Greg Fox thinks that he doesn't look big, so coaches may conclude falsely that he can't play a strong game. At six foot six and 200 pounds Mike can take care of himself, but as Fox says, "He looks one-eighty. Maybe that hurts him." Mike has to look out for himself. His trainer at Gold's Gym on 54th Street, Gary Prince, is trying to hook him up with a tryout for the Houston Rockets.

Mike names Dytanya Mixson, the coach of his West 4th Street team, as a positive influence on his life. "He's a few years older than I am, but we grew up together," Mike says. "We've been friends for fourteen years. When I'm out of town he keeps tabs on me by talking with my mother. Dytanya was always there for me. I can talk to him, and I trust his advice. And he's that way for many of his players— some of whom are not great players, by the way."

The New York City summer leagues keep him playing, and Mike appreciates the people who run these programs. "I played in four tournaments this summer. They were all tough, all competitive." The Cage at West 4th Street presents special challenges. "It helps your game. Because you are in such a small area, it is tougher. It teaches you to calibrate your moves, to be smart, to think. Everyone is watching and they can get to you real fast. You don't have the time you would on a bigger court."

How does he compare basketball in Italy with NBA basketball? "There's just no comparison. I love playing in Italy. The competition is good. I like the country, too, especially the food. But the referees in Italy aren't good. They are inconsistent. Nothing compares with the NBA," he says. For long-suffering Knicks fans, this may be hard to understand. After all, the Knicks left plenty of empty seats in the Garden last year when they fell back into their horrendous stand-around-and-watch-the-guy-with-the-ball games that went nowhere. Mike disagrees. "I don't know what was going on in those games. They were pretty bad. But you bring those guys out here with us, and I promise, they're going to smack someone around. They're good players, believe me."

Mike could get a reasonable job outside of basketball, but at the moment, he will not consider it. He is still hustling, hoping to get a spot this summer, preferably in Europe. Basketball is his life, and one thing Mike doesn't lack is focus. "I'll play somewhere," he says. "I just will."

## Smush Parker

Like Mike Campbell, Smush Parker did not come through a big-time basketball program, but he has connected at all the right times with the right people. Good point guards are rare on the playgrounds and in the NBA as well. He's had good advisers, and he is not involved with drugs. His body is developing rapidly, so he will still improve physically and mentally.

Two obstacles seem to have held Smush back. The most important is his lack of playing experience. Every year makes a difference for Smush, because his high school and college careers were cut so short. His other besetting demon is an over-the-top independence and moodiness that worries coaches and fellow players alike. He may lack the quarterback's instinct to encourage and reassure his teammates. In the NBA big stars can get away with an attitude, but rookies cannot.

Smush kept getting better over the summer. Because he did well in rookie camp, he was invited to the Cleveland Cavaliers veterans' camp in September. Coach John Lucas was assembling a young team, and Smush's raw talent appealed to him. The move was a gamble for both parties, because Smush had to turn down veterans' camp invitations from Memphis and Orlando to go with Cleveland.

While Smush was at the veterans' camp, he played his first exhibition game at the Civic Center in Albany, New York, against the New Jersey Nets. His mother and sister took the train up to see him. He didn't score much, but he was on the court for sixteen minutes. Lucas liked what he saw, so he kept Smush around. At twenty-one years of age it is hard to get a commitment from an NBA team, especially after being passed over in the draft. Rodney Parker remained hopeful: "The only reason he is in the NBA is because of his extraordinary talent. That is why teams hesitate to let him go."

Smush continued to play well, so he made the cut for opening day, signing a half-year contract with Cleveland for $175,000. At first he played infrequently, but his minutes increased through December and January. He showed flashes of real brilliance, so he was re-signed for the remainder of the year, doubling his half-year salary. Over the course of the season he played in sixty-six games, scored 408 points, and made 119 assists. On the other hand, he recorded 133 turnovers, the worst assist-to-turnover ratio in the NBA. Turnover problems are worrisome, but they are correctable. Coaches say that a high turnover rate signals bad judgment, and for a player whose temperament is suspect anyway, it can be fatal. Unfortunately for Smush, his raw talent wasn't enough. At the end of the year he blew up at his coaches for not giving him more playing time. The press picked this up, and shortly afterward he was released.

Since Smush's last year at Fordham had ended with arguments and recriminations, even Rodney worried that Smush was in trouble. He was now free to work out with any NBA team, but he got fewer tryouts—eighteen teams had already seen him once.

While he was waiting to be picked up, Smush played regularly in three New York tournaments during the summer. At Hunter College he had become a favorite of the crowd. On one occasion he scored 26 easy points, while thirty-six-year-old Speedy Williams, a famous playground money player, challenged him on every move. Smush kept his cool, he avoided careless turnovers, and he wasn't forced out of his game. He hit on his first four shots (for 10 points) and in the closing minutes of the game he made a brilliant behind-the-back assist underneath the basket that brought the crowd to its feet, screaming and high-fiving.

The difference in talent between good players and professional players is difficult to distinguish on the playground. Often it's simply a matter of size and strength; there are not many six-foot-six NBA forwards anymore. Campbell and Parker are close in talent level, but Parker is a split-second quicker, younger, and a better natural athlete. Any player who could combine Smush's talent with Campbell's attitude would be in the NBA today. Smush fits easily into the super-athletic youth movement that has captivated professional teams, but the mystique of his youth won't last forever. He has got to keep improving his game.

Purdue basketball coach Gene Keady once articulated a sound theory for young players like Smush. Keady realized that most players will never be superstars like Michael Jordan. Surviving at the professional level is achievement enough. Keady was fond of a journeyman professional named Steve Kerr, a shooting guard who had a long career with the Cleveland Cavaliers and the Chicago Bulls during Michael Jordan's greatest years.

"Michael Jordan is tremendous and we all love him because he is so entertaining to watch," Keady begins. "But your dreams shouldn't be to copy Michael Jordan. Your dreams should be to imitate Steve Kerr *because that's possible*. He worked his game. You shoot one hundred free throws a day. You shoot two hundred three-pointers after you run five miles. That sort of thing is possible for a player who is not a supertalent." Like most good advice, it sounds simple, but it is not easy to follow.

# chapter eighteen

# The Importance of Play

It is not only possible to say a great deal in praise of play; it is really possible to say the highest things in praise of it. It might reasonably be maintained that the true object of all human life is play. Earth is a taskgarden; heaven is a playground.

—G. K. Chesterton

**Playgrounds are different from** stadiums and arenas. Playgrounds are for players; arenas are for fans. The contention of this book is that what happens on America's playgrounds is more important than what happens in its big stadiums. Why is this true? First, it is better for a person to play than to watch. Most people at playgrounds are playing, not watching. Second, watching an amateur play, either a neighbor's son or daughter in a high school sport or a basketball game at West 4th Street, does more good for both parties than paying to see a professional perform. When you go to Madison Square Garden to watch Kobe Bryant, Kobe doesn't know you are out there, and nothing you do will make any difference to Kobe. You have no interaction. The media needs superstars to sell things. You, in your day-to-day life, do not need superstars, nor do you need to buy the things they sell. You need friends, family, and community. Those marvelous professional athletes are not your friends.

Recent medical studies support the age-old belief that playing sports helps you mentally as well as physically. The secret is the endorphins.

This is how medical people explain it: Exercise gets the endorphins flowing. And endorphins are natural body chemicals that have a euphoric effect on your brain. Endorphins reduce the anxiety that comes from stress, and they reduce your feeling of pain, too. They make many of your organs healthier (especially the brain), they improve memory, and they can offset the effects of aging. They may help your sex life too. The more often you produce endorphins, the better your outlook on life is likely to be.

The three best ways to produce these endorphins are regular aerobic exercise, meditation or prayer—just being quiet, collecting your thoughts—and laughter. Laughing always makes people feel better.

On a normal Saturday during the basketball season, the Garden might have two games involving forty-eight players, performing before twenty-five thousand people (assuming a separate crowd for the afternoon and evening games). If one of the games at the Garden is professional, then those men are not playing at all, they are performing. They have co-opted the word "play," but it may not describe their actions. They are more like paid performers. They compete with the Broadway theaters for cash and an audience. That is why tickets for the Knicks are $100 per seat. Professional athletes are more talented than the guys on the playgrounds, but what you watch at the Garden is a performance.

On the other hand, on any given Saturday at West 4th Street, a few hundred spectators will watch more than eighty players, and that doesn't count games at the Houston Street playground down the block, which are played before smaller crowds. Playgrounds are for players.

Play has always been a vital part of culture; indeed, leisure defines culture. We play, and we must celebrate the play of others. For the ancient Greeks, amateur athletic contests were taken seriously enough to be part of religious festivals. The Greeks freely recognized excellence, even in visitors, and there was nothing incongruous about play and competitiveness. The Greeks extended the idea of competition to theater and dance. But money—that is, being paid cash for a performance—would have corrupted the celebration's solemnity. The athletic contestants themselves were aristocrats, often princes and kings.

When Diomedes wins the chariot race at the funeral games in honor of Patroclus in the twenty-third book of the *Iliad,* he is awarded a beautiful slave woman and a richly adorned bowl. He already has slave women and precious things of his own. The honor in these prizes comes not from their monetary worth, but because Achilles offers them from his own store of treasure. They are prizes he has won in previous contests. The prizes are treasured because they are symbols of excellence and because they are acknowledged by a previous champion.

Because of the festival's solemnity, the Greeks could never believe that winning was everything. The twin qualities that distinguished the hero were prowess and honor, and honor was not based on winning. The simultaneous demonstration of character and skill was essential. In the *Iliad,* a dispute erupts over second place in the chariot race. Antilochus beats out Eumelus, but he is accused of interfering with the chariot of Eumelus, driving him out of the race. The challenge would be decided by instant replay in today's televised world, but the Greeks resolved the dispute by oath. Antilochus is asked to swear by the god Poseidon, with his hand on his best horse, that he has not defeated Eumelus by trickery. Unwilling to compromise his honor, Antilochus apologizes and returns his prize.

Why make such a fuss about the importance of play?

Because play in America is vastly underrated. Our free time is the object of relentless marketing, which tells us that only by spending money on objects can we enjoy ourselves. When did you last see anything on television encouraging you to spend your free time just thinking, taking a walk in the park, going to church, or playing dominoes with the kids before bedtime?

Leisure is not supposed to replicate the busyness and responsibility of one's weekday job; it should fulfill other needs. Leisure, along with its spiritual sibling, play, is intended to be a break from work. In order to express ourselves as human we must make full use of leisure and play in our lives. Work is essential and it will be with us forever, but it cannot define us as human beings. Work usually exists for the sake of something else, for the sake of the money and the leisure it brings. Play and laughter, which are available to all, differ from work in that they are intrinsically good; that is, they are good in themselves. The Greek philosophers agreed that anything that is good in itself must be a higher good than something that exists for something else. This explains why people can't allow work to be their only interest.

People perfect their nature through contemplation, laughter, and play. For this reason, Plato's ideal academy provided a place for athletics. Plato was not interested in training professional athletes, but he did want fully realized human beings.

For the X-Men's Brian Elleby, play at the Cage is a way to ease tension, to feel relaxed and calm. For Artie Lawyer it is a place to match wits and skills with players as good as or better than he, and to derive satisfaction from outsmarting a stronger man. For Kevin Dunleavy it is a place to "have a good run" and get away from the pressures of his Wall Street career. We need play in our lives, and if we can't play all the time, we should derive a secondary satisfaction from watching others play.

A skeptic might ask, "I can understand why it is better to play than to watch. But why would you want to watch people who are just playing at a park when you could watch better athletes in a big arena?"

The question has a couple of answers.

First, play itself is fun to watch. That's one reason grandparents watch grandchildren play. Certainly it is not for the child's excellence. Play by talented amateurs combines the best aspects of professional performance with the spontaneity of play. When the spectator knows the players, the joy is shared. There are people for whom the highlight of a close game is the celebration of the winners. They love to see the players jumping up and down and hugging one another. This joyful celebration is an essential part of play.

Play doesn't mean no one cares who wins. Some play is competitive; some is not. Games on playgrounds are competitive; they are played for respect and for local reputation as well as for the exercise. This is normal and healthy. Respect is part of life everywhere. If Bo loses enough games, the best young players will want to play with someone else, whereas they used to cozy up to Bo. Fans are aware of these subtleties too. People know what a victory means, and they recognize that the agony of defeat goes deeper than the league standings.

Playing basketball requires that a number of unrecognized skills not be taken for granted. At the high school and college level, performing well with a team takes self-discipline and concentration. You must be a good learner, and you will have to blend your game with the other four members of your team.

Even simple pickup games develop useful talents. Five players who do not know one another must figure out how to beat the other five guys if they intend to stay on the court. Improvised strategy and problem-solving skills are required to do this. In softball, for example, you do not need team play or a strategy; you need more hits. However, a basketball team performs together, so they must work out a system.

You must maintain control not only of your own play, but also of the game itself. Without referees, the group is in charge, and the group creates its own culture. Unspoken rights can be asserted, but concessions must be granted. Doing this well is a skill of its own.

Further, local rivalries have a long history, and often a neighborhood's reputation is on the line. From the beginning of time, athletic contests have pitted school against school, village against village. When the X-Men play against Brownsville, this *is* the Battle of Brooklyn. It's Bedford-Stuyvesant versus Brownsville. These neighborhood rivalries are not reported in the press, but they are still real. In the

1980s when Harlem USA came down to the Cage, every team in Brooklyn wanted to knock them off.

Each team here may only play eight or nine times in a summer, which heightens the importance of each game. An NBA team will play eighty-two times in a season, and then at the playoff level a series of seven more games. Compare this with NFL football, where the championship is decided in a single game, rightly called the Super Bowl. For the professional basketball player with close to one hundred games a season, how important can any one game be? No wonder so many NBA games are played without focus or enthusiasm.

The constant promotion of big-name athletes and their sports gear, the hallmark of professional sports, is the opposite of play. It is pure sales, so by definition it is all about money. Sportswriters and TV commentators are instruments of the selling process; that is why they are hired. In criticizing golf, Bruce McCall wrote in *Esquire* a few years ago, "Not even Barbra Streisand celebrates herself as tirelessly as golf celebrates itself." He could have said the same about almost any professional sport, and it certainly applies to the NBA. If you doubt it, just pay a visit to the NBA retail store on Fifth Avenue in New York. Not only does the NBA want to clothe every part of your body, it has NBA towels for your bathroom and NBA tableware for your dining room as well.

In Johan Huizinga's seminal study on the play element in culture, *Homo Ludens* (1944), the historian summed up the distinction we all feel, but find difficult to measure: "Really to play," he wrote, "a man must play like a child." This accurately describes the play of Mike Campbell or Brian Elleby at West 4th Street. They may be aging warriors, but they are wildly playful.

Perhaps it is wrong to be too hard on professional or near-professional sports (which would include Duke basketball, Ohio State football, and the like). Maybe it is enough to say, as Huizinga concludes, that today's big-time sports, which lack the spontaneity of pure play, have become a thing *sui generis;* they are neither play nor performance. One can still ask the question: Which events enrich our culture more? The college bowl games and the NBA playoffs, or the thousands of games played on our playgrounds?

Recently a woman in her early twenties raised a very telling question: Is not part of the reason so many kids play basketball, or any other sport, due to the influence of the highly publicized professional and college teams? Would there be as many kids on the playgrounds if there were no pro leagues to encourage kids and set an example? This question reveals misunderstandings that people have developed about the nature of play and the history of sports.

Play always precedes professional athletics. Kids will play no matter what. Rather than lead children's play, professional sports always exploit an existing interest.

A higher percentage of American boys played baseball before television existed—when no big-league teams were south of Washington, DC, or west of St. Louis—than play baseball today. The best baseball players came from the rural South and the American farmlands, where no big-league teams existed. Babe Ruth and Lou Gehrig, from Baltimore and New York, were exceptions. More representative were Shoeless Joe Jackson (South Carolina), Paul and Lloyd Waner, Pepper Martin, Mickey Mantle (Oklahoma), Walter Johnson (Kansas), Tris Speaker, Rogers Hornsby (Texas), Grover Cleveland Alexander (Nebraska), Ty Cobb, Bill Terry, Dixie Walker, Johnny Mize (Georgia), Mel Ott (Louisiana), Dizzy and Paul Dean, Preacher Roe (Arkansas), Casey Stengel (Missouri), Pee Wee Reese ("The Little Colonel," Kentucky), Enos Slaughter—whose nickname was Country (North Carolina), Bob Feller (Iowa), and Willie Mays (Alabama). The huge number of successful players from the Dominican Republic now in the major leagues makes the same point.

In the first half of the twentieth century, boys did not need organized Little League baseball to play the game, just as they do not need organized leagues to play basketball on city playgrounds. From fifth to eighth grade I remember coming home from school, changing my clothes, riding my bike to the Forest Avenue School playground, choosing up sides, and playing baseball until dark. If we only had five on a side we played "no hitting to right field." I couldn't imagine doing anything else.

Without television and cheap air travel, big-time professional leagues would not exist. Until World War II, all sports were local. For midwestern football fans, Michigan versus Ohio State was enough, just as Harvard-Yale and Army-Navy kept eastern fans fired up. Southern rivalries—Florida-Georgia, Alabama-Auburn—were even more ferocious. In rural America, minor league baseball, which was everywhere, compensated for the lack of access to big-league teams. People did not watch sports on television; they went to the ballpark.

Kids play sports because playing sports is fun. Basketball was a city game long before professional basketball had any real following; as a game, basketball was an instant success. Today a million American kids play soccer, but few watch soccer on TV. The networks can't exploit soccer commercially because they have trained their audience to have too brief an attention span to follow the game. Americans are no longer patient enough to watch a low-scoring game on TV.

Nevertheless, children will always play, and playgrounds are the birthplace of games, not the media.

Part Three

•••

# THE OFF-SEASON

# chapter nineteen

# A Bitter Winter for Kenny

**Everyone sees the glamorous** side of Kenny's life. After all, he runs the biggest summer basketball tournament in the city right in the heart of Greenwich Village, and he is a central figure in Rio de Janeiro nightlife.

Everyone wants to talk to him.

He sits in a director's chair, and he has a staff that waits on him.

He is in charge.

Twenty-five years' worth of good basketball players, perhaps five thousand athletes, go out of their way to greet Kenny on the streets, at major sporting events, and in late-night clubs and restaurants. He is invited regularly to go to championship fights in Atlantic City and Las Vegas. Driving a limo has made him an intimate observer of New York City nightlife. From businessmen to bartenders, from the doormen and bouncers to the ladies of the night, from messengers on bicycles to the advice-for-a-price attorneys who work the city's violations bureaus—everyone wants to be Kenny's friend.

But things can go wrong, and this winter, they did. It was to be a stern test of his ability to deal with bad fortune.

Kenny has money, but he's not a millionaire who can jet back and forth between continents without a care. Money can't cover up misfortunes. So Kenny has developed the instincts of a survivor, and survivors have to make the hard choices millionaires can muddle over for years.

## September

Some of Kenny's problems are easy to resolve. In late September, about one month after the final game at West 4th Street, Kenny returned from another happy vacation in Rio. But the bills in New York are always waiting. Up here, his financial clock never stops ticking.

The tournament had accounts to settle. The Brooklyn company that made the T-shirts had not been paid, and Rosy had to be reimbursed for the money he advanced to the staff. In collecting past-due receivables, West 4th Street has the same problems of any small business. When Kenny comes back to New York, he is a busy man.

"Our Internet guy still owes us a few thousand dollars. I sent him an e-mail, a nice one, reminding him that I'd like to get this money now. Mistic still owes us too. We even have to collect the balance of our funds from Nike. I talked to Brimmer about the money and he said he'd take care of it. I'm sure they'll all be good for the money, but I wish I didn't have to spend time after the season is over collecting it."

Kenny is satisfied with Rick. "Rick took over this year. I think Rick has developed into a good commissioner. I knew Arizona couldn't be around that much with the kids' tournament taking so much time. But I still don't want Rick negotiating for me—with sponsors or with other tournaments. I want to know what is going on and I want sponsors to know they have to deal with me before anything becomes final."

For the rest of the winter Kenny continued to shuttle back and forth between Rio and New York, staying roughly a month in each place. On Christmas Day he flew to Charlotte to visit his daughter, but he was back in New York the next day. During the month of December, he was hit with a big insurance bill for his limo, an increase of $1,400 from the year before. This was something he didn't expect. It seems every trip back has some unforeseen problem he has to deal with.

## February

Kenny returned from Rio again in February, right after a big New York snowstorm. Tournament finances were in good shape now, but there were other problems. While he was dropping off a customer at Penn Station, a police officer noticed that his limo did not have the diamond seal on the window that authorized him to pick up and drop off passengers in the city. Kenny's car is registered on Long Island, and he had not, in fact, bought the necessary sticker. He expected a warning, or at worst, a ticket. No such luck.

Kenny was issued a summons for picking up passengers in the city without a permit, and the officer then informed him that he was going to seize the car. While writing up the ticket the police officer noticed that Kenny's driver's license had expired two days before, so he received a second summons for driving without a license.

Kenny protested his car being taken, but to no avail. He argued that by impounding the car on the spot he would lose his source of livelihood for at least three days (it was a Saturday, and the car compound would be closed Sunday and Monday, Presidents' Day). He pointed out that he might win his case in court—he had won in a similar situation in 1998, and to take his car now would presume guilt, which hadn't been established. He wasn't soliciting fares, he was dropping off a passenger.

The officer was having none of it. The police drove his car to the city storage facility on the west side and charged him a $225 towing fee. Kenny was out of work for the three-day weekend.

On Tuesday he got up early and renewed his driver's license in downtown Brooklyn. This took extra time, because the city was digging out of twenty-five inches of snow. Kenny then took the subway to the Taxi and Limousine Commission courthouse in Queens to fill out the paperwork necessary to reclaim his car.

With so many summonses being issued to taxi and limo drivers, the place is always busy. In fact, three lawyers—one black, one Latino, and one who seems to specialize in Indian and Pakistani drivers—arrive every morning looking for business. Their arrangement seems to be that if a driver needs them to read a summons and explain alternatives, they will do that for free. But if a driver wants the lawyer to plead before a judge, then the driver pays. This is how men and women who can't afford to be out of work for long deal with the law.

The court system is designed to keep the trial burden light. The city wants a high percentage of guilty pleas with no hearings. In Kenny's case, he was told that in order to plead innocent, he would have to post a $1,500 bond. On the other hand, if he pleaded guilty he would get a $200 fine and he could get his car immediately. Kenny pleaded guilty. He waited two hours for the judge to sign his plea (lunchtime is a sacred rite for city workers), but he was then able to take the subway to Manhattan to claim his limo before the car compound closed.

The temporary building that houses the police office where towed vehicles are kept on the west side of Manhattan is as grim a public facility as you could ever imagine. Only prison could be worse. Six windows exist to deal with violators, but only two were open. The walls were the cheesiest of thin, worn-out, fake pine paneling, with two battered wall air conditioners, their backs removed and the plugs dangling uselessly to the floor.

The waiting room's artwork consisted of two dozen signs taped to the walls, all of which were emphatically negative: NO ENTRY, two signs. FIRE EXIT ONLY, one sign. NO SMOKING, five signs. NO PERSONAL CHECKS ACCEPTED, six signs. DO NOT COME TO THIS WINDOW UNLESS YOUR NAME IS CALLED, two signs. Five signs announced the payment rates for violations ($185 for a simple towing, etc.) and the storage charges ($20 per day). Over two dozen business cards of towing companies had been pasted randomly on doors and walls.

The only two signs that didn't tell you what not to do were pasted over the cashier's window. They announced: $100 FOR HAND GUNS, NO QUESTIONS ASKED. Perhaps this says something about what the city thinks of citizens who have their cars towed.

Kenny went to a window and presented his license, registration, and proof that he had paid his violation. After another ten minutes, the door to the back offices opened and a police officer asked Kenny to come back with him. It was then that he learned that there was a warrant out for his arrest in Queens. As it turned out, the summons was for a routine limousine violation. After being taken by the police to Queens, Kenny was released, but all this took up four hours.

"Unbelievable, man. Mind boggling," was the way Kenny began to recount his evening. "I waited for a couple of hours to get in front of a judge. The police were fair with me, but I was locked up with some desperate guys. A few of them were young, and some had been there for days. All brothers. Most of them had no idea how to represent themselves, and I felt bad for them. The system just doesn't seem fair. I talked to all of them—we got along real well.

"The ticket they arrested me for was issued in 1992, ten years ago! The summons was for soliciting rides at the airport without a permit. I couldn't believe I had not been told it was still outstanding. I was regularly having my license renewed and my permits validated. If my violation was on a computer, they should have picked it up a long time ago. You would think that at some time before now they would have told me about it.

"Anyway, when I got to the judge, she looked at the date and almost apologized. She said the old ticket never should have been handled this way. She told me to set a date to resolve the matter—she warned me not to miss that date—and then told me to leave."

Kenny grabbed dinner in the city, and around midnight he headed home.

## Trouble in Rio

Kenny's departure for Rio was delayed by one day while he got his car back, but at last he could get out of town. Good weather and good friends awaited him. With money in his pocket, he was ready to go.

During his first week there he ran a successful boat trip for eighty people. He still had rental commissions coming in, so he had plenty of money. Then, near the end of March, he sent a disturbing e-mail to a friend saying that he had run into trouble with the local police in Rio.

A few weeks later another e-mail arrived from Kenny, explaining that he had been arrested and jailed for six days, even though he had done nothing wrong. Kenny described how he had to hire a lawyer and spend $4,000 to get out of jail, but he remained optimistic that the charges would be dropped.

John Sullivan, a longtime friend who lives in Connecticut, has been traveling to Rio with Kenny for nearly a decade. He was there when Kenny had his brush with the law. "The whole thing was a setup, but Kenny took it well," he began. "Just the same, it was tough. The first cell they put him in must have had seventy to eighty guys in a space for thirty or forty. It was so crowded you had to stand up the whole time because there was no room to lie down. There was a hole in one corner where you could piss or take a crap, no toilet paper, and that was it. I think they fed them something once a day. Kenny was in there for two days. The first lawyer he got was a woman who was useless. I think she just showed up to collect a few hundred dollars from him, but she couldn't do anything. No one showed her any respect. We finally got two good lawyers and by Sunday night [Kenny was jailed on Friday] we got the right guys on the case. I worked with them. For the first two days, when I was not at the jail, I was at Mia Pataca [the restaurant where they all hung out] talking to people who could help. I was trying to get him moved to a better cell, and then out altogether. I'm a lawyer, as you know, and I knew I could figure out what was going on."

Kenny believed he was turned in by a cab driver who was jealous of his success. The arrest was built on the claim that Kenny had a minor on his boat and drugs were being sold. "I saw this girl, because I was on the boat when the cops came," John told me. "The girl was young, very pretty, and she was dancing up a storm when the police arrived."

As it turned out, she was carrying false identification. "This girl had made a boat party with me a few weeks before this, and I had asked her for her papers and checked them at that time," Kenny explained. "They looked fine to me. I had no idea that she was seventeen and she had doctored them. I liked her. She liked me. I was happy to have her around."

According to Sullivan, the cops checked everyone's ID first, saving the young girl for last. "I think they knew she was underage," John continued. "Shortly after they got to her, they summoned half a dozen cops in full battle gear, with helmets, nightsticks, and automatic weapons. That's when I got worried. Remember, the boat had not left the dock. We had just arrived, the music was blasting away, but people were just talking and meeting each other. Nothing illegal was going on. Then the cops claimed there were drugs on board, so they searched everybody. These guys with the automatic weapons were turning the boat inside out. As you know, Kenny has nothing to do with drugs, and to their great disappointment, the cops didn't find anything."

All this time the police were telling Kenny that he and the owner of the boat, a Dutch national, would have to come to police head-quarters. Kenny protested. He had done nothing illegal, they found nothing illegal on the boat, and he argued that if one girl had false identification they should simply take her off the boat and let the cruise continue. But they had other plans, and the officer told him that he had to go to police headquarters.

"That was my fatal mistake," Kenny recalled. "I should have insisted that I see an attorney right then. I didn't fully understand my rights, and I had no idea what they do to you when they lock you up. It's not like America. Once they get you inside the police station, you are theirs."

The police were determined to get Kenny off the streets right away. The story about Kenny's arrest—with his name but not his picture— ran the next day. Sullivan says the story was played up big. The story line was that the local police were routing out sin and corruption brought to Rio by the immoral Americans.

On Saturday a representative from the American embassy visited Kenny. By law, the embassy must be notified when an American is jailed or commits a crime. Kenny continued, "I told him my story, and he told me that this looked to him like an open-and-shut case. 'You should be out by Monday,' he told me." But the embassy did nothing; Kenny never heard from them again. "I did not ask for more legal help at the time because I did not think I needed it. By Sunday around noon I realized my woman attorney was not going to help. She told me that she would be back in three or four days—she was busy with other cases—and that it would take ten or fifteen days before the judge would look at my case. That did it for me. I knew I needed something better."

Kenny's new lawyers got him moved on Sunday night. Their fee was $3,500, but they got results. For an additional $500 Kenny and the owner of the boat were moved to a large cell with ten other men. All of them were living reasonably well. They had a hot plate, so they could cook their own meals. They could buy food, and with it they smuggled in marijuana and cocaine. Sullivan said that two of these guys were well-known Italian underworld figures in Rio. The men played cards until 5:00 A.M., during which time Kenny could sleep in their beds, since they were up all night. They smuggled in cell phones so they could conduct business. Because Kenny spoke Portuguese, he got along with everyone. His charm is so contagious that a couple of the guys he was locked up with asked to join his next boat ride.

All the news coverage was inaccurate, and a version of the bogus story even made it to the States. Frank Ski, a disc jockey for the Atlanta radio station V-103, was vacationing in Rio at the time, and he was told about Kenny's arrest by a cabdriver. Based on what he had heard from his friends in Rio plus the newspaper story, he filed an "on the scene" report from Rio in which he told the station's listeners that a "brother" was now serving ten years for a sex-and-drug sin cruise he had been running in Rio. Kenny found out about this radio report as soon as he got out of jail because one of his friends in Atlanta called him on his cell phone to tell him.

Kenny sent another e-mail to the States. "I'm okay. Been getting lots of support from the guys. The only thing I miss is doing the boat. I have enough guys here, but the boat is not available. I may be heading back next week. I know it is slow there, so I'm not worried about missing work. Talked with a few other limo drivers and they say things are bad in New York. As long as I have support, I'll stay here a week longer. I'll keep you posted. Kenny."

At Mia Pataca, Kenny was a returning hero. "It was gratifying," he reported. "These guys raised over four thousand dollars for me. I have a lot of friends here. I lost nearly fifteen pounds while I was in jail because I couldn't eat the food. And I still have to go back to appear in court. Plus, I have to explain to two judges back home why I missed both my court dates for my traffic violation in New York. If I don't do that, they will put out another warrant for my arrest. But the worst is over."

A few days later Kenny ran into Frank Ski, the Atlanta disc jockey. Kenny began by scolding Frank for putting out a false story about him, but before they parted, he got Frank to agree to set up a radio-station-sponsored basketball game between a WBLS squad from New York and Frank's station in Atlanta.

With the prospect of another deal in the works, Kenny was ready to return to Brooklyn.

# chapter twenty

# Winter in Brownsville:
# The Few Who Will Not Give Up

## The Housing Project

**The Noble Drew Ali** Plaza, which is located just down the street from the Brownsville Recreation Center, has been improving all year. These apartments are home not only for Bo Keene, but for dozens of other Brownsville basketball players as well. It is here that countless young men make the choice: a commitment to sports, a traditional career, or life on the streets. Over its thirty-year history, the project has mirrored Brownsville's good times and bad. The housing project got its name, Noble Drew Ali, from the early-twentieth-century founder of a church in North Carolina that blended Islam with Christianity and Black Nationalism. Ali was christened Timothy Drew, and after his spiritual revelation, Drew moved to Newark, New Jersey, where he founded his first Canaanite Temple in 1913. He established temples in Pittsburgh, Chicago, and Detroit, where one of his parishioners was W. D. Fard, an early founder of the Nation of Islam.

In 1970 entrepreneur Joseph Jeffries-el built the apartments where Bo lives, and they were regarded as first-class residential real estate. Greg Jackson and Keith Stroud were original tenants. "Jeffries-el was a true visionary," Jackson says. "He was as smart as they come. Mayor Lindsay was his man. He got money from Washington as well." (Jeffries-el also represented Fly Williams with the NBA and the ABA in the 1970s, but Fly's eccentric behavior made him almost unemployable.) Jackson believed the projects had great promise. "There was a tunnel under all the buildings for laundry machines. I think Jeffries-el originally planned to have shops down there. The whole place was beautiful. The central court was not paved like it is now. There was grass, and flowers all around it."

The properties decayed, and until recently, a company controlled by Louis Farrakhan, leader of the Nation of Islam, owned the buildings. Recently management of the five-unit housing project was transferred to Eshel Management in Coney Island, and the new company has been pouring money into the buildings all year.

At ten o'clock on a weekday morning, three or four groups of unemployed men and a few single women with baby carriages populate the central court area. The ponytailed security guard at the gate passes the time watching a tiny TV whose rabbit ears antennae produce a nervous, double-image picture. Young men come by his booth frequently to buy cigarettes, which he sells for fifty cents apiece. The courtyard is an uneven surface of cracked and frequently patched blacktop in four or five different tones of gray and black. It is an eyesore.

This central area is supposed to be resurfaced soon. Otherwise, the buildings have been substantially improved, and the project is in much better shape than it was earlier in the year. Some shrubs have been planted outside the buildings and the central hallways have been remodeled. Elevators that have not worked for ten years are back in operation. There are no broken windows.

Eshel has repaired most of these apartments, modernized the plumbing, installed new kitchens, and made the units clean and attractive.

In doing these renovations, the company has ousted previous non-payers or forgiven past debts, while insisting that new leases be signed. But the money that drives the renovations comes from converting the three rear buildings into apartments for the homeless, tenants whose rent is paid by a government agency. The city's Emergency Intervention Unit has placed hundreds of welfare recipients here. The rent is higher than before, and more important, the money is paid directly to the management company by the agency, so there are no collection problems. The new tenants are supposed to move to permanent housing within six months, but nobody knows if they will. As welfare tenants, they live with a number of restrictions, including evening curfews and security guards in every lobby. When they leave the complex, they must sign out.

Neighbors and longtime tenants are not sure they want so many homeless transients in their project, but the newcomers are not drug addicts or drifters, and they seem happy. It appears that more single mothers with young children live there than men or married couples. Since single women may not want to sleep alone every night, this is already causing problems. Still, the transients are an improvement over the nonpaying squatters who preceded them.

Construction workers and trucks with building materials come and go in the compound all day. Drug traffic, which had been a multimillion-dollar business in the projects from 1985 to 1998, is way down. This is true for the whole city, not just Brownsville. Residents of the Noble Drew Ali projects were looking forward to a peaceful winter.

But once again, the residents were to be disappointed. By the spring, circumstances had changed. Eshel was no longer running the project, and Louis Farrakhan's company was back in charge. The revenues continued to flow from the welfare tenants, but capital improvements were halted, and the center courtyard was never resurfaced. The residents are organizing to voice their complaints to the new management, and the project's future appears clouded. The residents will continue to struggle, as they always have.

••

Bo Keene continues to relive his final game at the Cage. "You want to know how we let the X-Men beat us and knock us out of the tournament?" he was asking, months later.

"One time-out did it," Bo began. "You know Shane was playing with the And 1 team uptown, and they had pros playing with them. Maybe it went to his head. But in the third period, we were beating the X-Men, and we had Mike Campbell all locked up. He didn't hurt us. In our previous time-out I told Shane, 'You're the difference. You keep blockin' shots. We can beat these guys. But you have to cover for guys who get beat.'

"Well, all of a sudden Shane decided to get mad, I guess. I don't know what got into him. But during that time-out, when the X-Men started to come back at us, Shane wouldn't get in the huddle. He said, 'You guys figure it out for yourselves,' and he just walked back and forth outside our huddle. I was tryin' to get the guys together. Keith was furious; he couldn't believe what Shane was doin'. He was tellin' Shane, 'This is our last go-round. Now's the time to get 'em.' But Shane wasn't havin' any of it. We broke down because Shane wasn't with us. Once we lost him, I was worried."

Bo had a point, but there was more to it. The problem went beyond Shane or the strategy of a single moment. Bo had tried all summer to assemble a team combining youth and age, but he couldn't get the right young players, and some of his most reliable veterans had migrated to other teams. Brent McCullum joined the CCC Eagles. Competing coaches Dytanya Mixson and Karriem Memminger picked up other Brownsville alumni. Rodney Stiles, a promising youngster, lost his effectiveness as the season wore on, and by the end he stopped coming altogether. Vinny Matos did not come to the last three games, and Jamal Faulkner never joined the team.

Bo wants to come back next year. He defends himself, pointing out that he was always there helping to break up fights; he was never in one. Should he take the blame for the misbehavior of his players? On the other hand, Bo has a new life. He's got a regular job and two boys who need him. Maurice, his ninth grader, was admitted to Teachers Preparatory School, an academic high school that gives students small classes and more personalized instruction. "My life has settled down. There's nothing dysfunctional about this family," Bo says with a smile. "We're all together." But winning West 4th Street championships will no longer be the center of his life.

A few days later, as Bo was leaving the Metropolitan Pool to go home for the evening, he got a call from his wife. She told him she was preparing to go to the hospital the next morning to stay with her sister, whose son was being operated on. Tragedy had struck once again. Bo's nephew, Lamont, had been shot the previous night. Bo speaks of all this in a most matter-of-fact tone: "He's seventeen, a big, strong kid, and he was arguing with a bunch of younger kids that were in a gang together. It was on New Lots Avenue in the early evening. One of the boys pulled out a gun and shot Lamont; I think the kid with the gun was fifteen. The bullet is lodged close to Lamont's spine, and tomorrow the doctors will have to remove it. They're giving him a fifty-fifty chance. If the operation is not a success, he won't be able to walk again. It's time for us all to pray for him."

It's hard to talk about a settled life in Brownsville.

## The Brownsville Recreation Center

The BRC has become Brownsville's unofficial town hall. This is the place where the Tenants Committee of the Noble Drew Ali housing projects meets to talk about their issues. Earlier this same afternoon, young women reading to small children occupied three classrooms on the second floor. At 4:00 P.M. a straight line of uniformed third graders filed quietly through the BRC lobby into another classroom, where a volunteer teacher awaited them. The weight room was packed: men getting stronger, and women in sweats losing weight on the treadmills. In the back room on the first floor, toddlers were playing with an old go-cart. Two half-court basketball games were going on in the gym, mixing players from fifteen to thirty.

This is a normal afternoon at Greg Jackson's BRC. Greg, known as Jocko here, is busy showing around a friend who has agreed to paint some furniture and rooms as part of a remodeling project. "Once you get the community involved, there's a lot you can do without spending a fortune. All this guy wants from me is the cost of the paint," he explains. "You want to know what my day is about? It's about getting things done. That's what I try to do, every day."

What's the new project?

"We are going to move the weight room to the back of the first floor," Jackson replies. "In what is now the weight room, we will bring some pool tables that we've never used and we'll make room for table tennis. I want to have some new space for preschool kids as well. The city is in an economic crunch now, but we can keep doing things if we use the community right. It's working out well. I tell you, I've been blessed."

Though Greg has lived in Brownsville all his life, he started working for the BRC part-time in 1985. He became a full-time employee in 1989, and he took over as director in 1997. His right-hand man is Darryl Glenn, who has been working with the center for seventeen years. Both men hold down two jobs. During normal working hours, from 7:00 A.M. until 3:00 P.M., Greg is an administrator at a nearby Brooklyn hospital, a job he has held almost twenty years. Glenn is the head custodian for the Bushwick District office of the board of education.

Many ambitious city workers have two jobs; this is the way getting ahead expresses itself in the city bureaucracy. Hammer has two jobs, and Keith Stroud has three. For each, the pay is adequate, but they all have a benefits package. Add a working wife, and you begin to understand what inner-city families must do to live a decent life.

Here Glenn mentors young kids and runs the youth basketball program. Greg boasts that Darryl runs the best youth basketball clinic in the city.

Unless Jackson and Glenn were physically strong, they could not work these long hours. Both men show up at the center five to six days a week. "Gangs would like to run this place," Jackson warns, "but as long as Darryl and I are here, it's not going to happen. We won't take that chance."

All the kids' programs are free, and the center serves thousands of adults as well. Jackson says, "We've done a good job in building up a family center, where a parent can come here to work out and leave the kids to us. We will help the kids with homework, or they can just play games. But single-parent families need this kind of place."

How does he survive the bureaucratic red tape and administrative fiats that often undercut grassroots programs like this? "I'm not sure," he says with a smile, "but I assure you, they are trying that stuff on us every day and we just keep going. I think part of it is that I have strong local support, at the center and in the community. When you get right down to it, the city doesn't want to mess up a good thing."

Jackson never runs out of projects. He's now working on a Brownsville Hall of Fame, and he will use the BRC as the museum for it. His next inductee is going to be Eddie Gregory, known as Eddie Mustafa Muhammad when he was Light-Heavyweight Champion of the World. "This is my dream, this building," he says.

He enlists the support of the entire neighborhood for the annual BRC Thanksgiving dinner. "We'll be cooking and serving a hundred twenty-five turkeys this year, just like we did last," he says. "I just ask people to bring one, and they do. Some people bring more. But you know, these are my friends; this is my neighborhood. We have a Christmas tree–lighting ceremony too. Just like Rockefeller Center, but since we don't have ice, we have roller-skating around the park. We close off the service road next to Linden Boulevard. We sing carols and serve hot chocolate inside."

The BRC was established in 1953 by the Brooklyn Dodger fan, advertiser, and local merchant Abe Starke. It comes under the direction of the New York City Department of Parks and Recreation, but much of its funding comes from federal grants and impromptu local donations. It has an enrollment of seven thousand, but Jackson thinks more than one hundred thousand people use his facility each year.

The training room is well equipped and the swimming pool is constantly in use. The second floor has three study rooms where kids are taken care of after school. A fully functioning recording studio is located in the basement. There are jazz dance classes for boys and girls. Girls develop dazzling skill in double-Dutch jump rope, kids can check out roller skates and trail bikes, and adjoining the center is a large paved playground for softball and touch football. A uniformed Muslim drill team practices its rigorous and precise marching on Saturday mornings.

The success of the BRC helps to explain how things get done in this neighborhood. In Greenwich Village and other more prosperous districts, improvements come from the city through the efforts of active, politically connected committees. In Brownsville, things get done through the leadership of a single individual. Greg Jackson has a huge network of friends, and he can say with confidence, "I know how things should be here. I was here when everything was good, when there was a deli on every corner and when the school system was among the best. It's not that way anymore. But since I have taken over the BRC, things have gotten much better."

Years before he made it to the NBA, Jackson started a youth basketball program called the Brownsville Jets that has trained thousands of young men over the years. To be a Brownsville Jet is like being in a service society, somewhat like the marines or the Guardian Angels. Jackson summons one of the workers in the center and asks him what it means to be a Brownsville Jet. The man, who is in his early thirties, responds without hesitation, like a Boy Scout. "To look out for one another, to help someone else, and not to want anything in return." Another man working at the center is wearing a Brownsville Jets T-shirt that says, FRIENDS FOREVER. Jocko continues, "This neighborhood is full of

Jets. And they all sound the same. We stick together and we take care of each other. All over Brooklyn, in every branch of government, you run into Brownsville Jets. And you don't jump one of the Jets. We don't start fights, but trust me, if you want to play that way, we don't mind."

One Saturday evening in October, the week before Halloween, Greg Jackson and Darryl Glenn were working late at the BRC. Jackson was moving around huge papier-mâché-adorned walls to be part of a haunted house he was building for the kids for Halloween. Glenn was sweeping up the gym. Both men had left the center the previous night at 2:00 A.M. There was a senior men's function at the BRC, and it ran late. Since the kids come early Sunday morning, the place had to be cleaned up before the doors closed. They would be the last to leave tonight as well.

At 10:30, Darryl took a break from his work to talk to a young boy and his mother, who had come to take the boy home. In Darryl's job, counseling never stops. When he talked to the boy, he was talking to his mother, too.

"It's easy to be good," Darryl was saying. "You may not have thought about it, but it's harder to be bad than it is to be good. You set goals for yourself and you follow them. When people say bad things about you, or try to put you down, you just stay with your plan. You try harder and you prove them wrong. You can do whatever you want; whatever you want to be, you can be.

"I know it's hard when it's just you and your mama," Darryl continues, "I grew up in a single-parent home. I had six siblings, but we had a lot of love for each other. And one thing I'll tell you, I never lied to my mother. Never. So don't you even think about doing that.

"Now listen here," he continues. "I need you here next Saturday morning for my basketball clinic. I need you. You know my methods and you can help some of the others. I expect to see you." He grabs the boy's head affectionately and presses him against his chest. "My love for you is strong, but I can't show you that love if you don't show up. Hey," he says, now holding the boy by the shoulders, "gimme some love. Gimme a hug. That's it. Now you come here next Saturday. Remember, I need you." The boy and his mother head for their car.

The evening is over. Almost. As the center is closing, two young boys wheel their bicycles out of the gym. One is sixteen, a high school dropout. The other is fourteen. They are here all day, every day. They literally live here, playing basketball or passing the time talking with older men. The BRC has become the center of their lives.

When it is close to midnight and all his work is done, Jackson leans back in a rickety swivel chair and recalls a sports story he likes to tell about Darryl Glenn.

"This is one of the best things I've ever done around here," he begins. "Years ago I needed trophies for kids who played in one of our basketball tournaments. I didn't have the money to buy any. So I called up some guys who had won trophies in the past, and I said to them, 'I need your trophy.' I mean I called guys like Pearl Monroe, Curtis Sumpter, and Fly Williams, who were legends around here. And I told them, I don't just want your trophy, I want you to come to the championship dinner and present the trophy yourself. I want you to tell the kid how you won it, and what it means to you.

"Now I would pick the kids who got these trophies, and I would try to match the boy with the man who was giving his trophy away. I wish I had the pictures here to show you. Some of these guys were real broken up giving these trophies away. I remember I got Darryl to give the Sportsmanship trophy away one year. He asked this little kid, 'How many points did you get?' And the kid said, 'Two. But we won.' Even Darryl, and you know how tough he is, couldn't hold back. As he hugged the kid and handed him his trophy, he said, 'Just like me.'"

# chapter twenty-one

# Springtime: Planning for California

**Kenny was not in** a good mood when he got back from Rio in May. Although he had been unfairly jailed for six nights in a police publicity stunt, he did not want to leave. He was mad at New York, not Brazil. In Rio, his distress had led to support and outpourings of friendship. He didn't have to ask for help, he just got it. But in New York, where he had missed his court date, the court clerk in Queens was hassling him while he tried to get his hearing rescheduled. It looked like this was going to be one more annoying episode with the bureaucracy.

America, he believed, harassed hardworking people with red tape, fines, and regulations; packed its jails with blacks; and oppressed poor nations all over the world. From Vietnam to Iraq, the results of American foreign policy were the same; things improved only when we left.

He did not always feel this way, and it's hard to explain the change. Certainly Kenny has reduced his personal investment in New York.

Twenty years ago his family was still around, he was working two jobs, he had basketball tournaments winter and summer, and he was the center of an active social scene. Today his family is scattered and his work is irregular. New York is a magical city for lovers, but it can also be aloof and unforgiving. The Copacabana district of Rio is cheaper, it faces a beautiful beach, and it doesn't cost big money to enjoy life. The longer one lives in Rio, the more harsh and stressful America appears. A Nigerian woman now living in New York summarized the contrast she experienced in moving here from Lagos. "In Nigeria you have no money, but you have your family and you have your friends. Here your family is more likely to be scattered, because they have to go wherever they can get jobs. You must have money. You are nothing without it." In a more sinister way, New York City itself can be like the Cage; the competition never stops.

In any case, when Adam Del Deo invited Kenny to Venice Beach, California, for a Memorial Day national street basketball championship to be held in his honor, Kenny's first reaction was that he didn't want to go. He was suspicious. "Adam cannot come up with enough plane tickets, enough hotel rooms, or any kind of money for the guys," he said. "I just don't want to be bothered."

Adam is calling this year's tournament "The Godfathers of Playground Basketball," and in addition to Kenny, he will invite Sonny Hill from Philadelphia, Lefty Boyd from Chicago, Ken Hicks from Venice Beach, Dino Smiley from Los Angeles, and Pops Cruz from Hoops in the Sun in the Bronx. It will be a six-team, three-day tournament.

After a few more calls and a little persuading, Kenny agreed to go. He immediately asked Dytanya Mixson, whose X-Men had won the tournament, to put together the team. Dytanya had never been asked to take a team out of the city. The chance to go to Venice Beach was a big opportunity. Sid Jones, Mark Figueroa, and James Ryans, the usual organizers, operate at a higher level of New York City basketball. They are at gymnasiums and parks all year round networking and recruiting players. Sid, Mark, and James have teams in the Nike Pro City at Hunter College, so they are used to working with professionals. Because they have a large network of players, they can produce top-flight teams on short notice. Dytanya knows players in his neighborhood, but not all over the city. Kenny was taking a chance.

Dytanya wanted to prove himself. "We're not goin' out there to play," he told Kenny. "We're goin' out there to win, to bring this championship back to New York where it belongs." Dytanya wanted his team—not a collection of all-stars—to make the trip. Mike Campbell was in Austria, and no one was sure if he would be back in time. In addition, he needed at least one big man. Dytanya came up with Jove Ford, a six-foot-eleven-inch center who once played with Nike One.

The buzz on the street was that Dytanya needed more big men, but no one went out of his way to help him. Kenny did not get involved in recruiting. One prominent coach said he had two good big men he could bring in from Europe, but in exchange he wanted to go along on the trip and assist with the coaching. Coaches who know good players don't want to lose them to other coaches. It's that competitive. Dytanya immediately began to run practices at the Van Dyke Recreation Center on Mother Gaston Boulevard in Brownsville.

Kenny turned to league friends to raise money and collect stuff. He worked on Antonio Brimmer for footwear. He got Steve Cronin, who had a team entered in his tournament, to pitch in a few thousand dollars to pay for extra tickets and a rental car. With this, Kenny planned to bring Ron Creth as the bus driver for the team. Joe Merriweather, Rosy Jackson, and Mike Williams also wanted to sign on.

On the Monday before the Friday departure, Adam called Kenny to make sure that he was coming out. "Well, I hope so," Adam said, "because I am trying to get you on national TV. We have *The Best Damn Sports Show Period* interested in bringing you and Sonny Hill on the program together." Adam got a film crew to fly from Los Angeles to New York to interview Kenny at West 4th Street, and talk to some of his players at their final workout on Thursday evening in Browns-ville. The same crew went uptown to film Pops Cruz as well.

The departure plans had some last-minute hitches. Ron Creth was having thyroid problems, so his doctor would not let him leave town. On that Wednesday Rosy Jackson was taken to Montefiore Hospital in the Bronx because of an arterial blockage that looked like it was moving toward his heart. A procedure was undertaken to unblock the artery, but Rosy stayed home.

Kenny did not expect his team to do well in California. Most teams that go there are all-star teams, and while the X-Men have plenty of solid players, they lack size, brilliance, and experience. The week before the team departed, the X-Men lost in the semifinal round of the Fireball winter tournament in Brooklyn. This was a bad sign.

But the trip was on. At 8:00 A.M. on Friday morning, the two New York basketball teams (West 4th Street and Hoops in the Sun from the Bronx) left a rainy JFK airport for the sun-filled beaches of southern California.

# chapter twenty-two

# Venice Beach

**The official proceedings of** the 2003 Hoops by the Beach Memorial Day Tournament began Friday evening with a coaches' meeting and a reception for the players at the Gotham Hall in Santa Monica. Gotham Hall is a New York–style club with hulking security guys dressed in black managing the velvet rope at the door. The club is on the second floor overlooking the Third Street Promenade below, and it has huge TV screens along with a dozen pool tables that can be rented for $14 per hour.

In addition to the usual assortment of singles looking to make connections, the place was full of publicists, agents, and event planners, all of whom had business cards they were quick to exchange. For media and entertainment entrepreneurs, mostly women, the objective is to get your name out there: for some it's music, for some it's athletics, and of course there is always Hollywood. The idea is to make the next hot scene or at least attach yourself to it. Smile and turn on the charm. Your own talent is not the issue as long as you are associated with something trendy. In part, that is what Adam Del Deo is doing with his tournament. Adam gets everything down on film, and this weekend he is promoting himself by getting control of a priceless piece of Los Angeles real estate: Venice Beach. On a beach that is all about being seen, this is where you want to be. In New York, everyone wants stuff. LA is all about press passes.

The coaches met for an hour before the players arrived, at which time Jim Bartolero, the tournament director and the man who hired all the referees, explained how the tournament would be run and answered questions on rules and procedures. Lester Jackson, who started this tournament eleven years ago, was there, along with the current promoter, Adam Del Deo, and his aide, Alex Lagory, a film major from American University in Washington, DC. Adam has been running and promoting the event for the last three years.

The official entertainment for the evening was watching *The Best Damn Sports Show Period,* which had been taped that afternoon and featured interviews with Sonny Hill and Kenny Graham. Tom Arnold, the host, did not get much mileage out of his guests. Hill and Graham were asked about famous stars who played in their league, but that was all they were asked. To fill in the time, each coach had been asked to bring a player. Mike Jordan (a good college player from the University of Pennsylvania) was with Sonny Hill, while Mike Campbell was with Kenny. The idea was for the players to each play a one-basket one-on-one game against the nonathlete host, Tom Arnold. The two athletes won easily. Watching at Gotham Hall, the coaches were happy enough to see four of their own get national TV exposure, but the show told its audience little about street basketball.

One of the old-timers watching the show was outspoken in his disappointment. "It was a disgrace to the network and an embarrassment to the guests," he began. "It was not serious at all. Arnold showed no interest in learning anything about playground basketball;

even though he had two guys, Ken Graham and Sonny Hill, who had spent thirty years running summer programs. Why not tell us what playground basketball is all about? How do they get sponsors? What is the crowd like? By his clowning around, he assumed these guys had nothing to say.

"What we got was the show's usual shtick, and Arnold condescendingly let these guys share in it. We saw a middle-aged man playing one-on-one basketball on an improvised little court against good players. Arnold gets his guests to drop a few names—Kenny mentioned Anthony Mason, and Sonny Hill talked briefly about Wilt Chamberlain. But what does that tell us? The name-dropping is all part of the shtick. Hill and Graham were never asked to sit down. Do professional athletes stand for their interviews? I thought the real message was that this show plays everything for laughs. The host doesn't care anything about you or about street ball. Thanks for coming—who's next?"

Mike Campbell may have shared this sense of impropriety, because his one-on-one game against Tom Arnold had a bit of an edge to it. Instead of just beating Arnold and making his shot, which is what Jordan did, Campbell made Arnold work. He dribbled between his own legs and then dribbled between Tom Arnold's legs. After that, he didn't take his shot. Campbell came back out and dribbled the ball slowly in front of Arnold again, making him sweat, challenging him to take the ball away. Finally, he passed the ball around Arnold's right side, collected it behind Arnold's left side, and took his shot. When the shot did not go in, Arnold leaped desperately to retrieve it (was there a chance for an upset?). Campbell tapped the ball delicately back to himself, and finished off the game with an easy layup. This was the most serious gesture of the show.

On Saturday each team would play two games, with the tournament's first game pitting Los Angeles against Chicago at 10:00 A.M. The games were short, four seven-minute quarters, so sloppy play was fatal. If you fell behind, you would not have enough time to make up a big deficit. Lefty Boyd had been bringing top-flight teams out here from Chicago ever since the tournament started eleven years ago, and he had another good team this year. His first opponent was Dino Smiley's crew from the Drew Middle School in Los Angeles. This league, with twenty-four teams, is probably the biggest tournament in Los Angeles, and it has been running for thirty years. Smiley, who counsels youngsters for the City of Los Angeles Parks and Recreation Department, has been in charge for the last eighteen years. Edmond "Tiny" Fournoy coached the team.

Los Angeles had the biggest team in the tournament, and they knew how to exploit their size. The offense was run by point guard Kenny Brunner, a standout at Dominguez High School in Compton, who played briefly at Southern Idaho Community College and then for one year at Georgetown. Coincidentally, Brunner and Smush Parker were both playing at Southern Idaho at the same time.

Los Angeles never utilized a second guard, or even a small forward. Instead, throughout the game they kept four big forwards and centers on the court with Brunner. Eric Holmes, a star at Pasadena High School; Greg Lakey, from Loyola Marymount University; Maurice Spillers, from Locke High School and Utah State; and Marcus Mason, from Xavier of Ohio, all ranged from six foot seven to seven feet. John Staggers, a dominant Los Angeles and Venice Beach playground player for over a decade—now thirty-three years old—was the starting power forward and one of the team's top scorers. When Staggers was a senior at Crenshaw High School in 1988, he never started a single game, yet he was voted the city's Player of the Year. Chicago played Los Angeles even for the first half, but the latter's size took its toll, and LA won comfortably, 63–53.

In the second game, Pops Cruz's Orchard Beach team from the Bronx took on Sonny Hill's All Stars from Philadelphia. This match showed the importance of recruiting a balanced team. Since good players may play on two or three teams during a summer, no coach can be certain that a player will go with him to big tournaments. Obadiah Toppin was the outstanding player in the West 4th Street all-star game, but he played regularly with Cruz in the Bronx, and at this tournament he again played with Cruz.

Sonny Hill is connected, and good athletes like to play for him. His top power forward was Kennedy Okafor, a native of Crown Heights in Brooklyn and a regular with the Ice Tea team at West 4th Street. He and Dytanya have been friends for years. Okafor played his college basketball at the University of Maryland in Baltimore, and he plays professionally in Spain. His agent hooked him up with the Philadelphia team for this tournament. He didn't know that Dytanya was bringing a team from Brooklyn until they met at Venice Beach.

Philadelphia had size with its starting center Alexandre Sazonov, seven foot one, a St. Joseph's graduating senior, who came to the States from Russia. But the offensive punch came from floor leader Mike Jordan. After a shaky first quarter, Philadelphia's balance proved too much for the Bronx team, and they won 55–46.

The short game times (twenty-eight minutes), the change in the temperature (early and late games can be thirty degrees cooler than games at noon), and the brief rest time between games means that upsets can happen easily, and that's just what occurred in the third game. At half-time the Los Angeles team was routing Ken Hicks's Venice Beach team, 37–18. Apparently, being warmed up and familiar with the court was an advantage. But LA's overconfidence, combined with a pressing defense in the second half, allowed Venice Beach to pull off a 54–53 upset of what appeared to be the best team in the tournament.

The X-Men played their first game against Philadelphia, and they suffered from first-game jitters. Philadelphia took a quick 14–7 lead. Jove Ford, the center for West 4th Street, missed some early chippies under the basket, and this may have undercut the team's confidence in its half-court offense. But with guard Reggie Roberson and Mike Campbell scoring clutch baskets, West 4th Street was able to finish the first half tied at 27.

When Brian Elleby scored on a post-up to start the fourth period the score was still tied at 38 and it appeared the X-Men were about to make their move. But amid a five-minute flurry of turnovers, missed shots, and offensive fouls, the X-Men found themselves down 45–41 with two minutes to play. Their defense held Philadelphia, but their offense had become ragged and inconsistent. On five consecutive offensive possessions, they failed to get a single shot. Philadelphia worked on denying Mike Campbell the ball, and he went scoreless in the second half. From two minutes and twenty-five seconds remaining until twenty-two seconds were left, the X-Men took just four shots, and they were all wide of the mark. Campbell missed a three-point attempt with a few seconds left on the clock, Roberson missed the tip-in, and the game was over. The score remained 45–41. The entire team had scored only 6 points in the third quarter (Elleby had four of those) and 5 points in the final period. "It was there for the taking," Dytanya said when it was all over. "This is a hard loss."

Indeed it was. Only one hour and thirty minutes later, after Chicago had routed Venice Beach 72–57, the X-Men would play their second game against their uptown rivals from the Bronx. Much of the day the temperature had been in the seventies, but for this game at 6:00 P.M., the temperature had dropped into the low fifties. Spectators were puffing on their hands to keep them warm in the late afternoon.

Javone Moore started the game for West 4th Street as the shooting guard, and he scored 7 of the team's first 10 points. But he could not transmit his energy to the other players, and a poor first quarter ended with the Bronx team leading, 15–10. Once again West 4th Street could not generate offense from its half-court game.

Kenny Graham said at halftime that his team simply did not have enough talent. "Roberson and Mike Campbell, and a few other guys, can play at this level. But most of this team can't compete with players of this caliber. Our guys are playing as well as they can, and they have nothing to be ashamed of, but they are not good enough. I think it is as simple as that." Kenny had a point. Mike Campbell had played in Austria professionally during the winter, but everyone else had been playing in Brooklyn recreation leagues. These leagues are good, but they don't prepare you to deal with professionals. The Bronx team was leading at the half, 26–14.

West 4th Street started slowly in the third quarter, but with a few minutes remaining in the period, Mike Campbell led a charge to get his team back in the game. Trailing 35–24, Campbell made a driving layup and was fouled. He made the free throw, thereby narrowing the lead to 35–27. On a one-on-one clear-out, he beat Jared Johnson, a star at Manhattan, to make the score 35–29. Campbell was fouled on his next drive and made one of two free throws. Then as the quarter ended, he made a tip-in to bring the score to 37–32. Campbell scored 12 points in the period.

With one minute left in the game the Bronx team was still leading by 5 points, 57–52. Elleby scored with twenty-four seconds remaining to bring the score to 57–54. Johnson and Campbell exchanged baskets, and the Bronx team added a free throw to go up by 4 points. Reggie Roberson got clear for a three-point attempt with five seconds remaining, but it was wide. Cruz's team held on for a 60–56 win. Campbell had 20 points, Reggie Roberson had 11 (all foul shots), and Javone Moore, who started so well, finished with 11 points. Having lost to the two teams in its division, the X-Men could not make it to the final rounds.

They had to play Los Angeles on Sunday morning at eleven A.M. Without elaborate scouting, preparing for street ball games begins and ends with a single question, "Who are their shooters?" The shooters are the guys you have to cut down. For Los Angeles, the strategy was simple: Stop Mike Campbell, or isolate him so he couldn't pass the ball to his teammates. If he got in close, make him take foul shots.

The strategy worked. Los Angeles built up a 39–20 lead at halftime and coasted to a 65–53 win. John Staggers had 13 points and guard Kenny Brunner led his team with 15. Mike Campbell finished with 24 points, but he was unable to get the rest of his team involved in the offense.

In the semifinals Los Angeles defeated Cruz's team from the Bronx and Philadelphia beat Chicago. On Memorial Day, Los Angeles won the championship, easily defeating Philadelphia 61–48. Kenny Brunner was selected as the tournament's Most Valuable Player.

As much as Kenny likes LA, Venice Beach is not his scene. He would rather show his friends a good time, which he does every day in Rio, than be seen, appear on television, or be applauded by people he doesn't know. He had left the opening-night party early, and he didn't spend a lot of time at the tournament when his team wasn't playing. But on his second night in LA, Kenny found his spot, La Bomba, a Brazilian club located amid some tired strip malls, a Pep Boys auto store, and a Target discount store. Kenny brought along Mike Williams, John Sullivan, and a couple of other friends.

If it were not for the huge crowd of people drinking and smoking outside, one could easily drive right by this place, but it is a busy club. La Bomba is run by an attractive Brazilian woman in her early thirties. In addition to an all-Brazilian staff, TVs are everywhere playing tapes from past Rio Carnivals. The club has live Brazilian music and customers can dance all over the club, not just on the small dance floor in front of the band. This means that wherever you are, someone is dancing around you. Kenny was quiet. He sat back and watched as two girls tried to teach a third girl a new Brazilian dance. Kenny can't get away from Brazil. Here in Los Angeles, with the beach scene, the fancy women, discos, and television cameras easily within his reach, he wanted La Bomba.

•••

After the final game, Dytanya was tired and disappointed. He was in no mood for a party. Back in his hotel room with his roommate Whyett Benn, his power forward, he shared a pizza and thought about the previous three days. "Kenny gave us a great shot, bringing us out here," he began. "We all appreciate that. But what I would like most is to be able to come out here again next year.

"I realize we did not have the talent with us to compete at this level," he continued. "Still, we were in every game, and I actually thought we could have won them all. After all, we lost those first two games by four points. They could have gone either way. We brought our regular team with a couple of supplements. I don't want to go with an all-star team either. I want to build a great team, a team that plays together all summer long and doesn't lose a game.

"I know we need more scoring power from the wings. Mike Campbell can't do it all. I would like to enter a team at Rucker so we can play on a big court. I want to recruit guys who will focus on coming back to Venice Beach. That is going to be our goal."

Whyett had another perspective. Because he is such a large, powerful man, his quiet intelligence and careful manner of speech seems out of character. He is a computer technician with Ziff Brothers, a sophisticated money manager in midtown New York. "There are more lessons to be learned from losing than from winning," he began. "We have been playing together for so long that I think we failed to realize that there are guys all over the country who take the game just as seriously as we do, and who are talented players. They are disciplined and well coached. It's easy to forget this if you don't get out of Brooklyn.

"I am not ashamed of the lessons we've learned out here. This game is still about talent and fundamentals." Whyett paused for a moment. "I don't like to be critical of And 1, the footwear and clothing company that has done so much to support street basketball. But I'm not sure they are sending the right message to city kids. This one-on-one stuff, and all the tricks, and the connection with rap and hip-hop—I'm not sure that is the best message to send.

"There are plenty of kids with great moves and great athleticism, but they don't have the fundamentals they should. Ninety percent of the people I play against are totally predictable, and they are predictable because they have not mastered the fundamentals. Guards that are right-handed will always go back to their right hand. The same thing happens to post-up players, and I play against them all the time. The first thing a right-handed player does is to look over his left shoulder. I know it's coming, and he either gets stripped, or I'm right in front of his shot and he has to pass the ball back out again. That's just one example of what I mean about building fundamentals. You've got to be able to go either way and be comfortable doing it. These skills don't show up on TV highlights, but they make you a better player. We learned out here that we have to improve our game.

"No," Whyett concluded. "We didn't win any games out here, but I would never say this was not a good trip, or a successful trip either. I'm glad we came. We learned a lot, and we are better for it."

# chapter twenty-three

## The City Game: Is Basketball Good for the Cities?

**Once upon a time,** certainly back in the 1960s when the Cage was drawing the best talent in the country for pickup games, basketball was a city game. It was a city game when Ed Warner and CCNY defeated mighty Kentucky for the national title in 1951. Basketball was a city game when the best players were Jewish—with Ed Roman (CCNY), Adolph Bigos (LIU), Connie Schaff (NYU), Jack Molinas (Columbia), and Ernie Beck (Pennsylvania). Nat Holman was a star in the 1920s. The great migration of blacks to the cities after World War II insured that basketball would remain a city game, as it was when Pete Axthelm wrote his wonderful book about it, *The City Game,* in 1970.

Big cities created modern basketball style. Bob Cousy and Dick Maguire (New York City) perfected deceptive passing and dribbling; they highlighted the importance of great ball handling. Wilt Chamberlain (Philadelphia) gave us the first modern big man. New York playground legends Jumping Jackie Jackson (Globetrotters),

Earl Manigault, Pee Wee Kirkland, and Herman "The Helicopter" Knowings pioneered feats of great leaping, and Julius Erving made the slam dunk the premier event of the professional game.

Don't look now, but the cities are no longer setting the pace. Larry Bird was from French Lick, Indiana. Michael Jordan grew up in North Carolina. Shaquille O'Neal was an army brat. Kobe Bryant grew up in Italy. LeBron James played in Akron, Ohio. Yao Ming came from China. As a matter of fact, the 2003 McDonald's USA All-American High School Basketball roster didn't include a single player from New York, Chicago, or Los Angeles. The cities set the standard for a long time, but it's not their game any longer.

In *The City Game,* a book about the 1970 championship season of the New York Knicks and the concurrent playground ball in the city, author Pete Axthelm reminds us that the Knicks won sixty of eighty-two regular season games because of "the perennial presence of that nightly Knick hero, the open man." Balance and teamwork, not one-on-one confrontation or the brilliance of a single player, were the hallmarks of the Knickerbocker style. Team play enabled the Knicks to take the NBA championship from a Los Angeles Lakers team that included Wilt Chamberlain, Jerry West, and Elgin Baylor. Indeed, the popularity of the Knicks and the success of Axthelm's book may have been based on the fact that the type of game the Knicks played was the kind of game the middle-aged fans understood and admired.

Michael Jordan changed all that. He won the first of six consecutive scoring titles in 1987, quickly becoming fabulously wealthy and the most popular athlete in the world. On the court he reestablished the hero as the "go-to guy," the unstoppable superman who could create his own shooting opportunities and deliver key baskets at crunch time. Unfortunately, Jordan's basketball intelligence and mastery of fundamentals were lost on many of his imitators. At the professional level, the disconnect now between the fans in the expensive seats and the players on the court is that these older fans did not grow up with today's highly individualistic style. Thus, the forty- to fifty-year-old fans are waiting to see a game the pros no longer play.

Whether basketball does more harm than good to inner-city kids is a most vexing question. Basketball is great fun, good exercise, and it can keep kids out of trouble. It is a useful socializing opportunity. On the other hand, too many ghetto kids think basketball is a substitute for schoolwork and a normal nine-to-five straight life. When they are finished playing, often before they graduate from high school, they have nothing to take with them but their attitude. A few years ago a study found that an astounding 66 percent of black youths between the ages of thirteen and eighteen believe they can earn a living playing professional sports. This ridiculous misconception of reality produces widespread disappointment. For many young black men, basketball becomes the centerpiece of an anti-intellectual life of protest against conventional middle-class values. Even worse, popular city playgrounds are regularly invaded by hoodlums, drug dealers, and neighborhood gangs.

New York public high schools have had epidemics of gang wars and drug-turf battles transferred to basketball games. At some schools in Brooklyn, police are armed and everyone must pass though a metal detector. For a while, games were closed to visiting fans. At some public high schools during the pregame warm-up period, there is a ritual entrance of the drug dealers, moving slowly and conspicuously through the gym doors, wearing the latest fashions in leather and fur, and loaded with gold necklaces and bracelets. They move lazily along the sideline to their seats, defying the guards. This blatant thuggery is often carried over to the playgrounds as well.

Basketball certainly means something different to a poor kid in a Brownsville housing project than it does to the country boy from Iowa, who has a normal family life, graduates from high school, and lives in a supportive, patriotic community. Just as the rural game emphasizes cooperation and teamwork, one-on-one style of play emerges naturally from the independent, inner-city ethos.

West 4th Street's acting commissioner, Rick Johnson, laments what he believes is the current ethic of the ghetto. "If you serve a few years in jail upstate, when you come out, you are respected. You are *the man*. If you do your homework and take school seriously, you are a mama's boy," he explains. "You may not like it, but that is the way it is."

Buddy Keaton has been refereeing at West 4th Street for decades, and he runs a basketball referee school. He directs the New York City Department of Parks and Recreation program in Brooklyn, and he is the guy who helped Bo Keene get a job. He loves basketball.

But Keaton still believes that basketball gets too much emphasis. "It's now a year-round program, and I'm not sure I like it that way," he says. "There are too many basketball tournaments and anybody can run them. Kids definitely need other outlets, other sports, something more than basketball. The basketball junkie generally has nothing to fall back on; he needs a mentor program.

"On the other hand, you need people to run programs for other sports. Without enough people, you get no follow-through. In our pools we teach kids to swim, but that's about it. We need people to develop competitive swimming programs, but we don't have them. There are not nearly enough tennis programs in Brooklyn; we need an expanded junior tennis league. If we had this, the kids would come; there's plenty of interest in the sport." Buddy's conclusion: "Ultimately, I think the local community has got to get involved." Community involvement, for Keaton, is at the heart of the successes and failures of youth programs. The city has the facilities, but the city can never have enough people to manage all the programs its parks could accommodate. In Brownsville, Greg Jackson has the same idea. "We have everything different sports programs have," he says. Basketball and boxing are balanced by chess and table tennis.

Mike Williams believes that without the discipline and direction provided at schools like his own, the hoodlum element would take over. Mike is defiantly old-fashioned, and he detests everything about the concept of "cool" or "hip" that so captivates youngsters and winds up destroying their lives.

Not long ago the great jazz trumpeter Wynton Marsalis said something similar on a TV program. He was talking with some black teenage boys who were nodding knowingly as Marsalis spoke to them about jazz. Yet it was apparent that these young boys were not so much listening to Marsalis as reveling in their own coolness, musing over how they might later tell their buddies about their afternoon hanging with the great Wynton. Marsalis spotted this, and he abruptly interrupted what he was saying and told the boys that when he was their age he never considered himself hip. As a matter of fact, he was a nerd.

Marsalis then said sternly, "I'll tell you boys something you probably don't know. Coolness is crippling. By being cool you maintain all your prejudices and ignorance, and you miss half of everything that happens."

Mike Williams respects intellectual achievement, doing homework, going to good schools. Mike deals with high school kids every day, and this has made him cautious. "I'm a little afraid of youth. You never know what they will do," he says. Kenny Graham concurs. He went through a period in the late 1980s and early 1990s when he would not run a league for sixteen- to eighteen-year-old boys. He felt that the gangs they brought with them were uncontrollable. The situation has improved. The coaches at West 4th Street control their players better, and the kids seem more focused on basketball.

"At Bishop Loughlin we have a positive message: Do something that's lasting," Mike continues. "Drugs are a short-lived way to make money. Kids are coming into the drug business every day. But they discover that dealing in drugs quickly becomes very competitive and very dangerous."

Ed Lacayo, captain of the Lehigh University basketball team and a Gaucho player in his teens, thinks that basketball is particularly harmful to young women. "From what I've seen," he says, "the better the women players get, the nastier they are. I don't mean to overgeneralize, but some sick women can be pretty good basketball players. I'm not sure basketball is good for them." Some experts say that professional women's basketball is beginning to adopt the bad habits of the men's league. Hot-dogging and individual stardom is crowding out the team game that made women's basketball popular.

College teachers make a similar point regarding women basketball players. An English teacher in the City College system explained, "Women already do much better breaking out of ghetto culture than the men. They adapt better to office work, and they are not afraid to develop useful intellectual skills. Getting them to adopt male activities, like basketball with its macho attitude, takes them away from more useful and productive interests. They don't need basketball to get ahead. In fact, it probably sets them back."

On the other hand, many of those who love basketball defend it. Mike Campbell claims that dedicated players learn to ignore the gang-ster element that collects around basketball playgrounds. "I don't even notice those guys anymore," he says. "You're crazy if you get sucked into that crowd. If you do, you probably never wanted to play basket-ball anyway. I want to play, to get better."

Kevin Dunleavy grew up playing basketball in Brooklyn with his older brother, Mike, who became a great NBA player and coach. For him, the dominant position of basketball in the city is inevitable. "You can't get away from it. Let me tell you why," he begins. "First, the game is cheap. All you need is a basketball and what does that cost? Twelve dollars? Equipment for other sports can be expensive. Even in tennis you need a racket, and that is expensive. Second, you have accessibility. There are so many places to play. There must be tens of thousands, maybe hundreds of thousands, of baskets in this city. But where can you play baseball? How many parks are there with baseball diamonds? Not that many. Third, basketball is self-entertaining. You can play alone, or one-on-one, or two-on-two. For the city, it is an ideal game."

••

One problem with basketball may be that it is too simple a game. That is, it's too easy for an athlete with a few superior skills or physical characteristics—quickness, leaping ability, or height—to dominate play. Most people agree that the passion for natural ability is behind the NBA's rush to draft boys right out of high school. Kobe Bryant was not a finished player at Lower Merion High School, nor was LeBron James. These boys are great natural athletes, and more than ever, pure athleticism is seen as the key to success in the NBA.

Joe Sterrett, the athletic director at Lehigh University, thinks it may not be the best sport for inner-city kids. His reasoning is that learned skills count for less here than in any other sport.

Sterrett makes the following proposition: If you take one boy with great quickness and leaping ability and stand him next to a boy of good athletic skills but lacking these talents, then give them each a basketball and tell them this is how their talents will be measured, the second boy has little chance to excel and he knows it. If peers over-rate basketball skills, then the second boy may regard himself as a loser, an athletic nobody. With too much time on his hands, he gets into trouble.

But if you put these boys on ice skates, or hand them each a lacrosse stick or a baseball bat, then everything changes. Now the boy with less physical talent has a chance. Skating is a skill, and it takes years to perfect. Skating skill replaces raw quickness and strength. Throw these boys into the deep end of a swimming pool and watch what happens to the better athlete's confidence. All of a sudden knowing how to swim becomes a life-saving skill.

Soccer, the world's most popular game, neutralizes pure strength because you can't use your hands. In addition, the soccer field is huge, so it is hard for one person to dominate. While basketball relies on frequent scoring and thereby provides frequent gratification, soccer makes scoring difficult, and this teaches patience and teamwork. A goal is a big event. Pelé, the greatest soccer player ever, averaged fewer than one goal per game.

The need for acquired skills rather than natural ability levels the playing field and gives less gifted competitors a chance. In ghetto neighborhoods, where opportunities for success are limited, basketball may be the worst possible sport to promote. The game is becoming dominated by raw athleticism and is producing a situation in which only the best natural athlete can win.

Pete Carril, the great Princeton University basketball coach, has another solution to save basketball for those of more average talent: Play a disciplined, cerebral game in which all players are grounded in all the skills. The recent success of well-rounded European players in the NBA suggests that Carril's ideal may be coming back into fashion. Carril doesn't like the game's specialization in which the one-guard always brings the ball up the court and the four-man is a power forward who should not dribble, and so on. He thinks all players should have all skills, and when this happens, the team can play a more varied offense.

In his book *The Smart Take from the Strong* (1997), he explains that when you take out the game's cerebral aspects, you remove the part that enabled a player with limited ability, but a head for the game, to contribute. When you force a player into a specialized role, you limit his ability to use his head. Modern coaching, and much of playground basketball, emphasizes this specialized role and tries to produce a more entertaining, individual style. When this happens, basketball becomes less of a game, less like play.

Carril loves the game and defends it against its detractors. He writes, "If you have a Congress unable to pass a budget, major stock market firms doing criminal things, an eight-billion-dollar drug problem, and we're giving helicopters to foreign countries for war, you cannot expect sports not to have problems. Sports are a reflection of our society."

Tom Konchalski, the high school scout, agrees. "The beauty of the game is that it can be played with an emphasis on self-expression, or it can emphasize team play. There will always be this tension in the game; that helps to make it interesting. And you know, it is hard to fight the culture."

Carril's final assertion can be taken one step further. Sports are frequently misused by interests within a society that support their own agendas. That's why big companies advertise during the Super Bowl, and that's why rap labels advertise at the Entertainers Classic at Rucker Park.

Great games, because they are the most visible expression of play, rise above the surrounding cultures. *Games may be second only to religion as a force that supercedes cultural conventions and political boundaries.* After soccer, basketball is probably the most popular sport in the world. Within nations, cultural advocates must win over sports if they are to win over the people.

The question for city basketball is: Which element of culture is it reflecting? It appears that inner-city basketball has been captured by hip-hop culture and is being used to support those values. But make no mistake: The rap industry needs basketball to sustain its own authority. Basketball does not need rap.

Rap attitudes remain credible if professional athletes accept them. In this, the rap industry is much like the sneaker industry; everyone wants a piece of the basketball star. Spike Lee sits courtside for Knickerbocker games because he wants to be perceived as being close to the players. He wants us to believe his world and their world overlap. But Michael Jordan sells Nike sneakers, not Morris Blackman. The sport is more important than the pitchman.

Basketball doesn't need the rap culture. The success of noncity players proves that basketball built on a Carril-style game, stressing intelligence and fundamentals, does work. Carril and his followers are using basketball to bring a different message. The urban style of play is changing to catch up with reality. The players have recognized a reverse correlation between the city game and NBA success. If you go to the best summer basketball programs, you will find more players developing fundamental skills. Basketball intelligence *does* matter.

While the Entertainers Classic at Rucker Park works to unite rap and street ball, the Nike Pro City and the Cage at West 4th Street do not.

Inner-city rap culture may claim Kobe as one of its own, but he is not. He accepts their claiming him for the same reason middle-class blacks accept the inner-city hard guy as their cultural paradigm. They do it because it pays. Kobe landed a gigantic Nike contract because the boys from the "'hood" admire him. Perhaps middle-class blacks are driven by guilt about their own success. They're afraid to acknowledge that their success has come from adopting conventional white attitudes rather than black attitudes. Perhaps the forty years of America's schools and black political leaders promoting the idea of the urban victim has sunk in, and blacks now believe it, without understanding how badly it is hurting them.

Or it may be pure romanticism. Shaft and his followers have replaced the Western cowboy as America's highest expression of raw masculinity. In part this image is true, and the truth has a power all its own.

# chapter twenty-four

# The Off-Season:
# Kenny's Legacy

**For summer league players,** winter is the off-season. Winter is when they resume their normal lives. Kenny can go to Rio, but everyone else goes back to work.

Lambert Shell is at his library in Queens. Iron Mike is greeting his Gristede's customers on Manhattan's Upper East Side. Karriem Memminger, still bloated with prescription drugs, is recuperating from his near-fatal disease. Brian Elleby juggles his time between basketball and his five children. Keith Stroud is helping kids in the city's juvenile justice system. Bo Keene is working at the pool in Greenpoint, while his nephew, Lamont, who recovered from his gunshot wound, is back in school.

In the off-season Rick Johnson sometimes resembles Lewis Carroll's White Rabbit—whenever you see him, he is always in a hurry to get somewhere else. Unlike many West 4th Street men, Rick is not rescuing anybody, and he has no dependents to wear him down. His principal activity seems to be promoting theatrical events throughout the city, and he is comfortable with the theater crowd—perhaps more comfortable than he is with the guys at West 4th Street. Theater managers and box office clerks give him a big hello and around curtain time he can be found anywhere in the city: at cabaret theaters in the Village, uptown at St. John the Divine Cathedral for gospel concerts, or at Carnegie Hall and Lincoln Center looking for people and handing out tickets. The beneficiaries of his largess are generally dignified middle-aged couples who appreciate good theater and good music. He sleeps in, but he returns his phone calls. He's quick to tell you, "I'm just glad to be alive. You know, life is good."

Most West 4th Street alumni have stayed in basketball, and several of them have returned to coach or work in youth programs. These men are basketball purists, and they use the game to reach out to children and make better kids.

Here is what four of Kenny's alumni are doing with basketball in their everyday lives.

### Pete Edwards: "The Kids Needed Someplace to Play"

Pete Edwards has created the best youth basketball program in the city. He created the program he now runs, and he's been at it for twenty years. "I grew up in this part of Queens, and we always had three or four good places to play," he explains. "When I came back here after college—during the wild eighties with all the drug stuff going on—there was nowhere to play. So I started up a little kids' tournament in the gym at Intermediate School 8. The kids needed someplace to play."

His program has grown steadily. The building itself has been spruced up and renamed the Richard S. Grossley Junior High School (a Beacon school in the New York system), but for locals it is, and always will be, IS 8. More important, Pete now runs four major high school tournaments a year here that draw teams from as far away as Minnesota, North Carolina, and Boston, and college scouts come from farther away than that. Tom Konchalski is a regular.

In September Pete's high school tournament runs for seven weeks and draws about forty teams. In January he has another tournament for three groups of kids—twelve-and-under, fourteen-and-under, and sixteen-and-under—that gets sixty teams. In April he runs a high school classic, and in July he has a tournament for returning underclassmen with sixteen to twenty teams. All these teams pay entry fees, so the program is financially sound.

Competition is fierce. LeBron James came here one January and in his first game of the tournament he scored only 2 points. "He ran into guys like Charlie Villanueva (Connecticut, six foot eleven), Jason Fraser (Villanova, six foot ten), Curtis Sumpter (Villanova, six foot seven), and Sebastian Telfair; he learned that you cannot just stuff the ball on anybody whenever you want," Pete recalls. "Of course he got better as the tournament went on, but it's tough out here. Our motto is 'Bring your game, not your name.' If you don't want to get hit, play checkers; don't come here to play basketball."

Pete's temperament is confrontational, but he doesn't like swearing, he expects players to respect their coaches, and he doesn't carry a grudge once the game is over. Pete has an intuitive sense of class. Darryl Glenn of Brownsville often had to cover him at West 4th Street, and he has great admiration for him as a person and as a player. "Pete never embarrassed me on the court. I'm sure he could have, because he had the talent. We played each other tough, and straight. There was no showboating. I respect him for that."

Nike is the principal sponsor of IS 8, and Pete acknowledges that without them the tournament could not continue. Like most good coaches, Pete tries to emphasize fundamentals and team play. "Today's pro game is horrible," he complains. "After Michael Jordan, I lost interest. I can't bring myself to watch it anymore. For the kids, there's been too much And 1 hype, too much video. New York high school basketball has fallen off big-time too. The high school players are now likely to be better out of state, where they're not pampered."

While the game has changed, Pete still recognizes it as a meal ticket for kids who are willing to work. "I always remind kids, this can produce a free education. You need that education to get the job you want. When you go to college, don't blow it. Someday your career will be over, but one thing I teach here is that you can't give up when it's over."

Pete is a living example of his own advice. After a successful career at Thomas Edison High School, he played Division II basketball for New York Tech in Old Westbury, Long Island, and for one year he teamed up with Curt Sumpter at the guard positions. Pete could have gone to UNLV after high school, and he realizes today that he should have accepted their scholarship. At the time, he thought Las Vegas was too far away. As it turned out, New York Tech got to the national Division II Finals in 1983, losing to Virginia Union in the final game. After college Pete received a bid from the CBA, but he turned it down because the pay was low ($7,500 for the season), and he was serious about earning a living. He took a job in the city, and for twenty years he has been a supervisor for the New York City Housing Authority.

Pete's father was a twenty-one-year navy veteran, and Pete still lives with his mother, who is eighty-three, just a few blocks from IS 8. He is happy to take care of young kids who need guidance and a place to come for tutoring and recreation, but he will chase after parents who drop off their kids all day and never pick them up or come to see them. "Parents have to understand they have a responsibility toward their kids. I tell them, there are a lot of ways a kid can be underprivileged; it's not always about money."

## Hassan: Back from the Ivy League

Hassan Duncombe could have parlayed his Ivy League education into a high-paying job with a big Wall Street firm if he had cared to. But Bo Keene's big center, a gentle giant off the court, preferred to work with kids and go back to the neighborhood. His coaching opportunity came at Kingsboro Community College, which is in the Manhattan Beach–Brighton Beach area of Brooklyn. This old Jewish neighborhood, as described in Neil Simon's play, *Brighton Beach Memoirs,* is remote from Manhattan, but it is economically healthy and relatively safe. The campus is modern and is surrounded on three sides by water. The gymnasium is first-class. Hassan began here as an assistant men's basketball coach five years ago. He worked without pay, and the athletic department never did hire him. Because the academic bureaucracy locked him out, the only way he could become a coach was to be hired as a campus peace officer. This is the position he holds today, though he spends most of his time as the head basketball coach.

The woman who gave him this opportunity was Kerri McTierney, a remarkable woman. Kerri was the head men's basketball coach here, and during her last three years, with Hassan at her side, her team won three New York City Community College championships. Today, she is the athletic director at the Fashion Institute of Technology on Seventh Avenue in Manhattan, another City College school. That's how Hassan, who is only thirty-three, became head coach.

Hassan is proud of his position. "If you look over America's head basketball coaches, you will see that few are this young," he says. "I like it here, but I think I have a great career ahead of me." Hassan is finishing his Penn degree; he left the school in the last semester of his senior year to play professionally. With an Ivy League degree and a winning record behind him, Hassan's coaching career should be in good shape.

Coaches at junior colleges are as much life-counselors as they are teachers of basketball. These schools do not get the top high school players, who are whisked off to the big four-year programs. This winter Hassan's tallest player is six foot five. Instead, the local junior colleges get players who didn't finish high school and are still playing on the playgrounds. In all likelihood they got their GED diplomas after they left school. Thus, twenty-one-year-old freshmen are common. Kingsboro has no dormitory system, so the players must live at home and work part-time jobs. They need coaches who understand the difficulty of their personal lives.

Hassan's father, who worked for the Metropolitan Transportation Authority in New York, got him interested in the game in the eighth grade; until then he preferred baseball. Coming from his home in the nearby Chilton housing projects, he would spend many winter hours mastering the game at the BRC under the watchful eye of Greg Jackson. "I met Gus Williams there [Gus averaged 17 points a game over eleven NBA seasons]," he recalls. "A lot of older guys helped me with my game." At home schoolwork remained a priority.

"I remember once I came home with what I thought was a pretty good report card. But I got an eighty in one subject," he recalls. "My father said that if I got one more report card like that he was not going to let me play basketball. I couldn't believe he would pull me out of sports for an eighty, but he was serious. My father said that as long as I could get As then I should. So I just said to myself, 'If that's the way you want it, then I'll go back to getting As.' And that's just what I did."

Hassan left the neighborhood to attend Westinghouse High School, a vocational school, which he selected because it was a basketball powerhouse. There he ran into three other players with whom he would play for the rest of his basketball life: Keith Stroud, Shane Drisdom, and Shannon Shell. They all played with Bo Keene in the summer.

When he was a high school senior, he remembers, he mentioned to one of the coaches that he might like to attend an Ivy League school. He says he didn't know much about them. "All of a sudden I started getting mail and phone calls from Ivy League coaches," he says. "First there was Cornell, and Penn, then Columbia. I was also looking at Wake Forest and Drexel in Philadelphia. I took the SAT tests and did well, so they kept calling. I finally decided on Penn because of their schedule. They played all the Big Five schools in Philadelphia, plus they played UCLA, UC Santa Barbara, and Indiana University on the road. The combination of an Ivy League school and a big-time schedule was just what I wanted."

At Penn, Hassan got what he bargained for and more. He was

selected as Most Valuable Player on the freshman team, but he was not allowed to coast. "Fran Dunphy was a real experience for me," he says. "We clashed at the beginning of my junior year, and he didn't let me start. He is an intense coach, and he wanted me to realize that no one man was above the team. It took me a while to learn this lesson. He got me in the best shape of my life. But most important, he got me to think not just about my game, but about the team. If we lost, I could only think about what I could have done better to prevent the loss. I didn't just think about how many points I scored. He changed my personality. I wanted to figure out how I could contribute." Hassan made all-Ivy that year.

Hassan's great disappointment came in his senior year when he became academically ineligible to play. "I couldn't deal with it, just sitting on the bench watching," he says. "I got depressed. That's when I left school for the Continental Basketball Association, and then on to Europe. At least I could play there. I wasn't in love with the overseas life; you make a good living but you don't get rich. After a few years, I decided that my professional playing days were over."

During his summers at Penn, Hassan played with Bo Keene. "One Saturday afternoon I was over at Shane's and he said, 'Come on with us over to New Jersey. Bo's got us playing in East Orange this afternoon.' So I just went. There was nothing else to it. Bo played me quite a bit and I had a great game. Afterward Bo told me I could play with him whenever I wanted to. He said he would help me with carfare from Philadelphia to New York too. You know, I didn't have much money then, and the round-trip train ride was pretty expensive. But Bo was good to me, and I respect him. I know that Bo does not have the money now he did years ago, but as far as I know, he has never asked one of his players for a dime."

Hassan had no trouble adjusting to Bo's coaching style, because Bo so closely resembled Coach Dunphy at Penn. "They were both real intense guys, and they would get right in your face. Bo knows the game; he has this hands-on way of teaching you. He wanted you to put Brownsville over all your other commitments. But he loves his players, and I'm still with him."

Like the coaches Fran Dunphy and Bo Keene whom he learned from, Hassan gives his players at Kingsboro intangibles as well as instruction in individual technique and team play. He wants them to be proud of their achievements and develop a mature perspective to deal with life's recurring challenges. He also advances their careers. Last year, four of his first five starters got scholarships to four-year colleges. He hopes to do as well this year.

"I've been offered other jobs," he says. "But I like it here. I plan to be around for a while."

## Mario Elie's Big Brother

For almost twenty years Clark Elie has been playing basketball every weekend and reporting for work every morning at the Frederick Douglass Children's Center. He looks young and he acts young (he is forty-seven). His kids, Bryce and Bria, are eight and one. To stay in shape he's got himself into a Sunday morning basketball league for guys thirty-eight and older. "We've got uniforms and an eighteen-game schedule. Games start at eight thirty in the morning and go until the middle of the afternoon. It's in the Schaumberg Junior High School on 128th Street between Park and Madison. Gus Williams is up there; a whole bunch of NBA types are there." He loves it.

Clark learned the game in the local playgrounds and with Louis D'Almeida's AAU team from the Bronx, the Gauchos. Clark went on to become an excellent point guard at CCNY in the 1970s under their famous coach, Floyd Layne. (Layne was a CCNY star under coach Nat Holman in 1950, but his career crashed with the point-shaving scandals of 1951.) Though the school played only Division III basketball, it was the best in its class. "For the three years that I played, we never lost to any CUNY teams, although we did lose games when we traveled and played Division One schools like West Virginia and Oklahoma. But I liked the competition."

Clark's little brother, Mario, is a wealthy and successful veteran of eleven NBA seasons in which he earned three NBA championship rings (two with Houston and one with San Antonio). Although Mario was best known as a defensive player, he scored over 6,000 points and maintained a lifetime free-throw percentage of over 85 percent. Now a coach with Golden State, Mario has all kinds of financial interests in Houston. He's offered Clark a job working for him in a retail shoe business he owns with Sam Cassell. The money would be nice, but Clark has chosen to stay where he is. "I can't see myself managing a shoe store and ordering shoes for a living," he says. "It's a good business, a five-store chain, but this job here is rewarding for me. Kids come here and they learn about life; then they go on to become constructive people."

His famous brother Mario comes home every year, and he always visits the center. "He'll work with kids in the summer program, and of course they all tell their friends, 'I've been taught by a pro.' Mario tells kids about people who helped him, how Magic Johnson showed him this, and showed him that. One summer he sponsored our 'Just Say No to Drugs' tournament."

The two brothers spent many summers at West 4th Street, and Mario was first taken on the Harlem USA team because he was Clark's little brother (Clark is nine years older than Mario). Clark recalls, "When Mario first came down to West 4th Street, I thought he still played a little timidly. But after a year or two in the Cage, he became a real tyrant. I remember early on he was getting pushed around and I said, 'Mario, let's get rough here.' Next time down the court he took this guy who was pushing on him and ran him into the fence and put his knee in his chest. After that, everybody got out of his way. Every once in a blue moon you've got to do that. You've got to just slam it on."

Clark has lived in the neighborhood since he was four, when his parents moved to New York from Haiti. He has spent nearly two decades working with young kids in the neighborhood youth center run by the Children's Aid Society of New York. As a national institution, Children's Aid has been around for one hundred fifty years, and it specializes in adoption and foster care, as well as recreation, health care, and the education of city children. The present facility was established in 1954, and it has always been a part of the Frederick Douglass housing project.

The neighborhood would be in tough shape without this children's center. "Every kid around here has one problem or another. This is one of the largest housing projects in the New York City Housing Authority, and you know we've got drug dealers on the corner right now," Clark explains. "It's hectic. It's got seventeen buildings, extends from Amsterdam all the way to Manhattan Avenue, and then it goes from 100th Street to 104th Street." There are over two thousand apartments in the project. No one is sure what the population is, but the streets are always busy.

"I have done everything in here. I've worked as the after-school coordinator and I've been the teen coordinator. My position now is assistant director. Hammer (Marvin Stevenson) is the recreational coordinator. He runs the 'Just Say No to Drugs' tournament we have in the summer, and he's responsible for getting all the coaches we need for all the things we are involved in.

"I always wanted to be a gym teacher because I was highly influenced by my own gym teacher at Louis D. Brandeis High School on 84th Street. His name was Mr. Lipchak. I went back to Brandeis to do my student teaching with him. When I was finished he said, 'Do you want a job here?' Of course I did, so I stayed there for two years before I came over here. I grew up here, and now I help to run the place. This is where I belong."

## Mike Williams: Thirty Years in the Cage

Among the West 4th Street alumni, Mike Williams is probably the most distinguished, although he is certainly not the richest. Mike was present at the creation, and as cofounder of the West 4th Street tournament, he and Kenny have been close for thirty years. Like many good friends, their personalities are not much alike.

He's a big man, fifty-two years old, six foot seven and 240 pounds with a booming baritone voice. A few years ago he suffered a mild stroke, so he moves slowly, but he has not lost any of his natural authority. Retirement is not far away. Like Kenny, Mike is thinking about leaving the city when his teaching days are over. He may go back to Colorado.

Mike has been fortunate enough to make his living in sports. In 1976 he became an assistant coach at Columbia University. From 1977 to 1980 he did the same at Fordham. Then he got his chance to be a head coach at Colorado College for three years. He resigned this job in 1983 and got out of sports, although he stayed in Colorado, working for the pharmaceutical company Meade Johnson, until 1987.

That summer the principal of Bishop Loughlin asked him to run its summer basketball clinic. Mike figures he must have done a good job, because when it was over, he was asked to join the school as athletic director. "I thought I was just stopping by for a cup of coffee; I assumed I would soon get back into college coaching," Mike says today. "But I'm still here. It has been a godsend for me. It's just a wonderful experience. This is a great school."

Bishop Loughlin takes seriously its mission to educate the children of poor and working-class families. Tuition is $5,400 and almost the entire student body is black or Hispanic. The school's socially conscious alumni give the school about $600,000 a year, and the Catholic diocese kicks in another $340,000 for scholarships. Mark Jackson, the NBA point guard, graduated from Bishop Loughlin, just as his daughter did last year.

About half the students are Catholic. The faculty likes to project a cheerful but no-nonsense image to the kids. For example, boys cannot wear baseball hats into the gym. You make your fashion statement outside the gym, or Mike himself will ask you to leave. The kids call him Coach Will, and when he is sitting around the gym watching a game, students are always touching him or hugging him. The principal, Brother Denis Cronin, calls him a loveable teddy bear, which is appropriate.

Mike's blend of realism and idealism makes him an effective athletic director. He feels that even the best-intentioned schools are not doing all they should to prepare young athletes for college. "Kids pick these great schools in the Midwest, but when they get there, they're lost. These subjects have to be talked about before they go away.

"In New York City, most things revolve around money. I don't want to say anything bad about unions, but running public programs in the summer, or anytime for that matter, is costly. To open up a building on a weekend you probably have to hire four or five people."

Mike visits the Cage only a few times a year. "After I had been away at Ithaca College I remember feeling that the park was like a home to come back to. Here you could always find out what was happening, sometimes things you didn't want to hear, like who had passed, or hopefully, who had finally gotten a break.

"Back in the early years there were always people standing by the fence, some of whom were coaches and scouts. There were years when guys from St. John's—and me too, when I was a coach at Fordham—were looking at the kids play, trying to figure out their age, if they were young enough to go to college.

"The park was always a community of its own. Every day, a guy named Gil, a retired parks department employee, would be there. He would always speak to me," Mike continued. "People who you thought never knew you would stop to talk.

"In the 1980s I became a head college coach in Colorado, and when I would come back in the summers I could see that 'little brother Kenny' had grown up. More or less, I had become a spectator. When I came back after leaving coaching, Kenny had become settled. He was no longer Kenny, or Graham Inc.; he was Mr. Graham. Everything started and ended with him. I also think Kenny would have made a great NBA ref, but he didn't take that path."

Mike is always thinking of ways to improve the tournament. "I think the league has to make an effort to get more white teams and white players in the league. We've got to do a little recruiting. Also, we may have too many young guys in the league. We shouldn't have a lot of nineteen-year-old kids. The league should stick with its older men, around twenty-five and older. The goal of the league should always be to make the game better, to be an operation with class, to keep the fans coming back."

Mike leans back in his tattered swivel chair, stares out his window overlooking the Bishop Loughlin playground, and allows himself an uncharacteristically sentimental moment. "Kenny and I were together from our youth, through our early adulthood, to being grandfathers. In that time with Kenny, I saw a lot of things that made me happy, and a lot of things that gave me pain. What came through was that Kenny put in hours down at that park. He had great dedication, and with the help of his friends, the tournament has flourished. To see that this tournament amounts to something, that it is well run and respected everywhere, has brought me so much pride and joy. . . ." Mike is still looking out his window. Silent. There is nothing more to say.

# chapter twenty-five

## A Conclusion in Which Nothing Is Concluded: The Next Season Begins

**The most compelling aspect** of a sport is that it never dies; it is always being reborn. The seasonal nature of West 4th Street brings fans and players back every year. One summer may end in disappointment or in victory, but the victors must prove themselves the following summer, and those who were defeated can try again. They can be reborn. In no other way are sports more like life. As long as men are biologically able, they will begin again. Each summer brings forth new fruit. On the asphalt of the Cage, a new crop of coaches and athletes arrives every summer. The cycle continues; West 4th Street is beginning its twenty-sixth summer.

This year Kenny has accepted five new teams, though some good teams of the past have dropped out. Bo Keene did not come back; his efforts to rebuild Brownsville were brave but draining. Nike One also dropped out. Like the dominant teams of the past—Harlem USA and Prime Time—Figueroa's day here may have passed. He'll keep his group together but will focus on other tournaments.

Raul Marti did not reenter his team, All Out, because, he explained, he had kept the team going to provide a place for Chris Sandy and Sidney Smith to play, but neither of them wanted to put in another summer on the concrete. Sandy graduated from Fresno State and he considers himself a serious NBA candidate, so he will give over his summer to preparing himself for NBA tryouts. Sidney Smith wants to play professionally, and he too is giving up concrete. They will play at the Nike tournament held indoors at Hunter College, where Smush Parker is their teammate in what is the best backcourt combination in that tournament. All three of them work out at John Jay College during the day, joining Shawn Couch's Pro-Style workouts. Yes, the NBA playoffs are still going, but for everyone else preparation for the new year has already begun.

The staff has changed too. John Clark, who is closing in on sixty, retired after twenty-three years of officiating at the park. He was honored at the midseason all-star game. One of the few white refs who preferred the Cage to all other city playgrounds, John considered West 4th Street to be his basketball home. He didn't work in the city, so he had to commute in from Livingston, New Jersey, for every game.

Moneybags, the regular "electronic scoreboard" at midcourt, never showed up this year. Blue told us that he heard Moneybags was in Maryland, but Rosy fears he may be in jail. No one knows for sure. Hopefully, he will reappear one day just as mysteriously as he disappeared.

After a seven-year absence, forty-year-old Tony Sherman came back to play briefly with Lance's Crew. Sherman has not played in Kenny's tournament since 1996, when he was shot in the leg. He's still the unofficial leader of the park's pickup games. Toward the end of the summer season he told Kenny, "Pretty soon you guys will finish up, and we'll get our park back." Playing from noon until five o'clock is not enough for Sherman; he'd like to go until dark.

In his first game at the park Dytanya Mixson made a statement. He won by 30 points with a team that is better than the one he had last year. A dozen guys showed up. It didn't take long for the meaning of his losses at Venice Beach to sink in. He has added Kareem Lewis, a power forward who played at Venice Beach with Cruz's Orchard Beach team, as well as Greg Hardin, another power forward who played with Mike Campbell at LIU.

Dytanya's big catch is guard Alvin Young, who led the nation in scoring with a 25.1 points-per-game average in 1999 when he was at Niagara. He plays in Italy during the winter months, and he is a quiet standout at the Cage. When Joe Merriweather first saw him play, he remarked, "I notice that players who play with their mouths shut generally play a better game."

Dytanya is using two other young guards: Greg Summer, now playing Division II college ball, and Miguel Million, who is playing junior college basketball in Kansas. James Williams (Sticks), a skinny small forward, has joined the X-Men, and he has led the team in scoring in a number of games. Vinny Matos, Bo Keene's point guard from last season, may become a regular with Dytanya. The trick will be keeping all these standout players together. If they don't get playing time, they will move on.

When new players arrive, established players leave. For years Dytanya kept the same group together, so this upgrading of talent has a personal downside. Benny Timmons, Aaron Walker, Henry Simpson, and Gerard Sampson all took spots with other teams. This strained the relationships Dytanya had with his players. The departed players feel they were cut, but Dytanya says they left because they feared they wouldn't be getting much playing time. Probably they are both right.

At an early-season Rucker game, Aaron Walker was playing with a team that included Lambert Shell, leader of the Shooting Stars at West 4th Street. On one trip down the court Dytanya made a critical remark from the sidelines when Walker was beaten by his man, who scored a layup. Walker didn't acknowledge the remark; perhaps he never heard it. But at the next time-out Lambert passed by Dytanya and said to him quietly, "He's with us now. You've got nothing more to say." The family has been broken up.

Dytanya is surrendering financial security to build a first-rate all-city team. Sid Jones, whose life revolves around playground basketball, has teams in four leagues during the summer, and he has between forty and fifty guys playing for him at one time. Sid is very tight with Nike, which gives him clout with the players. The cell phone hearing device he hooks onto his right ear is probably the first thing he puts on in the morning and the last thing he takes off at night. He's constantly juggling dozens of relationships.

"I think I can compete with guys like Sid and James Ryans, guys who regularly have pros playing with them," Dytanya says. "I'll never know if I don't try."

Dytanya lost Mike Campbell in the middle of the summer when he was invited to the Los Angeles Clippers' summer program for rookies and walk-ons. He didn't stick with the Clippers, but he did get hired to play in Europe, and that's where he finished his summer.

Chaz Dudley, whose team was eliminated early in last year's playoffs, has also used the winter to rebuild his team. He has added Shane Drisdom, Brownsville's center, along with Kennedy Okafor, who played with Philadelphia at Venice Beach. He started the season with Richie Parker, one of the city's most publicized guards when he was in high school, and who later played with Mike Campbell at LIU. Parker plays professionally now, and in his first game at the park he casually collected 22 points in the first half. Then, with the game in the bag, he spent the second half passing out assists to his teammates. He finished with 27 points, but he could have scored 40.

••

Smush Parker visits the the Cage almost every day. He was the property of the Cleveland Cavaliers until July 1, when he became a free agent. Because he will soon be back at NBA camps trying to make another team, nobody expects to see much of him during August. Once a week Smush is with the Uptowners at Hunter College, where local pros like Rafer Alston and Ron Artest play regularly.

When he is at West 4th Street, Smush is relaxed and cordial to everyone; he enjoys returning to his basketball home. He is greeted by dozens of people every day; the little kids are happy to shake his hand, the women give him a hug—and may ask for his phone number—and the men say something to maintain whatever bond they may have. When he broke a two-summer absence from the Cage to participate in the midsummer all-star game, he put on a terrific show, scoring 30 points and throwing down some sensational slam dunks. Everywhere he goes, he is the most exciting player on the court.

Later in the fall, Smush was cut from the Atlanta Hawks after having worked out with the team right up until opening day. Once again, it was said, his talent was not the problem. Some say that Smush would have a better chance with a team like San Antonio, where the David Robinson–Tim Duncan tradition doesn't tolerate immature foolishness. Pat Riley, another notorious disciplinarian, would be a good choice, and Detroit, with Larry Brown, could be an even better fit. After all, only one coach has to say yes. "Some people are saying Smush may be the greatest player that never was," one park regular lamented, "but I think they're wrong. It took Mario Elie five years to get into the NBA after he left college, and he was physically more mature. Don't count Smush out. His playing days are far from over."

Rodney Parker is at the park every day, but his interest is no longer the men's games at 6:00 P.M. He now studies the afternoon high school games that precede the men's division, and he will stay for the later game only if one of his prospects is playing. He still helps promising players move from high school to college. One thing Rodney can do for a young athlete is to put him with good coaches all over the city. Today he is staying to watch Raheem Boroughs, a promising point guard playing at Nassau Community College. After one more year he can transfer to a major four-year school, and Rodney will be helping him along the way.

Tom Konchalski is back scouting the high school kids who play before the men's games. Later in the summer he will be on the road, following the national AAU tournaments that the best high school players must participate in if they hope to receive a bid from a top college. Tom acknowledges that this travel culture detracts from academics and wrongly encourages a sense of entitlement: "Some of these kids think they are on a scholarship for the rest of their lives," he quips. Even at the high school level, professionalism has undercut the traditional summer programs.

This summer's new sensation is a five-foot-eight-inch point guard from Brooklyn called Fridge, whose real name is Jerome Holman. Fridge will be attending Wichita State (Missouri Valley Conference) this winter, and he brings a fresh excitement to the game. He is what Rodney Parker calls a low-risk point guard. He always looks for the pass. He rarely shoots unless he has a good shot, and he is a good shooter. He seldom turns the ball over and he doesn't foul out. He combines the speed and excitement of a superquick point guard with excellent judgment. He has fans who follow him wherever he plays, uptown or in the Village. Rodney thinks he can be a top-twenty draft pick in the NBA. Rodney amazes me with his peculiar reasons for liking a player: "I like him because he is slow-footed like Smush. His toes point way out when he walks. That's very important for a player; it means he can change direction quicker." An odd comment, perhaps, until one recalls Rudolf Nureyev moving across the stage at Lincoln Center. Rodney has a point.

• • •

Obadiah Toppin is back playing at the park—and at Nike's Hunter tournament and in the Bronx as well. He's a dominant player here, and his team is leading its division. Unfortunately, he will not be going to Manhattan College in the fall. Toppin was a star at Globe Institute of Technology in New York City last year, and he had hoped to get enough college credit there to transfer to a school with a bigger program. Manhattan College made a strong bid for him, including day-care expenses for his two young boys. But the twenty-four-year-old college sophomore stopped going to classes after his basketball season ended, so he didn't complete his semester and receive the credits that Manhattan required.

Two years under coach Bobby Gonzales could have helped him enormously. Gonzalez might even have made Toppin a local celebrity. "He could have scored 20 points against St. John's in the Garden, and that alone would have endeared him to enough Manhattan alumni to get him started on a career outside of basketball," one of his boosters told me. The Manhattan College alumni group is well connected in New York City, and intensely loyal to one another.

Perhaps more important, Gonzales could have strengthened Obadiah's game. As another of the park regulars explained, "Toppin is a great playground player. But he is only a playground player, and he needs more training and exposure to be prepared for the professional game. He's got to take that next step."

Why did Toppin stop going to classes when he seemingly had it made? Ronnie, his wife, said that she did everything she could to encourage him to go to Manhattan, but he didn't want to stay in school. "If he just won't do it, I can't make him stay," she explained. Toppin told his friends he wanted to get paid to play. He's talking with an agent and he hopes to get hooked up in France.

Who knows? It is sad whenever anyone throws away a wonderful opportunity. Obadiah is a delightful guy whom fans instinctively want to watch. He will be around all summer.

•••

Rick Johnson has taken undisputed charge of the tournament, and he's getting tougher on players who don't behave. The players need Rick and the tournament more than he needs them. After his mini-heart attack, Rosy is watching his diet and losing a few pounds, but he is at the park every day.

Joe Merriweather still sits just behind the scorer's table in his yellow director's chair and he is still outspoken on matters of decorum and good form. One hot afternoon when one of the announcers was resting his bare leg on the scorer's table, Joe asked him politely to take it down. "There are ladies present," Joe explained, "and this is not the way you should be sitting when you are a member of the staff." The announcer gave Joe some lip. "This is not the ghetto, you know," Joe responded. The leg came down.

The tournament lost its video sponsor this summer: Adam Del Deo will not be renewing his *Slam from the Street* option. But the sponsors will be back.

Kenny was at the park during the first few weeks, shaking hands and ensuring that things moved smoothly, but he plans to go back to Rio. He wants to set up an exhibition game there with a team from New York playing against a local Brazilian team. Rio today is much like New York was for Kenny in the early 1980s—a place of total engagement and endless possibilities. In the 1980s if you wanted to be seen, you played at Rucker or West 4th Street. But West 4th Street has peaked, and Kenny is less involved there than he once was.

One is tempted to imagine Kenny living full-time in Rio, without basketball, but the image doesn't quite stick. At least not yet. Duke Ellington used to say that music was his mistress. Kenny has a mistress too, which is basketball at the Cage. The Cage keeps him in New York.

## Another Lesson of the Greeks?

It is difficult to summarize everything that happens at the Cage over a one-year period. More is going on than guys shooting hoops. Kenny has created an institution that challenges many of the degrading aspects of today's inner-city life. He encourages the old-fashioned basketball virtues of solid fundamentals and team-oriented play. He expects players, coaches, and his staff to display courtesy and conventional good manners. Personally, he is independent and self-reliant, and he must refinance and organize his tournament every summer. His judgment is color-blind, and he has no time for whiners. Remember, this is a guy who has been working since he was twelve.

Kenny has intentionally surrounded himself with older directors—Joe, Rosy, and myself—and he constantly refers back to "West 4th Street traditions." Superficially, Kenny is fashionable and attuned to the latest trends, but his attitudes are backward-looking and conventional.

David Victor Hanson, a classics professor at California State University at Fresno, analyzed this same struggle between old and new, country and city. Because people do not change that much over time, it struck me that some of the lessons Hanson had learned from Greek history could shed light on inner-city culture today.

Back in 1995 Hanson published a book called *The Other Greeks: The Family Farm and Agrarian Roots of Western Civilization.* Despite its specialized, arcane title, the book was revolutionary in its field of classical studies. Its principal argument was that historians for centuries have been mistaken in attributing the origins of Western civilization and liberal thought to the Greek city-state, the *polis,* best exemplified in Athens of the third century BC. True, this was a great period of Greek culture, marked by dramatists Aeschylus, Sophocles, Euripides, and Aristophanes, by the historians Xenophon and Thucydides, and by the philosophical teaching of Socrates, Plato, and Aristotle.

But the foundation of this culture, Hanson argues, was the Greek family farm and tough-minded rural culture that provided the wealth and common sense that first created the *polis* and sustained it, economically and militarily. Hanson argues that classical Greece was built by an agrarian society of middling, autonomous farmers. Athens doesn't have the huge, lush agricultural expanses of Kansas or Iowa. Its fertile land is smaller and more hilly, so Greek farming consisted largely of vines and trees that yielded olives, figs, grapes, and fruits. With a vineyard or an orchard it takes four or five years before a farmer gets his first good crop, and becoming successful requires constant attention and great patience. This type of farming entails risk and requires a commitment to place. The farming culture produced the real community wealth, Hanson argues, and it was the independent farmers, not the politicians, financial middlemen, or the big thinkers of the city, who created the famous Greek ideals of private property, constitutional government, and individual rights.

Hanson has gone from his study of the ancient Greeks to argue in subsequent books that the decline of agrarianism in America has produced dire cultural consequences. American democracy, like its ancient Greek predecessor, depends on the virtues bred on the farm: self-reliance, honesty, hard work, accountability, and a healthy suspicion of urban sophistication. These Greek farmers made their own laws, fought their own battles, and could be bothersome, cantankerous, unpleasant oddballs.

Professor Hanson's thesis about the ethic of the independent farmer may provide a useful background when we think about the culture of blacks in America's cities. Blacks possess the gifts necessary to flourish in an agrarian society, and many started their lives here working on farms. They are capable of strenuous physical labor. Their family ties are strong and they often have extended families: aunts, uncles, and grandmothers all living under the same roof. Blacks are brave, and they are cautious. All these qualities were present in the early Greek independent farmer.

Yet by accident of history, blacks in America have never had an opportunity to own and operate independent farms. Their liberation came at a time when they were too poor to invest in land; blacks had no call on capital when they most needed it—in the late nineteenth and early twentieth centuries. Certainly being a slave on a Georgia plantation was a poor way to learn about independent farming: Most cotton and tobacco plantations were huge, overleveraged, inefficient monopolies.

Thus, blacks have been forced to define themselves in America's cities, which, Hanson argues, is a difficult place to develop the conventional virtues that come more naturally to an independent farmer. Cities are dominated by two conflicting mind-sets. One is extreme social stratification and large bureaucracies, which hamper mobility. Big banks and most big companies are highly bureaucratic, even though they may profess free-market ideals. In addition, the city government is a huge employer of black workers, and its bureaucracy is full of featherbedding, workers' compensation fraud, political maneuvering, counterproductive departmental infighting, union obstructionism, endless legal confrontations, and just plain laziness. All of this distances its employees—many of whom are black—from the agrarian ideal.

The other end of the New York spectrum is entrepreneurial extremism, emphasizing fast money, fashion, and rapidly shifting values, which favor a certain kind of social hustler. The show-biz rap culture and the drug trade flaunt this attitude on the streets, but big business participates in it. New York's wealthiest business leaders, the traders of goods and financial operators, will deny it, but people of the trading class and the money class tend to dissolve culture, not strengthen it. In ancient times the Phoenicians had this role, and the Greeks despised them. This class does provide wealth, but they are less likely to have group loyalty and they are not bound by place. They are too dependent on change, and too opportunistic.

Yet inner-city schools like Bishop Loughlin have helped improve poor neighborhoods because they have not moved out of the cities. They had little choice, so they held their ground and worked with whatever kids they got.

Hanson's major point is that cities generally provide a poor character-building environment.

The crowd at the Cage offsets this. The special trait of the men in this book is that they are bound to a particular place. Kenny Graham, Greg Jackson, Pete Edwards, Darryl Glenn, Bo Keene, Tony Sherman, Clark Elie, Mike Williams, Rosy Jackson, and most of the others in this book have never left the neighborhood. They grew up in Brownsville, Harlem, or around West 4th Street, and they are still here.

Another obstacle for inner-city kids is the widespread teaching of victimology, opportunism, and racial separatism at the expense of patriotism, respect for the law, and assimilation. Disrespect for learning, common among young black men, dooms their chances of success.

In another book he has written about Mexican immigrants, *Mexifornia: A State of Becoming* (2003), Hanson laments that it has become unfashionable for public schools to teach that America is an admirable country, with a way of life worth emulating. Hanson writes, "Rather than confess that mankind by its very nature is prone to be murderous, sexist, and racist—and that only liberal institutions of the West can rein in these innate proclivities—we instead demand instantaneous perfection of our own country and no other, both in the present and in the past." As long as "acting white" is considered bad, progress for blacks will be slow. Since big-city thinkers and the media are the leading proponents of victimology and reparation, it stands to reason that the cities will be the last place to discard these counterproductive ideas.

Yet there is no interest in victimology at the Cage at West 4th Street. The men here knew O. J. Simpson did it. To argue otherwise would be to insult their intelligence. More important, they are here to prove themselves, not complain. They are trying to win games, play better, maybe knock someone around a bit; that's enough for one day. When these men are not playing, they have real jobs. Many of Kenny's personal attributes—self-reliance, honesty, cranky possessiveness, flexibility, hard work, accountability, and skepticism—match those of the independent farmer, and the tournament here enforces these qualities. At times, the ancient farmers could be irritable and stubborn. But stop a moment and recall the people of West 4th Street: battlers like Bo Keene, Brian Elleby, and Tony Sherman; tireless organizers like Dytanya Mixson, Sid Jones, and Kenny Graham; hard-to-define characters like Rick Johnson and the eternal moralizer, Joe Merriweather. Are these people not oddballs in their way, but still the modern counterparts of the ancient Greek farmer?

The Cage doesn't create these people, but it supports and attracts them, and they feel at home here. The Cage draws in the same kind of person that produced the early Greek farms. This is what West 4th Street has in common with the Greek tree- and vine-growing culture. West 4th Street keeps these attitudes alive.

Kenny Graham has remained in control of this park and this tournament for nearly three decades. Who else could have done it? The legend of the Cage is a legend created by Kenny Graham. Though the personalities that dominate the Cage may appear to be bullying or self-centered, the tournament at West 4th Street has become a jewel of civility. Kenny doesn't beg for sympathy, he takes care of business, and he takes care of himself. He has made the lives of thousands of people better and happier.

Of course he is charismatic, but Kenny is more than talk and charisma. It's easy to understand why he is so widely liked. An ancient Greek maxim accurately describes it: Happiness is to wish to be what you are. That's Kenny, all the way.

# The Guy in the Suit, or How I Got Involved in West 4th Street

**On a hot July** afternoon in 1985, I climbed out of the E train stop at West 4th Street to catch my first complete basketball game at the park. At 6:00 the temperature in the subway was close to 100 degrees and at the park the humidity was in the 90s. My white shirt was soaked with sweat, my tie was crooked, and my feet were squeezed into wingtip Oxfords, tightly laced. Clearly, I was not dressed for the occasion.

Vice Squad was playing Les Pines's team, the Village Mustangs, whose top scorer was Gary McLain, a star from Villanova's NCAA championship team. He was an outstanding jump-shooter, and both teams played a game of style and finesse rather than brute power. It promised to be a great matchup. Because I arrived early, I was able to find a spot inside the fence in an alcove on the northeast corner of the playing area, far away from the scorer's table.

This was a good place to watch the game, and three or four of us were huddled together in this small space. Of course whenever the action became intense at the other end of the court I found myself drawn out onto the court to see what was happening. Finally Kenny, who was announcing the game through his megaphone, became impatient. He hollered at me, "Hey, suit, get back off the court!" So after one game, I got a nickname. I was "Suit," the guy from Wall Street who couldn't stay off the court.

During my first year of coming to games regularly, I started hanging around with Kenny and some of the players. We didn't have long conversations because we had little in common other than basketball, but we seemed to like one another just the same. For the first few years I tried to be helpful. I'd help set up and take down the chairs for the spectators and tables for the scorers and the staff. I'd run errands, and I raised small amounts of money for the tournament from friends and business associates.

I think Kenny liked the idea of having a middle-aged Wall Street guy in a suit hanging around his tournament. I was an institutional bond salesman at Lehman Brothers at the time, and that was considered pretty hot stuff in the 1980s. In Thomas Wolfe's 1987 bestseller, *Bonfire of the Vanities,* corporate bond salesmen at the big firms were called Masters of the Universe because of their presumptuous arrogance and the huge commissions they earned. That was my crowd.

Of course, whenever I was at the park, Kenny kept an eye on me, because he knew all too well that Wall Street or not, I was pathetically naive about New York City street life. I recall one Sunday afternoon Kenny sent me across West 3rd Street to get a blue T-shirt out of his car. After I had opened the trunk and had begun to rummage around the huge pile of stuff he had in there, a burly street wanderer leaned over me, reached a thick black forearm across my chest into the trunk, and said, "I'd like a nice bright orange. Size XXL."

"I can't give you a shirt," I stammered.

The big man ignored me and started tossing shirts around in the trunk of the car, picking at them so he could read the size that was printed on the labels. "Nice shirts," he mumbled.

I was frantically looking for the correct size in the blue shirt Kenny had asked me to get, holding my position over the open trunk as best I could, hoping to deny my intruder free access. He disregarded my efforts. "Those blue ones look nice too. I'll take a couple of those," he said.

As he extended his reach farther into the trunk, his body pressed heavily against mine. Turning to me with a potent whiskey breath, he whispered hoarsely, "Kenny and me go way back." He gave me an evil, nicotine-stained smile.

I didn't feel like a Master of the Universe.

Just then I spotted the shirt Kenny wanted and I grabbed it. "I have to close the trunk now," I said. "You'll have to talk to Kenny if you want a shirt."

I was looking down to see how far I could close the trunk without slamming it on his arm, which would anger him. He looked up, glanced across the street, and then looked down at me scornfully.

Should I slam the trunk on his arm? Scream for help? Or just let him have the shirts and explain later?

Gradually, he reduced his pressure against me and straightened his body. His arm slid slowly out of the trunk. Casually, he moved away, down West 3rd Street. I was amazed. Maybe I could handle these street guys after all.

As I returned to the court, I looked across the street, over at the park gate. There, with their arms across their chests and motionless, but staring right at me and my intruder, were two of Kenny's security people, Iron Mike and Big Pete Simmons. They were leaning back against the park fence, glaring. Their eyes were narrow and intensely focused. Apparently my intruder had taken a quick look at the park before deciding to make his move, and he decided it would be better if he backed down quietly.

When I crossed back to the park with my blue shirt in hand, Pete and Mike smiled faintly at me but said nothing. I mentioned to Kenny what had happened, and he said that he had asked Pete to keep an eye on me "just in case, no big deal."

..

Kenny has always believed that a quality tournament should have quality awards to give away to its top players and championship teams. He likes to give away T-shirts, sneakers, jackets, watches, athletic bags—anything with the West 4th Street name on it that others will covet. A single player on a winning team can get prizes worth more than the total team entry fee. Kenny loves stuff: the more the better, and the bigger the better. "When other tournaments were giving out four-foot trophies to the winning team, we were giving out six-foot trophies. We were the first to go to eight-foot trophies too."

Back in the late 1980s Kenny went to Nobody Beats the Wiz to pick up four television sets to be given out as prizes at the end of the final playoff game. The big retailer, which had provided trophies every year, had a store just down the block from the court, and Kenny was supposed to collect the televisions Sunday morning, the day of the final game. But when he got to the store, no one knew they were supposed to give him four TVs.

Although he didn't have the money to pay for the TVs, Kenny gave the store manager his credit card, charging them all to his own account. Most street people do not spend their own cash if they have some way around it. They are used to getting stiffed, and a big company like Nobody Beats the Wiz could easily forget its obligation after the televisions had been paid for. Furthermore, no agreement had ever been put in writing.

But for Kenny, his pride and reputation with the best of New York's basketball elite, most of whom would be playing or watching that afternoon, made compromise impossible. He didn't moan or hesitate; he bought the TVs and gave them away as planned. On Monday, The Wiz reimbursed Kenny, just as he expected.

After three years Kenny began to discourage me from setting up chairs and tables. Perhaps he felt I should be treated as a special league friend, so whenever I came to the park, he would have Bean or one of the other guys get a director's chair for me. I think I was Kenny's string of pearls, his touch with corporate sophistication, suburbia, and the money people. He wanted everyone to know that I was important to him, and I was entitled to their respect.

During the playoffs of the 1989 season, I officially joined the league to sponsor Tony Hargraves's team, Prime Time, for the following year. This entails paying the referees after each game and the entry fee at the beginning of the season. That year Hargraves recruited Anthony Mason, thereby beginning a three-year championship run. When the awards were handed out each year, Tony would call me onto center court and present me with the same trophy the players received.

During the winter of 1992, Kenny had a health scare—he was lethargic and low on energy. Because he was so weak, he felt he could not continue to run the league and he would not be able to withstand the hot July and August afternoons in the park. Along with two of Kenny's closest friends, Joe Merriweather and Rosy Jackson, I met with him to figure out how to keep the tournament going. It meant too much to all of us to let it fold. This was a big test for West 4th Street basketball.

We all did our part to help Kenny while he rested and rebuilt his strength. Friends took him down to see a doctor in Philadelphia, and they spent extra time with him in Brooklyn. But figuring out how to run the league without Kenny was a bigger chore. Joe Merriweather was to work with the city and handle administrative matters. I watched the money and filed the tax returns, and Rosy took care of equipment and supplies. Bill Motley, whose Harlem team had brought such dignity and respect to the league for over a decade, was asked to become commissioner. This was the hardest job to fill because managing the tournament on a daily basis took so much time. Motley asked Denis Britain, who had once played for him with Harlem USA, along with Arizona Pearson, who had been playing with Prime Time, to help.

Every couple of weeks the directors and Bill Motley would meet to anticipate problems. Sometimes Kenny would come to these meetings, and sometimes he would not. All the normal helpers showed up at the park as they always had. Since the tournament did not have a major sponsor that year, the promise of stuff—money, T-shirts, sneakers, and the like—was less certain. Just the same, the staff members did their jobs and the games went on.

Almost twenty years later I still visit the Cage regularly. They don't call me Suit anymore; now I am Golden Pond. On the other hand, while most of my retired friends have moved south, I am not satisfied by quiet sunsets over the seventeenth fairway. My view of the good life more closely resembles the Cage at West 4th Street; I think it is important to stay in the game, even if the game has to change a bit.

The players here have something that is missing in the bright young men becoming overnight millionaires on Wall Street. After my first West 4th Street game I wondered what Lehman's young MBAs would have thought if they measured themselves against the best young men at West 4th Street. I saw in young players like Sherman and Mario Elie an inspiring toughness, a raw masculinity, and a deep-rooted personal pride. The better players have grit and a capacity for physical exertion that our increasingly feminized society does not want to face directly. Men here play with a controlled violence that is easily undervalued.

Kenny admits that he is a hustler—but not in a devious way—and frankly, this is part of city life. His personal habits are clean. He doesn't drink, smoke, or do drugs. He eats prudently, and he works out regularly, even in Rio. Most important for his tournament, he is honest, persevering, and tactful. These qualities are not often exemplified in national politics and city government. We don't find them in Hollywood, on television, or in professional sports. Even Little League and the Olympics have become suspect. After the Enron-Global Crossing-Adelphia-WorldCom-Tyco scandals, we don't see these good qualities exemplified by the captains of industry.

All of a sudden the question, whom do you trust? has become a difficult one for many Americans to answer. Well, at the Cage, everybody trusts Kenny. So Nike gives him equipment and money because the company knows he won't squander it. His staff gives him loyalty. His players and coaches give him respect.

Each year at West 4th Street brings a new struggle. New teams and new players come to assert their place. There is respect to be earned and trophies to be won. The players here care about what they are doing. These are men who are fully engaged in life. They are exposed, and they keep taking chances.

**Wight Martindale Jr.** has followed the West 4th Street tournament for twenty years, and for the last decade and a half has served as one of four of its managing directors. He was a finance editor at *Business Week* until he shifted his attention to Wall Street, where he was a senior vice president at Lehman Brothers. He has taught at Temple, Villanova, and Lehigh Universities, studied at Oxford and Cambridge, and holds a PhD in English literature from New York University.